TOURISM, TRADE AND NATIONAL WELFARE

CONTRIBUTIONS
TO
ECONOMIC ANALYSIS

265

Honory Editors:
D. W. JORGENSON
J. TINBERGEN †

Editors:
B. Baltagi
E. Sadka
D. Wildasin

ELSEVIER

Amsterdam – Boston – Heidelberg – London – New York – Oxford
Paris – San Diego – San Francisco – Singapore – Sydney – Tokyo

TOURISM, TRADE AND NATIONAL WELFARE

Bharat R. Hazari
and
Pasquale M. Sgro
*Deakin Business School, Deakin University, Melbourne,
Victoria, Australia*

2004

ELSEVIER

Amsterdam – Boston – Heidelberg – London – New York – Oxford
Paris – San Diego – San Francisco – Singapore – Sydney – Tokyo

ELSEVIER B.V.	ELSEVIER Inc.	ELSEVIER Ltd	ELSEVIER Ltd
Sara Burgerhartstraat 25	525 B Street, Suite 1900	The Boulevard, Langford Lane	84 Theobalds Road
P.O. Box 211, 1000 AE Amsterdam	San Diego, CA 92101-4495	Kidlington, Oxford OX5 1GB	London WC1X 8RR
The Netherlands	USA	UK	UK

First edition 2004

Library of Congress Cataloging in Publication Data
A catalog record is available from the Library of Congress.

British Library Cataloguing in Publication Data
A catalogue record is available from the British Library.

ISBN: 0 444 51707 3
ISSN: 0573 8555

⊗ The paper used in this publication meets the requirements of ANSI/NISO Z39.48-1992 (Permanence of Paper).
Printed in The United Kingdom.

Dedications

To Joshua, Carrie and Diane
– *for their love and support*

Pasquale

To Chandra and Ravi

Bharat

INTRODUCTION TO THE SERIES

This series consists of a number of hitherto unpublished studies, which are introduced by the editors in the belief that they represent fresh contributions to economic science.

The term 'economic analysis' as used in the title of the series has been adopted because it covers both the activities of the theoretical economist and the research worker.

Although the analytical method used by the various contributors are not the same, they are nevertheless conditioned by the common origin of their studies, namely theoretical problems encountered in practical research. Since for this reason, business cycle research and national accounting, research work on behalf of economic policy, and problems of planning are the main sources of the subjects dealt with, they necessarily determine the manner of approach adopted by the authors. Their methods tend to be 'practical' in the sense of not being too far remote from application to actual economic conditions. In addition they are quantitative.

It is the hope of the editors that the publication of these studies will help to stimulate the exchange of scientific information and to reinforce international cooperation in the field of economics.

The Editors

ENDORSEMENTS

This is an important contribution by two of today's most prolific international economists. It illuminates a subject of growing importance.

Jagdish Bhagwati
University Professor
Columbia University

Professors Hazari and Sgro have an uncanny ability: they succeed in incorporating new important elements (usually treated as separate issues) into trade theory in a consistent and convincing way. They did this in their previous book (Migration, Unemployment and Trade, Kluwer, 2001) as regards legal and illegal migration. In this book they repeat the feat as regards tourism: here trade theory is extended to incorporate all types of mobility: goods, factors *and* *consumers*. The brilliant and simple idea is to deal with tourism as "a temporary movement of consumers from one country into another to consume non-traded goods and services, for example, the Eiffel Tower in Paris and the Twelve Apostles on the Great Ocean Road in Australia".
Another welcome addition to international trade books.

Giancarlo Gandolfo
Professor of Economics
University of Rome "La Sapienza"

This is an impressive book that provides unique analysis of tourism within the context of international trade theory. They have succeeded in extending our knowledge of tourism and trade far beyond the current limits. Their book is unrivalled in its originality, depth of analysis and contribution to opening up new frontiers in research on this important subject.

Thea Sinclair
Professor of Economics and Tourism
Christel DeHann Tourism and Travel Research Institute
Nottingham University Business School

ACKNOWLEDGEMENTS

This book is based on research on tourism and trade theory that we have undertaken over the last decade. Several parts of the book have been presented at seminars at the Universities of Lille 1, Sorbone Paris 1, Rome, Venice, John Hopkins Bologna Centre, City University of Hong-Kong and at tourism conferences in Cyprus and Sardinia. We thank the participants for providing comments. As is clear from the introduction, some of the research has been carried out with Jean-Jacques Nowak and we thank him for his insights, hard work and for sustaining our interest in this area of research. Jean-Pierre Laffargue read the entire manuscript and provided extremely detailed, critical and insightful comments, for which we are greatly indebted. Bharat Hazari thanks both the University of Lille 1 and CEPREMAP for providing a stimulating environment for research during his sabbatical. Pasquale Sgro thanks the University of Rome "La Sapienza" for providing research facilities in October/November 2002 when some of this work was carried out. Comments received from Chi-Chur Chao, Vijay Mohan and Eden Yu are gratefully acknowledged. Our thanks are also due to the following journals for allowing us to use material from published research: The Journal of International Trade and Economic Development, Pacific Economic Review and the Journal of Developing Areas.

Finally, and most importantly, we thank Lillian Barrie for preparing the manuscript. She suffered through the typing of many drafts and did an excellent job.

Bharat Hazari and Pasquale Sgro

CONTENTS

CHAPTER 9 TOURISM, INCREASING RETURNS AND WELFARE 171

CHAPTER 10 TOURISM AND GROWTH IN A DYNAMIC MODEL OF TRADE 185

CHAPTER 11 OPTIMAL GROWTH AND TOURISM 197

CHAPTER 1

Tourism and Trade

1.1. Introduction

Tourism is a growing and important industry in both developed and Third World countries. According to Luzzi and Flückiger (2003a, p. 239), 'between 1950 and 1999 the number of international arrivals increased from a mere 25 million international arrivals to the current 664 million which corresponds to an average annual growth rate of 7%. Such a growth rate is much higher than those observed in other activities'. Tourism in many countries is also an important source for earning foreign exchange and employs domestic labour, guest workers and illegal migrants. In spite of its importance as an exportable good and the presence of a large body of empirical research on tourism, it has not been fully integrated into the real theory of trade. This book represents a pioneering attempt at systematically integrating tourism into the pure theory of international trade.

Traditionally, trade theory has concerned itself with determining the pattern of commodity trade and then deducing the welfare consequences of such trade. Ricardian and Heckscher–Ohlin (henceforth referred to as HO) models of comparative advantage explained the pattern of trade on the basis of differences in technology and factor endowments, respectively. They also implicitly established that free trade in commodities, in the absence of distortions, necessarily raised welfare. This is a straightforward application of the first fundamental theorem of welfare economics. The HO model, which became the cornerstone of trade theory (until the arrival of new trade theory), was later extended to include one and/or all of the following: non-traded goods, factor mobility and intermediate goods, in both competitive and distortionary models.

The Komiya (1967) extension of trade theory to include non-traded goods is both unrealistic and unsatisfactory as in this model the international terms of trade fix the relative price of non-traded goods. It is well known that even in the small country case the relative prices of non-traded goods change for a variety of reasons – hence, the need to use models of non-traded goods that allow for flexible prices. There are several ways of achieving this objective. Flexible prices for non-traded goods can be introduced by using the well-known dependency model and/or the specific factor model of trade. Samuelson's 'guns and butter' production possibility curve in his elementary textbook on economics is an excellent example of the specific factor model. By appropriate choice of models, most of this book will treat the relative prices of non-traded goods as flexible.

Tourism represents a temporary movement of consumers from one country into another to consume non-traded goods and services, for example, the Eiffel Tower in Paris and the Twelve Apostles on the Great Ocean Road in Australia. It is not possible to move these non-traded goods across boundaries (in technical terms the transport cost of moving these goods is extraordinarily high or infinite). This book therefore extends trade theory to include temporary consumer mobility to consume non-traded goods and services. Trade theory can then be viewed as incorporating all types of mobility: goods, factors and consumers. Guest workers, illegal migrants and students also consume non-traded goods, hence, our analytical approach also applies to all categories of temporary movement of individuals.

Flexible prices for non-traded goods are of critical significance in the case of tourism as they allow for the presence of a distortion, specifically, monopoly power in trade. In the two justly celebrated papers by Bhagwati and Ramaswami (1963) and Bhagwati (1971), four distortions in terms of consequences were introduced:

(1) DRS = DRT ≠ FRT
(2) DRS = FRT ≠ DRT
(3) DRS ≠ FRT = DRT
(4) Shrinkage of the production possibility locus

The term DRS stands for domestic rate of substitution, DRT for the domestic rate of transformation and FRT for the foreign rate for transformation.

Distortion (1) represents the case of monopoly power in trade. It is a constant theme of this book that foreign demand for non-traded goods (assuming flexible prices) by tourists necessarily creates a monopoly power distortion. Even in small open economies which take the terms of trade as given, tourists influence domestic non-traded goods prices – hence, the presence of monopoly power in trade. It is this feature that makes tourism different from other goods and it is the exploitation of this characteristic that integrates tourism into the main body of trade theory. While in the case of goods it is very easy to work out the optimal tariff, this is not the case for tourism. Tourists consume many goods, hence, there are several optimal taxes depending on the elasticity of demand in each market. Alternatively, one could view a visa fee as a mapping of all these taxes to correct the distortion created by monopoly power in trade.

1.2. Organization of the book

As remarked earlier, there is a large body of empirical literature on the economics of tourism; however, tourism has not been integrated into the pure theory of trade. In Chapter 2 we provide a systematic and self-contained treatment of trade theory (to make this book accessible to non-trade theorists and specialists in tourism). A reader familiar with trade theory can skip this chapter. However, specialists in other areas will hopefully find this chapter useful in coming to grips with the analysis in the rest of the book. Chapter 2 presents the two-sector general equilibrium model for a small open economy. Both the primal and dual approaches to trade theory are discussed. The Rybczynski and Stolper–Samuelson theorems are explained as both theorems are used in later parts of the book. The first best solution of the small open economy is also discussed along with a very brief introduction to distortion theory. Most of the geometry and algebra required for understanding this book are also developed in this chapter.

Chapter 3 builds on the pioneering paper of Hazari and Ng (1993) which introduced tourism as the temporary movement of agents to consume non-traded goods and services. Using the dependency model, Hazari and Ng discuss the interdependence between monopoly power in trade and tourism. This chapter represents a complete development of the ideas contained in the 1993 paper (including correction of a few errors). The dependency model is fully elaborated and the consequences of large country assumption on the concavity of the consumption possibility locus explored. The model in this chapter demonstrates for the first time (to our knowledge) how international prices can affect the consumption possibility locus. The introduction of tourism in this model leads to some paradoxical results, for example, it is shown that as a result of monopoly power in trade, a certain type of demand shift (tourism boom) may be immiserizing. This immiserization arises from a demand side shift and such immiserization is present in Bhagwati and Johnson (1960) and Kemp (1969) in the traditional two-sector model of trade. This chapter then shows how their results can be extended to the tourism literature.

Chapter 4 develops the ideas of Hazari and Nowak (2003) and endogenizes tourism in a two-country model of trade. A simple model is developed in which tourism is introduced in the extreme form of a differentiated product produced in one country only. In this context, the following remarks of Luzzi and Flückiger (2003b, p. 289) are worth quoting: 'Tourism is not really an industry but rather a collection of activities in which foreigners partake and which are also available for consumption by local residents. Tourism is thus a bundle of goods and services that can be viewed, for analytical purposes, as a single complex and differentiated product. It is complex because it includes a wide variety of goods and services and differentiated because each destination has unique features'. Since the non-traded good is produced in one country only, it can only be consumed by movement of consumers (tourists). It is established that under such conditions, tourism *necessarily* creates monopoly power in trade, hence, the need for taxing tourists to arrive at an optimal solution. This chapter, for the first time, shows how supply side expansion in tourism in the presence of a distortion may lead to immiserization. This is a very important policy result for tourism specialists who put great faith in increasing the supply of tourist facilities without realizing that such expansions in a distortionary framework may be immiserizing. Chapters 3 and 4 have been concerned with analysing tourism with monopoly power in trade, that is, DRS = DRT $\neq$ FRT. In Chapter 5 the foreign distortion is removed and replaced by a domestic distortion. Specifically, a production monopoly is introduced which creates the distortion DRS = FRT $\neq$ DRT. As the monopoly is in the production of non-traded goods and services, it is not eliminated by opening the economy to free trade. The monopolist also practises price discrimination between domestic consumers and tourists. The chapter demonstrates that an increase in tourism may lead to an increase in resident welfare. Welfare increases provided that the crowding out effect of tourism expansion is outweighed by the favourable movement in the relative price and output of the non-traded good consumed by the tourists. The term 'crowding out' is used in a different way to the manner in which it is often used in macroeconomics. Price discrimination by the monopolist represents optimal pricing and if the tourists are paying more, then the extra payment may be viewed as a tax on tourists – only, in this case, it arises from the presence of monopoly in production.

The next two chapters of the book deal with guest workers and illegal migrants. The chapter on guest workers is based on a paper by Hazari and Nowak (2003) and the chapter on illegal migrants on an unpublished manuscript of McArthur (2003). Both illegal workers and guest workers transform non-traded into traded goods (just like tourists). Their welfare is not part of the local residents' welfare – hence, there are two agents in the economy: residents and guest workers, or residents and illegal workers. Hazari and Nowak (2003) establish an appropriate technique for analysing guest worker consumption by using microeconomic foundations. This technique is used in both chapters. Chapter 6 extends the analysis of Chapter 5 by considering a model in which there are guest workers as well as tourists. It is shown that a tourist boom in the presence of guest workers may result in the immiserization of the resident population. This result arises from two effects: first, a favourable terms-of-trade effect from the tourist boom and second, an unfavourable terms-of-trade effect of guest workers consumption of the non-traded goods and services. If the second effect is greater than the first, then the host country is immiserized. Optimal policies for avoiding immiserization are also derived and explained.

Chapter 7 extends the basic tourism model to include illegal migrants and analyses the implications for domestic residents of such a phenomenon. Illegal migrants are assumed to be tolerated by the local residents – hence not policed. Future research could introduce policing into this framework. The analysis demonstrates that when an economy experiences a boom in tourism, the presence of illegal migrants may improve the terms of trade in the non-traded goods sector and hence have a positive effect on the rate of domestic employment. These results point towards positive gains from the presence of illegal migrants. The welfare effect is ambiguous, but it is possible for illegal migrants to have a positive impact on the domestic economy, for example, reduced unemployment and also increased welfare. Although not discussed, the granting of amnesty to illegal workers is a possible way of avoiding illegal worker induced immiserization.

In Chapter 8, tourism is introduced in the Hazari and Sgro (1991) generalized Harris–Todaro model. In this model, two urban and two rural goods are produced. A distinguishing characteristic of this model is that the urban non-traded good is not consumed in the rural region and, similarly, the rural non-traded good is not consumed in the urban region. Tourists are also located in one of the two regions, in other words, urban tourists do not visit the rural region and vice versa. This assumption can be relaxed without any loss of generality of the results. The tourist's utility function in this case would have to incorporate location decisions. The most important result obtained in this framework is that a tourist boom in the urban region may immiserize the rural area. Hence, the welfare interests of rural and urban consumers may be in conflict as a result of tourist expansion in the urban region. Rural region tourism is always welfare increasing. These results arise due to the asymmetric structure of the model.

Chapter 9 is a variation of the setup in Chapter 8 and is based on the work of Nowak *et al.* (2003). The urban region now produces only manufactured goods, while the coastal and/or rural region produces two goods: an agricultural good and a non-traded good. Thus, the rural sector has the same structure as the rural region in Chapter 8. The most important change in the model is the introduction of increasing returns to scale in manufacturing. This creates two distortions: (1) DRS = FRT $\neq$ DRT and (2) shrinkage of the production possibility locus. A third distortion also comes into play in this chapter, namely, the monopoly power in trade associated with tourists' consumption of the non-traded good. This is the only chapter in the book where three distortions operate simultaneously. This model highlights the role of sectoral interdependencies and captures the tension between development led by tourism and traditional agriculture. It also incorporates the effect of such development on the urban manufacturing sector. It is established that, under certain conditions, welfare and manufacturing output may fall as a result of an increase in tourism. This occurs when the non-traded goods is more labour intensive than the agriculture good, a not unreasonable assumption that is supported by empirical evidence. Both theoretical and empirical studies tell us that these general equilibrium effects can be quite substantial and therefore they need to be taken into account in assessing the net benefits of tourism to an economy. The distortion literature establishes that a tax-cum-subsidy policy is required to correct the distortion. Note, however, that owing to the monopoly power in trade in tourism, an additional source of tax emerges. Tourism tax receipts could be used to subsidize the manufacturing sector.

Chapters 10 and 11 analyse the consequences of tourism in dynamic models of trade. Chapter 10 uses the framework of descriptive growth theory while in Chapter 11, tourism is analysed in a Ramsey-type growth framework. Chapter 10 is based on the work of Hazari and Sgro (1995) and Chapter 11 is an important generalization of an unpublished conference paper of Hazari *et al.* (2003c). The main result presented in Chapter 10 is that tourism acts as a time-saving device in a growth model. The closed economy steady-state capital labour ratio will be attained in a shorter time. Chapter 11 presents several interesting and important results. First, it shows that tourism is capable of generating sustained growth without the endogenous growth framework. Hence, in a dynamic context, tourism in poor countries may generate sustained growth that may ultimately reduce poverty. The second important result is that the country receiving tourists (host country) should seek to increase the degree of differentiation of its tourism product; the more differentiated its product the higher is the potential for increasing the economy's long-run growth rate. In other words, the degree of monopoly power in trade, as measured by the price elasticity of the export demand, exerts a strong influence on the magnitude of this transmission; the less elastic its export demand (and therefore the more differentiated its tourism product) the more the host country can benefit from the foreign country's growth. A necessary condition for the above result is monopoly power in trade; therefore, the presence of such power is important both in static and dynamic models.

The final chapter is in the tradition of applied work in tourism. It runs against the theoretical theme of the book which is based on tourism and monopoly power in trade in both static and dynamic models of trade. The chapter, based on Hazari *et al.* (2003b), analyses a data set for 19 OECD countries for competitiveness in tourism- and travel-related services. Variations in the real exchange rates have been shown to be of significance in influencing competitiveness. This chapter has been placed in the book as an example of applied work in tourism.

1.3. Conclusion

As remarked earlier, this book integrates temporary movements of consumers (defined as tourists) into the main body of trade theory. First, it is established that tourism, even in a small open economy, may be associated with monopoly power in trade, giving rise to the possibility of demand and/or supply side immiserization of the residents. Second, it is shown that tourism may occur in the presence of other distortions, again leading to some pathological trade results. Third, it is established that guest workers, students and illegal migrants share a common feature with tourists, namely, the conversion of non-traded into tradables, giving rise to the possibility of monopoly power in trade. Finally, dynamic models with distortions are also considered. Given the presence of a plethora of immiserizing results, one *may* be inclined to think or deduce that the message of this book is negative. This would constitute a misrepresentation of this work. The message of this book is loud and clear: follow optimal policies and remove or correct distortions and then tourists, guest workers and illegal workers will all raise national welfare.

References

Bhagwati, J.N. (1971), "The generalized theory of distortions and welfare", in: J.N. Bhagwati and R.W. Jones, editors, *Trade, Balance of Payments and Growth: Papers in International Economics in Honor of Charles P. Kindleberger*, Amsterdam: North-Holland, Chapter 12.

Bhagwati, J.N. and H.G. Johnson (1960), "Notes on some controversies in the theory of international trade", *Economic Journal*, Vol. 70, pp. 74–93.

Bhagwati, J.N. and V.K. Ramaswami (1963), "Domestic distortions, tariffs and the theory of optimum subsidy", *Journal of Political Economy*, Vol. 71, pp. 44–50.

Hazari, B.R. and A. Ng (1993), "An analysis of tourists' consumption of non-traded goods and services on the welfare of the domestic consumer", *International Review of Economics and Finance*, Vol. 2, pp. 43–58.

Hazari, B.R. and J.J. Nowak (2003), "Tourism, taxes and immiserization: a trade theoretical analysis", *Pacific Economic Review*, Vol. 8(3), pp. 279–288.

Hazari, B.R. and P.M. Sgro (1991), "Urban–rural structural adjustment: urban unemployment with traded and non-traded goods", *Journal of Development Economics*, Vol. 35, pp. 187–196.

Hazari, B.R. and P.M. Sgro (1995), "Tourism and growth in a dynamic model of trade", *Journal of International Trade and Economic Development*, pp. 143–252.

Hazari, B.R., M. Sahli and P.M. Sgro (2003), "Tourism specialisation: a comparison of OECD destination countries", Paper Presented at Tourism Conference, Cyprus.

Hazari, B.R., J.-J. Nowak and M. Sahli (2003), International Tourism as a Way of Importing Growth. Mimeographed, pp. 1–16.

Kemp, M.C. (1969), *The Pure Theory of International Trade and Investment*, Englewood Cliffs, NJ: Prentice Hall.

Komiya, R. (1967), "Non-traded goods and the pure theory of international trade", *International Economic Review*, Vol. 8, pp. 132–152.

Luzzi, G.F. and Y. Flückiger (2003a), "Tourism and international trade: an introduction", *Pacific Economic Review*, Vol. 8(3), pp. 239–244.

Luzzi, G.F. and Y. Flückiger (2003b), "An econometric estimation of the demand for tourism: the case of Switzerland", *Pacific Economic Review*, Vol. 8(3), pp. 289–314.

McArthur, C. (2003), Illegal Migrants, Terms of Trade and Resident Welfare. Mimeographed.

Nowak, J.J., M. Sahli and P.M. Sgro (2003), "Tourism, trade and domestic welfare", *Pacific Economic Review*, Vol. 8(3), pp. 245–248.

CHAPTER 2

A Two-Sector General Equilibrium Model of a Small Open Economy

2.1. Introduction

This chapter provides a systematic treatment of a two-commodity (two-sector), two-factor general equilibrium model of an open economy which is widely used in several real models of trade and growth.[1] This model is the cornerstone of the Heckscher–Ohlin, the Ricardo–Samuelson–Viner–Jones, the Harris–Todaro and many other models that are widely used in the trade and development literature.[2] It can also be extended to incorporate non-traded goods, economies of scale, imperfect competition and externalities. The framework of this model also provides the foundations for deriving optimal policies in the presence of distortions. This chapter is motivated by the desire to make this book as self-contained as possible for students, professionals and others working in the area of

---

[1] The term 'real' or 'pure' is used to emphasise the fact that these models are not concerned with monetary phenomena.

[2] It turns out that most of the useful results in international trade theory can be made in the framework of two countries, two commodities and one or two production factors since the majority of questions in trade theory involve issues of composition, distinguishing between gainers and losers among countries, expanding and contracting sectors in the economy or the intensive use of factors in one sector of an economy but not the other. This is not to say that general equilibrium analysis of higher dimensional cases is not useful, in fact for such issues as the aggregation problem and price changes, it is crucially important. It also turns out that a number of results from 'two-ness' type models retain their validity in higher dimensional cases. In fact, two-dimensional models cannot only provide building blocks and a firm foundation for multi-dimensional models, but also present a standard of comparison against which multi-dimensional results can be appreciated (Jones (1977)). Some of the trade theorems have been extended to the $n \times n$ framework. This book will not be concerned with such extensions. References to this line of work include Uekawa (1971), Uekawa et al. (1973), Ethier (1974), Kemp and Wan (1976), and Sgro (1980).

tourism who may not necessarily be familiar with the tools of trade theory. The model is presented in both the primal and dual forms as both types of presentations are widely used in this work and trade literature in general. This chapter can be skipped by readers who are already familiar with real trade theory.

2.2. A two-sector model of a small open economy

We consider an economy that produces two commodities, X_1 and X_2. The aggregate utility function for the country as a whole is given by

$$U = U(D_1, D_2) \tag{2.1}$$

where U indicates total utility and D_i ($i = 1, 2$) the consumption of commodity X_i ($i = 1, 2$). The utility function is assumed to be strictly concave and $U_i = \partial U / \partial D_i$, the marginal utility of consuming good i is assumed positive. It will suffice to assume that the utility function is quasi-concave but for geometrical reasons the assumption of strict concavity will generally be maintained throughout the book. The aggregate utility function is assumed to possess both behavioural and welfare significance.

It is important to provide some comments on the above utility function. An aggregate utility function can be generated only on the basis of stringent assumptions.[3] In this context, one can pose the question: why do we need to use an aggregate utility function? Such a utility function is not required if the economist's interest is only in making positive statements, for example, national income increases in response to a boom in tourism. However, if as social scientists we are also interested in examining the welfare consequences of parametric changes, for example, the effect of a terms-of-trade shock, a boom in tourism, pollution abatement, factor accumulation and so on, then there is the obvious need to use an aggregate indicator of welfare and a utility function happens to be one of these. As social scientists, one of our responsibilities is to make policy judgements and recommendations. The aggregate utility function is frequently used in economics and it will be used in this book in order to establish normative results in the presence of various distortions. It should also be made clear at

---

[3] See the paper by Samuelson (1956) on this issue.

this stage that aggregation is not a problem of the two-sector framework alone and also arises in other frameworks. In macroeconomic models an aggregate consumption function requires aggregation over individuals. A well-behaved aggregate consumption function also requires stringent microeconomic assumptions – a fact often ignored in macroeconomics text books.

An important departure will be made from this aggregate utility function in discussing tourism where two agents domestic residents and tourists will be introduced. This disaggregation will clearly show that welfare results which hold in a one-agent (representative agent) framework are not *necessarily* valid in multi-agent setting where agents may have heterogeneous (different) preferences. A similar disaggregation will also apply in the case of guest workers and illegal immigrants. Such differences in preferences are exceedingly important in actual policy making. Standard trade theory has generally avoided this issue by appealing to the compensation principle. Becker (1985, p. 336) in this context states that "some of the pioneers claimed that a policy is beneficial as long as gainers could compensate losers, regardless of whether compensation were actually paid. This view is untenable except when the political process has equalized the marginal social 'worths' of gainers and losers, which begs the question of what determines actual policies. Nevertheless, distribution concerns continues to be neglected by most assessments of the harm from monopoly and other 'market failures', and by most evaluations of public policies; these essentially consider only whether gainers could compensate losers.". The results in several chapters of this book highlight both the need for and difficulties of evaluating welfare in a multi-agent setting.

Given utility maximization and a position of interior equilibrium for the representative agent, it follows that

$$\frac{U_2}{U_1} = \frac{P_2}{P_1} = P \qquad (2.2)$$

where U_i and P_i $(i = 1, 2)$ denote the marginal utility and the ith price, respectively. In a small open economy the terms of trade, P, are given exogenously. This condition shows that, in a position of utility maximizing equilibrium, the domestic rate of substitution in consumption equals the ratio of commodity prices and is the national counterpart of the condition of individual maximization in the theory of consumer behaviour. It should also be mentioned that the tangency condition in Equation (2.2) implies that maximizing national income is the same as maximizing an aggregate utility function.

Ever since the publication of the book by Dixit and Norman (1980) duality theory has been very popular in trade theory.[4] Although it has added little in terms of obtaining significant new results, nevertheless it has made important contributions in terms of writing elegant and simple proofs of many results in the theory of trade. Corresponding to the utility function we now introduce two concepts: first, that of the indirect utility function, and second the expenditure function.

We first define the indirect utility function. Assume that the consumer has maximized utility subject to a budget constraint and that his/her demand functions are denoted by D_i^* ($i = 1, 2$). These demand functions depend on prices and income, hence, the indirect utility function can be written as

$$V = V(P_1, P_2, I) = V(D_1^*(P_1, P_2, I), D_2^*(P_1, P_2, I)) \qquad (2.3)$$

where I denotes nominal income. The indirect utility function V is non-increasing in prices, P_1, P_2 and non-decreasing in income, I. In certain problems it is more elegant and useful to use V rather than U. The indirect utility function can be used to perform all the functions that are accomplished by using the direct form, for example, the function can be used to generate the ordinary demand curves by using Roy's Identity.

In addition to the indirect utility function the concept of an expenditure function is also widely used in trade theory. This function is derived by minimizing expenditure subject to a specified

---

[4] Duality is easily defined in terms of sets and propositions relating to those sets. Consider sets A and B and operators α and β on these sets. If a given proposition is valid, then sometimes it might be possible to obtain a second valid proposition from it by interchanging the sets *(B* for *A)* and the two operators *(β* for *α)* as well. Mathematically this states that $\alpha A \leftrightarrow \beta B$. This is satisfied in the case of Rybczynski and Stolper–Samuelson theorems. When this is possible, we usually refer to the original propositions as the primal and the second as its dual. The Rybczynski and Stolper–Samuelson theorems satisfy the duality relationship.

level of utility at a given level of prices. It is denoted as

$$e = e[P_1, P_2; \bar{U}] \tag{2.4}$$

where e denotes expenditure at prices given by P_1 and P_2 such that the specified level of utility $\bar{U}$ is attained. The expenditure function is concave, linearly homogeneous and, by Shephard's lemma, its partial derivatives provide the Hicksian or income compensated demand functions.

In an open economy, local supply and demand are not equal to each other. Throughout this book we shall generally assume that commodity one (denoted by 1) is imported and good two (denoted by 2) is exported. Hence,

$$D_1 = X_1 + M_1 \tag{2.5}$$

$$D_2 = X_2 - E_2 \tag{2.6}$$

where X_1 indicates the level of output, M_1 imports of good 1 and E_2 exports of commodity X_2. This book is not concerned with an analysis of the pattern of trade; hence, for most of the book this pattern of trade will be assumed to prevail. However, when dealing with one-sector models and/or with two-sector models of growth where one of the goods is non-traded, the assumption about the pattern of trade will be suitably amended. In an open economy, markets need not clear locally and excess supply or demand can be met in the international markets as shown in Equations (2.5) and (2.6). In contrast with aggregate models, inventory accumulation (decumulation) is also omitted in Equations (2.5) and (2.6). Thus the markets, via price flexibility, adjust instantaneously. Non-traded goods are also introduced in this book. These are defined as commodities, which are cleared in the local market and not traded internationally. No attempt will be made to explain why certain goods become non-traded. In other words, the system will not be solved for the endogenous emergence of non-traded goods in a multi-good framework. In subsequent chapters, tourism is intro-duced as the consumption of non-traded goods by tourists. Thus, consumer mobility transforms non-traded into traded goods. This also holds for consumption of non-traded goods by foreign students, illegal migrants (workers) and guest workers. This adds a new dimension to trade theory, which has been presented historically in terms of commodity mobility and in recent years extended to include both labour and capital mobility. However, consumer mobility broadly defined to include temporary movement of other agents (students, guest workers) and its consequences for welfare have not been extensively explored in the literature.

It is appropriate now to specify the production side of the economy. The production relationship for the *i*th good is written as

$$X_i = F_i(K_i, L_i), \qquad i = 1, 2 \tag{2.7}$$

where K_i and L_i denote the amount of capital and labour allocation to the *i*th industry. Note that we have assumed the absence of externalities in specifying Equation (2.7). It is assumed that the production function satisfies the conditions of homogeneity of degree one, indispensability of factors of production and the Inada conditions. Given homogeneity, the production function in its intensive form is given below:

$$X_i = L_i F_i\left(\frac{K_i}{L_i}, 1\right) = L_i f_i(k_i), \qquad i = 1, 2 \tag{2.8}$$

The Inada conditions are

$$\lim_{k_i \to 0} f'(k_i) = \infty$$

$$\lim_{k_i \to \infty} f'(k_i) = 0$$

$$\lim_{k_i \to 0} f(k_i) = 0$$

$$\lim_{k_i \to \infty} f(k_i) = \infty$$

where $f'(k_i)$ denotes the marginal product of capital in the *i*th sector.

The intensive form of the production function is widely used in trade and growth literature and will be utilized in several chapters.

Initially both the factor and commodity markets are assumed to be perfectly competitive. These assumptions will be relaxed in later parts of the book when, for example, monopoly production, and/or monopoly power in trade, are introduced. Given the further assumption of profit maximization and an interior solution, it follows in equilibrium that the reward of each factor equals the value of its marginal product. These are now defined in real terms.

Good X_1 has been taken as the numeraire. Hence,

$$r = f'(k_1) = Pf'_2(k_2) \tag{2.9}$$

$$w = f_1(k_1) - k_1f'_1(k_1) = P[f_2(k_2) - k_2f'_2(k_2)] \tag{2.10}$$

where r denotes the rental on capital, w the wage rate and $P = P_2/P_1$ denotes the internationally given terms of trade. Later in the book the bracketed (k_i) will be dropped from the functions for notational convenience. From Equations (2.9) and (2.10) it follows that the ratio of factor rewards, ω, equals

$$\omega(k_i) = \frac{w}{r} = \frac{f_i(k_i)}{f'_i(k_i)} - k_i,$$

$$i = 1, 2 \text{ where } \omega = \frac{w}{r} \text{ (wage–rental ratio)} \tag{2.11}$$

These equilibrium conditions can also be written in an alternative form by exploiting the homogeneity property. By using this property the unit isoquants are expressed as

$$1 = F_i\left[\frac{K_i}{X_i}, \frac{L_i}{X_i}\right] = F_i[a_{Ki}, a_{Li}], \qquad i = 1, 2 \tag{2.12}$$

where the a_{ij}s denote the Leontief variable input coefficients. The two-sector model in the a_{ij} notation can be written in terms of the following equations:

$$c^1[w, r] = a_{L1}(w, r)w + a_{K1}(w, r)r = 1 \tag{2.13}$$

$$c^2[w, r] = a_{L2}(w, r)w + a_{K2}(w, r)r = P \tag{2.14}$$

In the equations below, the dependence of a_{ij}s on the factor prices has been dropped for mathematical convenience.

The terms c^1 and c^2 depict the cost functions which are concave in w and r. Equations (2.13) and (2.14) clearly show that the a_{ij}s are functions of the wage and rental rates. Given factor price flexibility, it follows that the two inelastically supplied factors of production are fully employed:

$$L_1 + L_2 = a_{L1}X_1 + a_{L2}X_2 = \bar{L} \tag{2.15}$$

$$k_1L_1 + k_2L_2 = a_{K1}X_1 + a_{K2}X_2 = \bar{K} \tag{2.16}$$

This model assumes that the aggregate supplies of labour and capital are given exogenously and that these inputs can be allocated between the sectors in a costless manner.

To complete the presentation of the dual side of the model one more concept needs to be introduced. It is the notion of a revenue function. In standard trade theory there are two commodities X_1 and X_2, and two inelastically supplied factors of production, capital K and labour L. The revenue function is the maximized value of $P_1 X_1 + P_2 X_2$ subject to the constraints of technology and factor endowments. Thus

$$\underset{X_1, X_2}{\text{Max}} \, P_1 X_1 + P_2 X_2 = P_1 F_1(K_1, L_1) + P_2 F_2(K_2, L_2)$$

subject to

$$L_1 + L_2 = \bar{L},$$

$$K_1 + K_2 = \bar{K}$$

The formal solution to this problem provides us with optimal values of K_i's and L_i's in terms of factor prices and endowments and we can obtain the revenue function in terms of goods prices and factor endowments. Let this be denoted as

$$R = R[P_1, P_2; \bar{K}, \bar{L}] \tag{2.17}$$

This function is convex in prices and concave in factor endowments. The function is also linear homogeneous in terms of the set of parameters $((P_1, P_2)$ and $(\bar{K}, \bar{L})$ taken separately). The revenue function has important and useful properties. These are given below:

(P1) $\dfrac{\partial R}{\partial P_1} = R_1 = X_1(P_1, P_2; \bar{K}, \bar{L}) = $ supply function for X_1 (2.18)

$\dfrac{\partial R}{\partial P_2} = R_2 = X_2(P_1, P_2; \bar{K}, \bar{L}) = $ supply function for X_2 (2.19)

(P2) $\dfrac{\partial R}{\partial \bar{K}} = R_{\bar{K}} = r = $ rental rate on capital   (2.20)

$\dfrac{\partial R}{\partial \bar{L}} = R_{\bar{L}} = w = $ wage rate   (2.21)

Thus, by differentiating the revenue function with respect to its arguments, P_1, P_2, $\bar{K}$ and $\bar{L}$ we can obtain the supply functions for X_1,

X_2 and the rewards of factors of production r and w. By taking second order derivatives of the above functions we obtain

$$\text{(P3)} \quad \frac{\partial^2 R}{\partial P_1^2} = R_{11} = \frac{\partial X_1(P_1, P_2; \bar{K}, \bar{L})}{\partial P_1} \geq 0 \tag{2.22}$$

$$\frac{\partial^2 R}{\partial P_2^2} = R_{22} = \frac{\partial X_2(P_1, P_2; \bar{K}, \bar{L})}{\partial P_2} \geq 0 \tag{2.23}$$

$$\text{(P4)} \quad \frac{\partial^2 R}{\partial \bar{K}^2} = R_{\bar{K}\bar{K}} = \frac{\partial r}{\partial \bar{K}} \leq 0 \tag{2.24}$$

$$\frac{\partial^2 R}{\partial \bar{L}^2} = R_{\bar{L}\bar{L}} = \frac{\partial w}{\partial \bar{L}} \leq 0 \tag{2.25}$$

Properties P3 and P4 follow from the assumption of the convexity of the revenue function in prices and concavity in endowments. The economic meaning of these conditions is that the supplies of output are non-decreasing in commodity prices and factor returns are non-increasing in factor supply.

From Young's theorem (also known as the Samuelson reciprocity condition) it follows that

$$\text{(P5)} \quad \frac{\partial^2 R}{\partial P_1 \, \partial \bar{L}} = \frac{\partial^2 R}{\partial \bar{L} \, \partial P_1} \tag{2.26}$$

Hence,

$$\frac{\partial w}{\partial P_1} = \frac{\partial X_1}{\partial \bar{L}} \tag{2.27}$$

$$\frac{\partial w}{\partial P_2} = \frac{\partial X_2}{\partial \bar{L}} \tag{2.28}$$

$$\frac{\partial r}{\partial P_1} = \frac{\partial X_1}{\partial \bar{K}} \tag{2.29}$$

and

$$\frac{\partial r}{\partial P_2} = \frac{\partial X_2}{\partial \bar{K}} \tag{2.30}$$

These relationships show the dual relations in the trade model and are nothing other than the Rybczynski–Stolper–Samuelson theorems.

These will be discussed in detail in Section 2.3. This completes the specification of the two-sector general equilibrium model and its tools. We now proceed to provide a treatment of the important relationships in trade theory.

2.3. Important relationships

Given the restrictions on the production functions, it is obvious from Equation (2.11) that the capital–labour ratios, k_i $(i = 1, 2)$ are uniquely determined by the wage–rental ratio. The relation between k_i and ω is obtained by differentiating Equation (2.11) with respect to ω:

$$\frac{\mathrm{d}k_i}{\mathrm{d}\omega} = -\frac{(f_i')^2}{f_i f_i''} > 0, \qquad i = 1, 2 \tag{2.31}$$

Equation (2.31) states that an increase in the wage–rental ratio results in an increase in the capital–labour ratio. The economic explanation follows from profit maximization (cost minimization) and the assumptions regarding the production functions. An increase in the wage–rental ratio represents an increase in the relative price of labour, so that profit maximizing firms substitute capital for labour, the relatively cheaper factor for the relatively dearer factor, leading to an increase in the capital–labour ratio.

Having established the monotonic and unique relation between the wage–rental ratio and factor intensities, we now proceed to explore the relation between the relative price of commodities and the wage–rental ratio. From Equation (2.9) it follows that

$$P = \frac{f_1'(k_1)}{f_2'(k_2)} \tag{2.32}$$

The right-hand side of Equation (2.32) is only a function of the wage–rental ratio ω. Let this function be denoted by $P(\omega)$. By differentiating $P(\omega)$ with respect to ω, we obtain

$$\frac{\omega}{P}\frac{\mathrm{d}P}{\mathrm{d}\omega} = \frac{\omega(k_1 - k_2)}{(\omega + k_1)(\omega + k_2)} \tag{2.33}$$

From Equation (2.33) it is clear that $(\omega/P)(\mathrm{d}P/\mathrm{d}\omega)$ is positive or negative, according to whether k_1 is greater or less than k_2. Therefore, the wage–rental ratio and commodity price ratios are related to each other via the physical factor intensity of the two sectors.

Figure 2.1. **(a) Factor intensity, wage–rental ratio and commodity prices for $k_1 > k_2$**

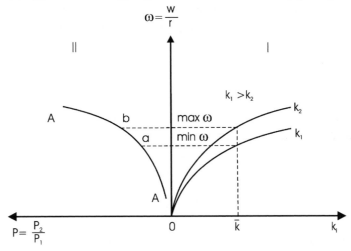

(b) Factor intensity, wage–rental ratio and commodity prices for $k_2 > k_1$

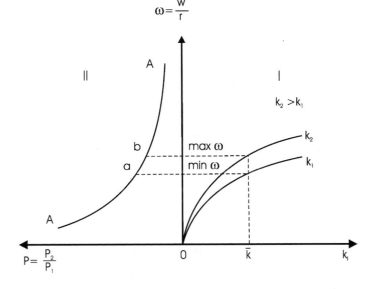

We are now in a position to construct the back-to-back diagram in which the relation between factor intensity, wage–rental ratio and commodity prices are all presented in one diagram. In Figure 2.1 we present the above relationship. An explanation of Figure 2.1(a) and a heuristic explanation of the result contained in Equation (2.11) follows. In quadrant I, the interrelationship between capital intensities, k_1 and k_2, and the wage–rental ratio ω is represented.

An increase in the wage–rental ratio results in an increase in the capital intensity in both sectors. This is shown by the curves k_1 and k_2. In quadrant II we present the relationship between the commodity–price ratio P and the wage–rental ratio ω. Given that $k_1 > k_2$, we know from Equation (2.33) that this is positive. The curve AA illustrates this relationship. The increase in the wage–rental ratio affects the relative price of the labour-intensive sector 2 proportionately more than that of the capital-intensive sector 1. Therefore, the relative price of commodity 2 rises more than that of commodity 1, hence, AA is positively sloped.

It is important here to draw attention to the fact that some points in Figure 2.1(a) are not feasible. The feasible points are obtained by imposing the full-employment condition on the model. Suppose the overall capital–labour ratio is given by $\bar{k}$. Let $O\bar{k}$ represent this ratio in Figure 2.1(a). It follows immediately that the range of variation (for incomplete specialization) in the wage–rental ratio is then given by points between minimum ω (min ω) and maximum ω (max ω). Obviously the economy is completely specialized in producing X_1 if min ω prevails and in producing X_2 if max ω becomes the established wage–rental ratio. The range of commodity price ratio for which the economy remains incompletely specialized is indicated by points that belong to the open internal $]a, b[$ that is, at points that are between a and b in quadrant II of Figure 2.1(a).

In trade theory the most difficult relationship to derive is between the relative price ratio and the movements in the outputs as it involves most of the equations that have been presented. It is important to note here that this is not the case when duality is used. This relationship can be presented either by using primal (as in Hazari (1986)) or by using the dual and hat calculus. We will derive it from the latter. By differentiating Equations (2.15) and (2.16) we know that

$$\lambda_{L1}\hat{X}_1 + \lambda_{L2}\hat{X}_2 = -[\lambda_{L1}\hat{a}_{L1} + \lambda_{L2}\hat{a}_{L2}] \qquad (2.34)$$

$$\lambda_{K1}\hat{X}_1 + \lambda_{K2}\hat{X}_2 = -[\lambda_{K1}\hat{a}_{K1} + \lambda_{K2}\hat{a}_{K2}] \qquad (2.35)$$

where $\wedge$ denotes proportional change and λ_{ij}s the factor shares. By totally differentiating the relation that each λ_{ij}s is a function of the wage rate and rental on capital, we obtain

$$\hat{a}_{Li} = \frac{wc^i_{ww}(w, r)}{c^i_w(w, r)}\hat{w} + \frac{rc^i_{wr}(w, r)}{c^i_r(w, r)}\hat{r} \tag{2.36}$$

$$\hat{a}_{Ki} = \frac{rc^i_{rr}(w, r)}{c^i_r(w, r)}\hat{r} + \frac{wc^i_{rw}(w, r)}{c^i_w(w, r)}\hat{w} \tag{2.37}$$

We know from microeconomic theory that the cost functions, c^i, are linearly homogeneous; hence, it follows that their derivatives, c^i_w, c^i_r are homogeneous of degree zero. Hence,

$$wc^i_{ww} + rc^i_{wr} = 0 \tag{2.38}$$

$$rc^i_{rr} + wc^i_{rw} = 0 \tag{2.39}$$

We now define the elasticity of substitution in alternative but equivalent ways:

$$\sigma = \frac{\hat{K} - \hat{L}}{\hat{w} - \hat{r}} = \frac{(\hat{K} - \hat{X}) - (\hat{L} - \hat{X})}{\hat{w} - \hat{r}} = \frac{\hat{a}_K - \hat{a}_L}{\hat{w} - \hat{r}}$$

$$= \frac{c^i(\cdot)c^i_{rw}(\cdot)}{c_w(\cdot)c_r(\cdot)} \tag{2.40}$$

By using the above equations it can be easily established that

$$\hat{a}_{Li} = -\theta_{Ki}\sigma_i(\hat{w} - \hat{r}) \tag{2.41}$$

$$\hat{a}_{Ki} = \theta_{Li}\sigma_i(\hat{w} - \hat{r}) \tag{2.42}$$

where $\theta_{Ki} = ra_{Ki}/P_i$ and $\theta_{Li} = wa_{Li}/P_i$, that is the relative shares of capital and labour in the price of good i.

By differentiation Equations (2.13) and (2.14) and the use of hat calculus we obtain

$$\theta_{L1}\hat{w} + \theta_{K1}\hat{r} = 0 \tag{2.43}$$

$$\theta_{L2}\hat{w} + \theta_{K2}\hat{r} = \hat{P} \tag{2.44}$$

By solving Equations (2.43) and (2.44) we obtain

$$\hat{w} = -\frac{\theta_{K1}\hat{P}}{|\theta|} \tag{2.45}$$

and

$$\hat{r} = \frac{\theta_{L1}\hat{P}}{|\theta|} \tag{2.46}$$

where $|\theta| = \theta_{L1}\theta_{L2}(k_2 - k_1)$. Hence, $|\theta| > 0$ (< 0) as $k_2 - k_1 > 0$ (< 0).

From Equations (2.45) and (2.46) it is clear that

$$\hat{w} - \hat{r} = -\frac{\hat{P}}{|\theta|} \tag{2.47}$$

We are now in a position to re-write Equations (2.34) and (2.35) in the following manner:

$$\lambda_{L1}\hat{X}_1 + \lambda_{L2}\hat{X}_2 = \beta_L\hat{P} \tag{2.48}$$

$$\lambda_{K1}\hat{X}_1 + \lambda_{K2}\hat{X}_2 = -\beta_K\hat{P} \tag{2.49}$$

where

$$\beta_L = \lambda_{L1}\theta_{K1}\sigma_1 + \lambda_{L2}\theta_{K2}\sigma_2 > 0 \qquad \text{and}$$

$$\beta_K = \lambda_{K1}\theta_{L1}\sigma_1 + \lambda_{K2}\theta_{L2}\sigma_2 > 0.$$

By solving the system of equations (2.48) and (2.49) we obtain

$$\hat{X}_1 = -\frac{\lambda_{K2}\beta_L + \lambda_{L2}\beta_K}{|\theta||\lambda|}\hat{P} \tag{2.50}$$

$$\hat{X}_2 = \frac{\lambda_{K1}\beta_L + \lambda_{L1}\beta_K}{|\theta||\lambda|}\hat{P} \tag{2.51}$$

where $|\lambda| = \lambda_{L1}\lambda_{L2}(k_2 - k_1) > 0$ and $|\theta| = \theta_{L1}\theta_{L2}(k_2 - k_1) > 0$.

From Equations (2.50) and (2.51) it is clear that $\hat{X}_1 < 0$ and $\hat{X}_2 > 0$, hence, the respective supply curves are upward sloping. Note that duality makes it very easy to establish that the supply curve is upward sloping. The only reason for presenting this alternative way of deriving the supply curves is that it is still widely used in the trade literature.

2.4. Duality relations in the small open economy model

In this section we present two important propositions, the Rybczynski and the Stolper–Samuelson theorems, which are duals of each other. Consider the subsystem consisting of Equations (2.7)–(2.10) and (2.15)–(2.16). This subsystem consists of eight equations in eight unknowns: X_1, X_2, L_1, L_2, k_1, k_2, w and r as in the case of a small open economy ($P \equiv P_2/P_1$) is exogenously given. This sub-system describes the production side of the economy. Two different questions can be posed about this system. First, what happens to outputs when factor endowments change (either $\bar{K}$, $\bar{L}$, or both) at constant commodity prices (constant P_1 and P_2 and in some interpretations P). These are known as factor endowment theorems. Second, what happens to factor prices when commodity prices change (either P_1, P_2 or both) and factor endowments are held constant (i.e. $\bar{K}$ and $\bar{L}$ are kept at a fixed level)? These are known as price-factor income relationships (theorems).

We shall first examine the factor endowment–output relationships and then take up the price–factor income relationship. Let us first consider the implications of an increase in the capital stock $\bar{K}$ on levels of output at constant prices. This can be accomplished by differentiating the production function with respect to $\bar{K}$. With prices held constant, it follows that the optimal capital–labour ratio will remain undisturbed as long as both industries have positive outputs. Hence, by differentiating Equation (2.7) with respect to $\bar{K}$, we obtain

$$\frac{\mathrm{d}X_i}{\mathrm{d}\bar{K}} = f_i \frac{\mathrm{d}L_i}{\mathrm{d}\bar{K}}, \qquad i = 1, 2 \tag{2.52}$$

and from the factor endowment conditions (2.15) and (2.16) we obtain

$$\frac{\mathrm{d}L_1}{\mathrm{d}\bar{K}} = \frac{1}{(k_2 - k_1)} \tag{2.53}$$

$$\frac{\mathrm{d}L_2}{\mathrm{d}\bar{K}} = -\frac{1}{(k_2 - k_1)} \tag{2.54}$$

Substituting from Equations (2.53) and (2.54) into Equation (2.52) we obtain

$$\frac{dX_1}{d\bar{K}} = -\frac{f_1}{(k_2 - k_1)}, \qquad \text{or} \qquad \hat{X}_1 = -\frac{\lambda_{K2}}{|\lambda|}\hat{K} \qquad (2.55)$$

$$\frac{dX_2}{d\bar{K}} = \frac{f_2}{(k_2 - k_1)}, \qquad \text{or} \qquad \hat{X}_2 = \frac{\lambda_{L2}}{|\lambda|}\hat{K} \qquad (2.56)$$

Similarly

$$\frac{dX_1}{d\bar{L}} = \frac{k_2 f_1}{(k_2 - k_1)}, \qquad \text{or} \qquad \hat{X}_1 = \frac{\lambda_{K2}}{|\lambda|}\hat{L} \qquad (2.57)$$

$$\frac{dX_2}{d\bar{L}} = -\frac{k_1 f_2}{(k_2 - k_1)}, \qquad \text{or} \qquad \hat{X}_2 = -\frac{\lambda_{L2}}{|\lambda|}\hat{L} \qquad (2.58)$$

From Equations (2.55)–(2.58), the Rybczynski theorem is easily obtained. Note that the alternative expressions in hat calculus have been derived by using the structure of the model written in terms of the unit cost equations.

Theorem 2.1 (Rybczynski theorem). *In an incompletely specialized two-factor, two-commodity economy, an increase in the endowment of any factor, at constant prices, results in an increase in the output of the industry that uses the factor intensively and a decrease in the output of the other industry.*

This is a remarkable theorem, for it shows that an increase in the endowment of a factor does not lead to an increase in all outputs, but to the contrary leads to an absolute increase (decline) in the output of one industry and a decline in the output of the other industry. The intuitive explanation of the above result can easily be brought out by analyzing the following equation regarding the factor endowments (from Equation 2.16):

$$k_1 \frac{L_1}{\bar{L}} + k_2 \frac{L_2}{\bar{L}} = \frac{\bar{K}}{\bar{L}} = k, \qquad \text{or} \qquad k_1 l_1 + k_2 l_2 = k \qquad (2.59)$$

Note that $l_1 + l_2 = 1$ where l_i ($i = 1, 2$) indicate the proportion of labour allocated to each sector, and therefore, are less than unity at the point of an interior equilibrium. If we suppose that $\bar{K}$ increases, then the expression on the right-hand side of the above equation (k) rises, hence, the left-hand side must also rise. At constant prices k_1 and k_2 cannot change, and hence, all adjustments must occur through changes in l_1 and l_2. Assuming that $k_1 > k_2$, then the only way the left-hand side can rise is through an increase in l_1 which implies that l_2 must fall. It is obvious from the production function for X_2 that a decrease in l_2 with constant k_2 implies that the output of X_2, the labour-intensive sector, must decline.

The Rybczynski theorem is presented geometrically with the help of either the isoquant diagram or the box diagram. Both types of diagrams are presented in Figure 2.2(a) and (b).

Consider Figure 2.2(a) first. An explanation is only provided for the isoquant diagram. However, in later parts of this book the Edgeworth–Bowley box diagram is used in several places. Let us suppose that at factor prices given by the slope of line CA, production equilibrium occurs at points R_1 and R_2 where the unit isoquants of commodities X_1 and X_2 are tangential to the line CA. The factor intensities of commodities X_1 and X_2 are indicated by the slope of the lines OR_1 and OR_2. Since X_1 is the capital-intensive commodity the slope of OR_1 is greater than that of OR_2. Point E indicates the endowment point (sum of vectors OR_1 and OR_2), that is the overall availability of capital and labour. Now suppose that capital stock increases from $A'E$ to $A'E'$, so that the new endowment point becomes E'. Given fixed commodity and factor prices, which imply unchanged factor intensities, the new production equilibrium must occur along the rays OR_1 and OR_2. The production equilibrium compatible with full employment is given by points R'_1 and R'_2 (isoquants have been omitted). The point R'_1 indicates a higher output of the capital-intensive commodity X_1 and R'_2 lower output of the labour-intensive commodity X_2. The same result is depicted in Figure 2.2(b) in terms of the box diagram.

We now proceed to examine the relation between changes in individual (nominal) commodity prices and factor rewards. We have already established that an increase in the commodity price ratio results in an increase (decrease) in the wage–rental ratio if sector 1 is capital-intensive (labour-intensive) compared with sector 2 and that the elasticity of this relation is greater than -1 and less than 1.

Figure 2.2.   (a) The Rybczynski theorem

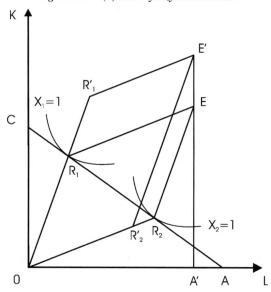

(b) The Edgeworth–Bowley box diagram and the Rybczynski theorem

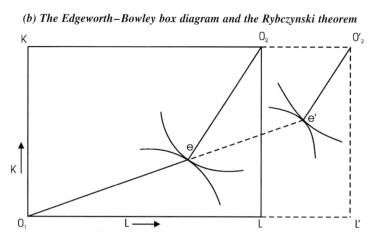

Sometimes this is used as a version of the Stolper–Samuelson theorem. Another version of the Stolper–Samuelson theorem relates movements in individual (nominal) commodity prices to individual factor rewards rather than to the ratio of factor rewards. By differentiating Equations (2.9) and (2.10) logarithmically with respect to P_1 and P_2 we obtain

$$\frac{\text{d}\log r}{\text{d}\log P_1} = -\frac{(k_1 + \omega)}{(k_2 - k_1)}, \qquad \text{or} \qquad \hat{r} = -\frac{\theta_{L2}\hat{P}_1}{|\theta|} \qquad (2.60)$$

$$\frac{\text{d}\log r}{\text{d}\log P_2} = -\frac{(k_2 + \omega)}{(k_2 - k_1)}, \qquad \text{or} \qquad \hat{r} = -\frac{\theta_{L1}\hat{P}_2}{|\theta|} \qquad (2.61)$$

$$\frac{\text{d}\log w}{\text{d}\log P_1} = -\frac{k_2(k_1 + \omega)}{w(k_1 - k_2)}, \qquad \text{or} \qquad \hat{w} = \frac{\theta_{K2}}{|\theta|}\hat{P}_1 \qquad (2.62)$$

$$\frac{\text{d}\log w}{\text{d}\log P_2} = -\frac{k_1(k_2 + \omega)}{w(k_1 - k_2)}, \qquad \text{or} \qquad \hat{w} = -\frac{\theta_{K1}}{|\theta|}\hat{P}_2 \qquad (2.63)$$

Equations (2.60)–(2.63) clearly demonstrate that the movements in individual factor rewards and individual commodity prices depend on the factor intensities of the two sectors. The hat calculus version of the theorems is derived from the unit cost equations. For example, an increase in the price of commodity 1 raises the rental on capital and lowers the wage rate provided $k_1 > k_2$. The reverse holds when $k_1 < k_2$. Moreover, the elasticity of these responses, specifically d log r/d log P_1 and d log w/d log P_1 are greater than 1 when $k_1 > k_2$ while d log r/d log P_2 and d log w/d log P_2 are less than 1 for $k_1 > k_2$. Similar results can be stated for $k_1 < k_2$.

We state the Stolper–Samuelson theorem below:

Theorem 2.2 (Stolper–Samuelson theorem). *In an incompletely specialized two-factor, two-commodity economy an increase in the price of any commodity raises the real reward of the factor used intensively in the production of the commodity of which the price has increased and decreases the reward of the other factor.*

This theorem is demonstrated diagrammatically in Figure 2.3 by the use of price isoquants. Let $P_1 = 1$ be the unit-price isoquant for commodity 1 and P_2 be the price isoquant for commodity 2. These isoquants show the combinations of wage and rental on capital such that the same price is maintained along the entire isoquant. The point of intersection between the two isoquants provides the initial equilibrium values of r and w which are denoted by r^* and w^*. It is assumed that commodity X_1 is capital intensive. Let us suppose that the price of the labour intensive good increases. This is shown by the shift in the price isoquant from P_2 to P_2'. At the new equilibrium

Figure 2.3.　Factor prices

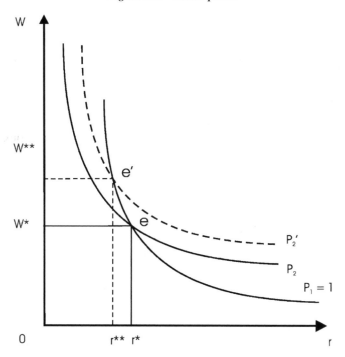

point as shown by e' the rental on capital falls from r to r^{**} and the wage rises from w to w^{**}. Furthermore, the marginal product of labour rises in terms of both the commodities and the marginal product of capital falls in terms of both commodities. This is indeed a remarkable result because of the way in which it avoids the index number problem in obtaining the impact of a change in commodity price on factor rewards. However, it is difficult to avoid the index number problems in more generalized models where there are many factors and goods.

Having established both the Rybczynski and the Stolper–Samuelson results our remaining task is to show that the theorems are duals of each other. The duality between the Rybczynski and Stolper–Samuelson theorems follows from the fact that

$$\frac{\mathrm{d}w}{\mathrm{d}P_j} = \frac{\mathrm{d}X_j}{\mathrm{d}\bar{L}}, \qquad j = 1, 2 \tag{2.64}$$

and

$$\frac{\mathrm{d}r}{\mathrm{d}P_j} = \frac{\mathrm{d}X_j}{\mathrm{d}\bar{K}}, \qquad j = 1, 2 \tag{2.65}$$

2.5. A digression: the production possibility curve

We have presented above the major results of a two-sector model of a small open economy. However, all this has been achieved without introducing the production possibility curve (also known as the transformation curve). Many results in trade theory are either proved or illustrated with the help of the production possibility surface. In this section we take a digression to establish this concept. The production possibility curve shows the various combinations of the two commodities, which might be produced under certain market conditions. Given our assumption of competitive markets, it represents the maximum possible output of one commodity given the output of the other that is $X_1 = X_1(X_2)$.

The production possibility curve is generally derived with the help of the Edgeworth–Bowley box diagram.[5] Since the two factors of production are fixed in supply, a box can be constructed, as in Figure 2.4, the dimensions of which represent the total supply of factors of production. Given our assumptions about the nature of production functions the level of output can be measured by the distances of their isoquants from the respective origin. The diagonal O_1O_2 measures the overall capital–labour ratio, $k = \bar{K}/\bar{L}$. This diagram plays an important role in the derivation of the production possibility schedule. Each point of a particular isoquant represents the same level of output, and hence, the output of each commodity can be measured by the intersection between the isoquant and the diagonal of the box. For example, the output of the first commodity X_1, represented by isoquant X_1 and X_1', is indicated by O_1a_1 and O_1a_1', respectively. The points O_2b_2 and O_2b_2' can be interpreted in a similar manner. Given these interpretations of points along the diagonal, a movement away from O_1 towards O_2 represents an increase in the output of the first commodity X_1 and a decline in the output of the second commodity X_2 and vice versa.

By introducing the Pareto optimality criterion, the contract locus and the production possibility curve is derived. This criterion states that a production point is efficient if every other feasible reallocation of inputs results in a decrease in the output of at least one commodity.

---

[5] This technique was first introduced by Savosnick (1958).

Figure 2.4.   *From the Edgeworth–Bowley box to the production possibility frontier*

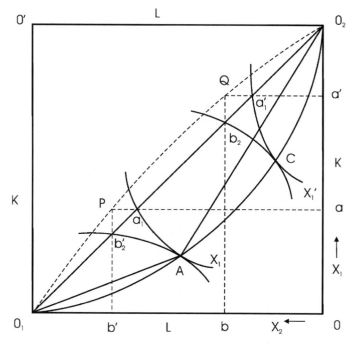

In view of this criterion, efficiency in the allocation of the two resources labour and capital can be attained at points such as A and C, where the isoquants of the two-commodities are tangential to each other. The locus of all tangency points, the curve O_1ACO_2, is called the contract curve or the efficiency locus.

The position of the contract curve in the box depends on the assumption regarding the capital intensity of the two sectors. The contract curve in the diagram lies below the diagonal because of our assumption that sector X_2 is capital-intensive relative to sector X_1. Hence, the slope of O_1A (the capital–labour ratio in X_1) with respect to the O_1O axis is less than the capital–labour ratio in X_2, which is given by the slope of O_2A with respect to O_2O' axis. If, instead of X_2, X_1 was the capital-intensive commodity, then the contract curve would be entirely above the diagonal. If the capital intensities of the two sectors are identical, then the diagonal in effect becomes the contract curve and also the production possibility locus.

The production possibilities curve can be derived from the contract curve. We have already established that various points on the diagonal represent different levels of output of each commodity.

If we transform this measuring scale to the vertical and the horizontal axis with the origin O, the transformation curve can be obtained. For example, the output levels of X_1, given by points a_1 and a_1' on the diagonal, can be projected towards the OO_2 axis to points a and a', respectively. Since the production functions are assumed to be homogeneous of degree one, the distance $O_1 a_1'$ is in exactly the same proportion by which Oa' exceeds Oa. Similarly the output of X_2 can be projected to obtain the points on the horizontal and vertical axis. The output associated with point A is given, respectively, by Oa and Ob'. The output combination given by points a and b' determines the point P in the commodity space. In similar fashion the output combination at C is associated with point Q in the output space. The locus of all such points is called the production possibility curve, which is given by $O_1 PQO_2$. The production possibility curve is concave towards the origin. This is due to our assumption of constant returns to scale, differences in the factor intensity of the two sectors and the applications of Pareto optimality criterion. Note that if $k_1 = k_2$ then the economy has a straight-line transformation curve as stated earlier.

So far we have concentrated on deriving the shape of the production possibility locus. However, we have not determined the point at which production equilibrium occurs. By differentiating Equation (2.7) totally, we obtain

$$dX_1 = \frac{\partial F_1}{\partial K_1} dK_1 + \frac{\partial F_1}{\partial L_1} dL_1$$

and

$$dX_2 = \frac{\partial F_2}{\partial K_2} dK_2 + \frac{\partial F_2}{\partial L_2} dL_2$$

From Equations (2.9) and (2.10), we know that $r = (\partial F_1/\partial K_1) = P(\partial F_2/\partial K_2)$ and that $w = (\partial F_1/\partial L_1) = P(\partial F_2/\partial L_2)$. It also follows from the full employment conditions that $dL_2 = -dL_1$ and $dK_2 = -dK_1$. By making appropriate substitutions, we obtain

$$-\frac{dX_1}{dX_2} = \text{DRT} = P$$

where $-dX_1/dX_2$ represents the slope of the production possibility schedule and is defined as the domestic rate of transformation (DRT).

The condition derived above shows that in competitive equilibrium the slope of the production possibility curve equals the commodity–price ratio. This also equals the slope of the social indifference curve as at a point of utility maximization the ratio of marginal utilities, DRS, also equals P, hence, DRS = DRT = P

Figure 2.5.   (a) Autarky equilibrium

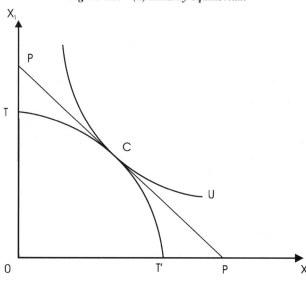

(b) Free trade equilibrium

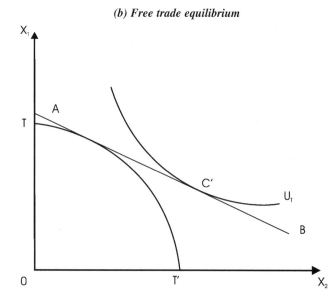

where P is the domestic price ratio. This is shown in Figure 2.5(a) where the competitive equilibrium is at point C.

In Figure 2.5(b), AB represents the world price ratio and for a small open economy this equals FRT. This is different from the autarky price ratio. The equilibrium point is now obtained where the slope of the social indifference curve, U_T, is tangential to AB. Hence, DRS = FRT which in turn equals DRT. This is shown by the point C' in the diagram. At this point the ratio of international prices equals the domestic rate of transformation (DRT) which in turn equals the domestic rate of substitution (DRT = DRS = P = FRT).

The concavity of the production possibility curve, coupled with the equilibrium condition that the ratio of prices equals the domestic rate of transformation, implies that an increase in the relative price of X_2 results in an increase in the output of commodity X_2, a result that has already been established from duality. It should be pointed out here that the concavity of the locus is not a sufficient condition for the positive relationship between own price change and output movements. For instance, in the case of wage differentials perverse price output movements can occur in spite of the concavity of the production possibility locus.

2.6. Trade and distortion theory

The results obtained so far have been based on the assumption that markets are competitive both on the factor and commodity side. However, many markets are known to be non-competitive. These market imperfections or distortions may be captured in terms of the following four distortions:[6]

(1) DRS = FRT $\neq$ DRT
(2) DRS = DRT $\neq$ FRT
(3) DRS $\neq$ DRT = FRT
(4) Shrinkage of the production possibility locus

Throughout this book the relation between temporary mobility to consume non-traded goods and distortions will be highlighted and

---

[6] This terminology was introduced by Bhagwati and Ramaswami (1963)

Figure 2.6.　Shrinkage of the production possibility frontier

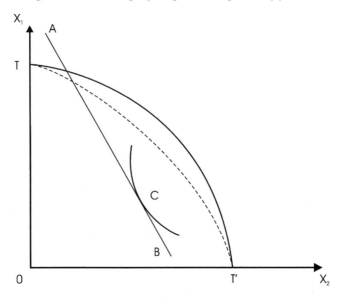

exploited for deriving both positive and normative results. In several chapters, for example, it will be demonstrated that tourism creates monopoly power in trade. The implication of this distortion will be discussed and analyzed both from a theoretical and policy perspective. It is this feature of tourism and temporary mobility that will be a dominant theme of this work, hence, the need for providing a brief discussion of distortion theory in this chapter.

Distortions (1) and (4) sometimes occur together, for example, in the case of a wage differential and a binding real minimum wage constraint. In this case DRS = FRT ≠ DRT and the production possibility locus shrinks. This distortion is shown in Figure 2.6 (extensively elaborated in Hazari (1978)) where TT'dashed represents the shrunken locus and DRS = FRT ≠ DRT. This is a case of a domestic distortion. Distortion (2) arises in the foreign market either by the presence of monopoly power in trade or in the case of a small country by the imposition of a tariff. The monopoly power in trade case is represented in Figure 2.7(a) and (b). In Figure 2.7(a) it is shown that at the equilibrium point C, DRS = DRT ≠ FRT as the slope of the indifference curve at point C is not equal to the slope of the offer curve OO'. The marginal and average terms of trade are not equal to each other. Hence, and

Figure 2.7. *(a) Monopoly power in trade*

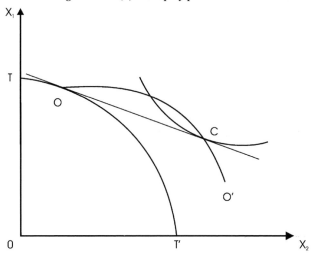

(b) Optimal tariff

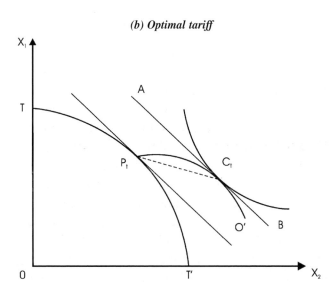

importantly, free trade is not the optimal policy. This distortion can be corrected by using an optimal tariff as shown in Figure 2.7(b) where the imposition of an optimal tariff brings into equality the three rates of substitution, namely, DRS = DRT = FRT. The wedge between the slope of AB and P_tC_t is the rate of optimal tariff. It will be shown in this book that tourism generates monopoly power in trade and if this distortion is left uncorrected, then all the perverse results of distortion theory apply to the analysis of both supply and/or demand side booms associated with global tourism.

2.7. Conclusion

This chapter provides an introduction to major results in trade theory utilizing a two-sector general equilibrium model. Its main objective is to make this book self-contained for economists and tourism specialists who are not familiar with trade theory. We will draw on the material presented in this chapter in later parts of the book.

References

Becker, G.S. (1985), "Public policies, pressure groups, and dead weight costs", *Journal of Public Economics*, Vol. 28, pp. 329–347.
Bhagwati, J.N. (1959), "Protection, real wages and real incomes", *Economic Journal*, Vol. 69, pp. 733–748.
Bhagwati, J.N. (1964), "The pure theory of international trade: a survey", *Economic Journal*, Vol. 74, pp. 1–78.
Bhagwati, J.N. (1971), "The generalized theory of distortions and welfare", in: J.N. Bhagwati, R.W. Jones, R.A. Mundell and J. Vanek, editors, *Trade Balance of Payments and Growth, Papers in International Economics in Honour of C.P. Kindleberger*, Amsterdam: North Holland Publishers.
Bhagwati, J.N. and V.K. Ramaswami (1963), "Domestic distortions, tariff and the theory of optimum subsidy", *Journal of Political Economy*, Vol. 71, pp. 44–50.
Bhagwati, J.N., A. Panagariya and T.N. Srinivasan (1998), *Lectures on International Trade*, Cambridge, MA: The MIT Press.
Caves, R.E. (1960), *Trade and Economic Structure: Models and Methods*, Cambridge: Harvard University Press, pp. 169–174.
Chipman, J.S. (1965), "A survey of the theory of international trade. Part 2. The neoclassical theory", *Econometrica*, Vol. 33, pp. 685–760.
Chipman, J.S. (1970), "External economies of scale and competitive equilibrium", *Quarterly Journal of Economics*, Vol. 34, pp. 347–385.
Dixit, A. and V. Norman (1980), *Theory of International Trade*, Cambridge: Cambridge University Press.
Eisenberg, E. (1961), "Aggregation of utility functions", *Management Science*, Vol. 7(July), pp. 337–350.
Ethier, W. (1974), "Some of the theorems of international trade with many goods and factors", *Journal of International Economics*, Vol. 4, pp. 199–206.
Hare, R.M. (1964), *The Language of Morals*, London: Oxford University Press.
Hare, R.M. (1965), *Freedom and Reason*, London: Oxford University Press.

Hazari, B.R. (1978), *Distortions and the Pure Theory of International Trade*, London: Croom Helm.

Hazari, B.R. (1986), *International Trade: Theoretical Issues*, London: Croom Helm.

Jones, R.W. (1965a), "Duality in international trade: a geometrical note", *Canadian Journal of Economics and Political Science*, Vol. 31(August), pp. 390–393.

Jones, R.W. (1965b), "The structure of simple general equilibrium model", *Journal of Political Economy*, Vol. 73(December), pp. 557–572.

Jones, R.W. (1971), "A three-factor model in theory, trade and history", in: J.N. Bhagwati, R.W. Jones, R.A. Mundell and J. Vanek, editors, *Trade, Balance of Payments and Growth: Essays in Honor of C.P. Kindleberger*, Amsterdam: North Holland Publishers.

Jones, R.W. (1977), "Two-ness in trade theory: costs and benefits", *Special Papers in International Economics*, No. 12, Princeton: Princeton University Press.

Kemp, M.C. (1969), *The Pure Theory of International Trade and Investment*, Englewood Cliffs, NJ: Prentice Hall, Appendix to Chapter 1.

Kemp, M.C. and H.Y. Wan (1976), "Relatively simple generalizations of the Stolper–Samuelson and Samuelson–Rybczynski theorems", in: M.C. Kemp, editor, *Three Topics in the Theory of International Trade, Distribution, Welfare and Uncertainty*, Studies in International Economics, Vol. 2, pp. 49–59, Amsterdam.

Kolm, S. (1996), *Modern Theory of Justice*, Cambridge, MA: The MIT Press.

Krauss, M.B., H.G. Johnson and T. Skouras (1973), "On the shape and location of the production possibility curve", *Economica*, Vol. 40, pp. 305–310.

Melvin, J.R. (1971), "On the derivation of the production possibility curve", *Economica*, Vol. 38, pp. 281–294.

Melvin, J.R. (1974), "On the equivalent of community indifference and the aggregate consumption function", *Economica*, pp. 442–445.

Mussa, M. (1979), "The two-sector model in terms of its dual: a geometrical exposition", *Journal of International Economics*, Vol. 9, pp. 513–526.

Rybczynski, T.M. (1955), "Factor endowment and relative commodity prices", *Economica*, Vol. 22(November), pp. 181–197.

Samuelson, P.A. (1953–1954), "Prices of factors and goods in general equilibrium", *Review of Eco Studies*, Vol. 21, pp. 1–20.

Samuelson, P.A. (1956), "Social indifference curves", *Quarterly Journal of Economics*, Vol. 701(February), pp. 1–22.

Savosnick, K.M. (1958), "The box diagram and the production possibility curve", *Ekonomisk Tidskrift*, Vol. 60(September), pp. 183–197.

Sgro, P.M. (1980), "Price distortions, joint production and some international trade theorems", *Welwirtschaftliches Archiv*, Vol. 116, pp. 657–668.

Stolper, W.F. and P.A. Samuelson (1941), *Protection and Real Wages, Review of Economic Studies*, Vol. 9, pp. 58–73. Reprinted in *International Trade*, J. Bhagwati, editor, Baltimore: Penguin, 1969.

Uekawa, Y. (1971), "Generalization of the Stolper–Samuelson theorem", *Econometrica*, Vol. 39, pp. 197–217.

Uekawa, Y., M.C. Kemp and L.L. Wegge (1973), "P- and PN-Matrices, Minkowski- and Metzler-Matrices, and generalizations of the Stolper–Samuelson and Samuelson–Rybczynski Theorems", *Journal of International Economics*, Vol. 3, pp. 53–76.

CHAPTER 3

Non-traded Goods and Tourism in the Pure Theory of Trade

3.1. Introduction

This chapter modifies the two-sector general equilibrium model already presented in Chapter 2 to include non-traded goods and tourism. Tourism is a growing economic activity and many countries promote tourism as a device for earning foreign exchange and promoting domestic welfare and growth. Typical examples of countries which significantly depend on tourist-generated income include: Singapore, Thailand, Hong Kong, Cyprus, Fiji, Caribbean Islands and Tunisia. In Cyprus, for example, tourism accounts for nearly 20% of its gross domestic product. In all these countries the non-traded goods (internationally not traded) and services are consumed by both domestic residents and tourists. Examples include hotels in resort areas of Cyprus, Thailand and Fiji, taxis, food establishments and public transportation. Tourists also consume public and club goods both free and priced, for example, the famous Twelve Apostles on the Great Ocean Road in Australia and the Louvre in France. Tourism, in essence, is the theory of trade of non-traded goods and services. Tourism shares this feature with guest workers, illegal migrants and international students, all of whom transform non-traded goods into traded goods.

An important difference between the consumption of non-traded goods and services by local residents and by tourists is that the latter convert the non-traded goods and services into an exportable. However, these non-traded goods and services are not an exportable in the traditional sense of the term because their price is determined in the local market and not in international markets. Moreover, for the purpose of consuming the product, it is the consumer who moves rather than the product itself. Such a movement of agents can be a possible source of externalities, such as petty crime and congestion. To consume the splendour of Notre Dame, the tourist has to visit Paris as the transportation costs of moving Notre Dame are infinite. Note that Notre Dame is a quasi-public good and is available for consumption by tourists free of any charge. However, the French residents pay for it via taxes. In this book we do not analyse the problem of free-riding by tourists. Tourists' consumption of non-traded goods and services has an impact on the relative price and availability of the non-traded goods and services for the domestic consumers. In the tourist-receiving country the relative price of the non-traded good is determined by foreign plus local demand and domestic supply. Hence, there is an element of monopoly power in trade as the average and marginal terms of trade need not be identical due to the demand by tourists. All countries are not the same and offer different non-traded goods and services to the tourists. It should be noted here that in many countries price discrimination is also practised – locals and tourists are charged different prices for the same good or service. The presence of discriminatory pricing represents an imperfection in the market. This aspect of tourism will be highlighted in a later chapter. It is important to stress here that if foreign tourist demand leaves the price of non-traded goods and services unchanged, then tourism is identical to exporting any other good. In this case there is no need for a separate analysis of tourism in trade theory. It should also be emphasized that countries that are small in trading goods may not be small in tourism, for example, Singapore is small in trading traditional goods but is not small in tourism. To incorporate the above points, we begin our analysis with the dependency model of trade. The main motivation for using the dependency model comes from its simplicity. Pedagogically, it represents an excellent model for understanding tourism as a transformation of non-traded into traded goods. We now proceed to develop the dependency model both analytically and geometrically.

3.2. The dependency model

It is assumed that two goods, a non-traded and an exportable, are produced in the home (or tourist-receiving) country. The exportable good is not consumed in the home country, an assumption that will be relaxed later in the book. These goods are produced with the help of the two inelastically supplied primary factors of production, labour and capital. On the consumption side, a representative agent consumes two goods: a non-traded good and an imported good, which are not produced locally. Thus, the exported good is not consumed domestically while the imported good is not produced locally. On the basis of this model, we shall demonstrate several significant features of the dependency model. The first feature is the determination of endogenous prices. The model has three relative prices: the terms of trade, that is, the relative price of exports in terms of imports (P_2/P_1), which are exogenously determined in the small country case; the ratio of producers prices (P_N/P_2) (which guides production) where P_N/P_2 is the relative price of the non-traded good and P_N/P_1 the ratio of prices that consumers face and which are endogenously determined. Thus, the model has both fixed and flexible prices – a feature absent in the Komiya (1967) model of non-traded goods and trade. This is a significant omission in the non-traded goods literature as it ignores the role of relative prices and their impact on resource allocation. It is this omission by Komiya that made the introduction of non-traded goods into trade theory less interesting and possibly trivial. In most small economies, non-traded goods prices change frequently without movements in the price of internationally traded goods. The second feature is the consequences of the difference between consumption and production space and finally we shall introduce tourism into this model.

The utility function for the country as a whole is normally given by $U = U(D_N, D_1)$. However, in the dependency model the autarky solution occurs at a corner point. Hence, a utility function that allows for zero consumption of one of the goods must be used. The specific form of the utility function chosen is

$$U = D_N^\alpha + D_1^\beta, \qquad 0 < \alpha < 1, \ 0 < \beta < 1 \tag{3.1}$$

where U indicates utility, D_N the consumption of non-traded good and D_1 the consumption of the imported good. The elasticity of substitution between the two goods is greater than 1. As usual, we assume that the marginal utilities U_i $(i = N, 1)$ are all positive and diminishing, that is, the second-order derivatives are negative.

Given the assumption of utility maximization and (at a point of an interior solution) it follows that

$$\frac{\alpha D_N^{\alpha-1}}{\beta D_1^{\beta-1}} = \frac{P_N}{P_1} = P_N \tag{3.2}$$

where the imported good is treated as the numeraire and its price, P_1 is set equal to 1. Thus, at the point of interior equilibrium, the relative price of non-traded goods equals the ratio of marginal utilities. Corner solutions occur at $D_1 = 0$ or at $D_N = 0$, while an autarky equilibrium occurs when $D_1 = 0$.

To obtain equilibrium in the markets for non-traded goods and imports of commodity 1, the following conditions must be satisfied:

$$D_N = X_N \tag{3.3}$$

$$D_1 = M_1 \tag{3.4}$$

where X_N represents the output of the non-traded good and M_1 the imports of commodity 1 which equals its consumption in the domestic market.

On the production side of the model, it is assumed that two commodities X_N and X_2 are produced with the help of two primary factors of production, capital, K, and labour, L, which are assumed to be in inelastic supply. Each production function is assumed to be linearly homogenous with constant returns to scale and diminishing returns to factors so that

$$X_i = F_i(K_i, L_i) = L_i f_i(k_i) \qquad (i = N, 2) \tag{3.5}$$

where L_i, K_i represent the allocation of labour and capital to the ith sector and the term k_i the capital–labour ratio in the ith sector.

The economy is assumed to be competitive so that, in equilibrium, the unit cost of production equals their price, hence:

$$c^2(w, r) = a_{L2}w + a_{K2}r = P_2 \tag{3.6}$$

$$c^N(w, r) = a_{LN}w + a_{KN}r = P_N \tag{3.7}$$

where a_{ij}'s denote input coefficients, w the wage rate, r the rental on capital, P_N the relative price of good X_N and P_2 the price of good X_2. The input coefficients are functions of the wage and rental rates as outlined in Chapter 2.

We define real income in terms of good 1 in the following manner:

$$I = D_1 + P_N D_N = PX_2 + P_N X_N = w\bar{L} + r\bar{K} \tag{3.8}$$

which states that income equals expenditure, which in turn equals the value of production and that in turn equals the sum of factor payments (the terms $P = P_2/P_1$ and $P_N = P_N/P_1$). Autarky equilibrium is characterized by the following equation (this occurs when $X_2 = 0$ and $M_1 = D_1 = 0$):

$$I = P_N D_N = P_N X_N = w\bar{L} + r\bar{K} \tag{3.9}$$

Similarly, in a trading equilibrium, if the country exports all of X_2 in exchange for M_1, then the economy will be characterized by the following solution:

$$I = D_1 = PX_2 = M_1 = w\bar{L} + r\bar{K} \tag{3.10}$$

It will be demonstrated later that the existence of corner solutions in this model can produce pathological welfare results.

Finally, it is assumed that both factors of production are fully employed:

$$a_{L2} X_2 + a_{LN} X_N = \bar{L} \tag{3.11}$$

$$a_{K2} X_2 + a_{KN} X_N = \bar{K} \tag{3.12}$$

Before presenting the model geometrically, a few remarks need to be made about closing the model and the price ratios that determine production, consumption and trade.

Remark 3.1. In the economy under consideration two goods X_2 and X_N are produced and their production is guided by the relative price ratio P_N/P_2. However, commodity X_2 is not consumed and therefore its price cannot *directly* affect the consumption of the two commodities consumed.

Remark 3.2. In free trade the commodities consumed are D_1 and D_N, hence, the relative price of the non-traded good in terms of the imported good along with income determine the consumption decision. Consumption occurs on the consumption possibility frontier, which is not the same as the production possibility frontier and is generated by using the terms of trade. Also note that P_2/P_1 is endogenously determined. This represents a distinction between prices that govern production from those that govern consumption – a feature that acquires some significance in introducing tourism in this model. This is also a feature that does not exist in the standard Heckscher–Ohlin (henceforth called HO) model of trade, where, as shown in Chapter 2, the prices that determine production are the same as those that determine consumption in the two-sector general equilibrium model.

Remark 3.3. Since this is an open economy model, the terms of trade are given by the price ratio $P_2/P_1 = P$. This price ratio plays the role of transforming the production space into consumption space which are different from each other. Thus, in the dependency model there are three price ratios: (P_N/P_2) which supports production; (P_N/P_1) which guides consumption (along with income); $(P_2/P_1 = P)$ the terms of trade. It is most important to note that the price ratios (P_N/P_2) and (P_N/P_1) are endogenously determined, along with the rest of the endogenous variables.

3.2.1. A four quadrant diagram and the determination of equilibrium with non-traded goods

In this section we develop a four-quadrant diagram for representing the dependency model. This diagram highlights the determination of all the endogenous commodity prices, but more importantly, demonstrates the significance of the dichotomy between the production and consumption spaces. Initially, we shall assume that the country is small and takes the terms of trade $(P_2/P_1 = P)$ as given. In Figure 3.1, in the left-hand top quadrant I, the production possibility locus TT' is represented. It is drawn with the assumption that the exportable sector, X_2, is more capital-intensive than the non-traded good sector, X_N, that is, $k_2 - k_N > 0$. The production possibility curve TT' is concave to the origin and the production possibility set is strictly convex. In the bottom left-hand quadrant II, exports are indicated by the horizontal axis X_2 and imports by the vertical axis M_1. The terms of trade, P, are represented by the slope

Figure 3.1. The dependency model

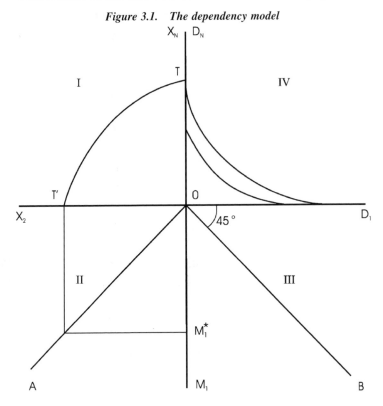

of the straight line OA in quadrant II. Given the small country assumption, the slope of OA translates or transforms the exportable good into an importable good, M_1. This is the foreign offer curve and its slope represents the FRT. For example, it shows that OT' of good X_2 can be exchanged for OM_1^* of the importable good. The line OB in quadrant III is a 45° line which transforms the M_1 vertical axis to the D_1 horizontal axis. The right-hand top quadrant IV shows the social indifference curves associated with the utility function. The information presented so far is not enough to determine the equilibrium; for this purpose we have to introduce a consumption possibility schedule.

3.2.2. Consumption possibility schedule

Using quadrants I–III a consumption possibility locus is derived in Figure 3.2. Let the terms of trade be given by the slope of the line OA. If production occurs at point T', then these terms of trade allow us to

Figure 3.2.   Consumption possibility schedule

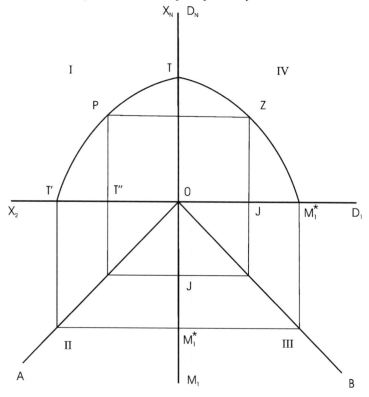

import OM_1^* of commodity M_1 in exchange for OT' of commodity X_2. By using the 45° line OB in quadrant III, we obtain OM_1^* of imports in the consumption space in quadrant IV. Let us now choose another point on the production transformation locus and let this point be denoted by P. At this point the economy produces OT'' of commodity X_2 which transforms to OJ units of the importable good M_1. By using the 45° line this transforms itself to point Z in the consumption space in quadrant IV. By using this procedure for all points in quadrant I, the consumption possibility locus TZM_1^* is generated. The separation between the production and consumption possibilities sets is clearly shown by this diagram. This separation arises because the commodities that are produced are not the same as the commodities that are consumed.

The diagram is now complete with production being shown in quadrant I, the terms of trade in quadrant II and the consumption

Figure 3.3.   Autarky and free trade equilibrium

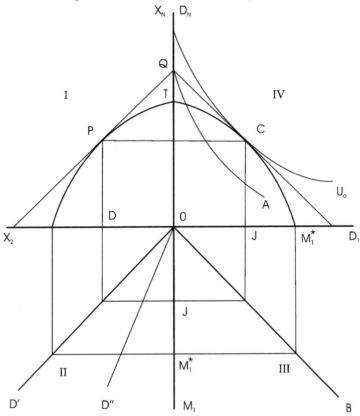

possibilities in quadrant IV. The equilibrium values of all the endogenous variables can now be determined. Autarky equilibrium is shown by point Q and the autarky welfare level by the indifference curve QA in Figure 3.3. The economy is completely specialized in the production of the non-traded good at point Q. Trade occurs as a result of the tangency between the indifference curve U_0 and the consumption possibility locus TM_1^* at point C which indicates the consumption equilibrium. The consumers are maximizing utility by consuming CJ of commodity X_N and OJ of the imported commodity M_1. This consumption equilibrium at point C in turn determines the production equilibrium at point P in quadrant I. In this model consumption and production decisions are not independent of each other.

On the production side, PD of good X_N is produced along with OD of good X_2. It is important to note that the production of commodity X_N, the non-traded good, exactly equals the consumption of the non-traded good $(CJ = PD)$. The output OD of commodity X_2 is transformed into imports OJ of commodity M_1 by using the terms of trade, which is given by the slope of the line OD'. The price ratio facing consumers, P_N, at point C equals the slope of the line QC, while the price ratio facing producers and consumers, commences from the same point Q on the X_N axis. The equilibrium position indicates that national income from the production side must equal national income from the consumption side, i.e.

$$D_1 + P_N D_N = PX_2 + P_N X_N \qquad (3.13)$$

Thus, given the terms of trade and other information, we have determined all the endogenous variables. It should also be noted that due to the form of the utility function used, the economy could also completely specialize in producing X_2 and consuming M_1 only. This is shown in Figure 3.4 as point A'.

3.2.3. The difference between production and consumption sets

This section presents the well-known result that for a small country, an improvement (deterioration) in the terms of trade raises (lowers) welfare. An improvement in the terms of trade occurs when for the same quantity of exports, more imports can be obtained. A favourable movement in the terms of trade as indicated in Figure 3.5a and b by a change in the slope of the lines AA and $A'A'$. However, in the dependency model, the change in the slope of the terms of trade is shown in quadrant II of Figure 3.3 by a shift from OD' to OD''. This results in a shift of the consumption possibility frontier from $T\tilde{T}_t$ to $T\tilde{\tilde{T}}_t$ as shown in Figure 3.5b. In the case of a deterioration of the terms-of-trade, the consumption possibility locus shrinks and in the limit, the consumption possibility locus will merge with the vertical line showing that only X_N is produced. If M_1 consumption was essential for the economy, then a deterioration in the terms of trade could result in a loss of entitlement to this good.

This is in contrast to the HO model where all the action takes place on the given production possibility locus. Note that quadrants II and III have been omitted in Figure 3.5. The production possibility

Figure 3.4. Specialization

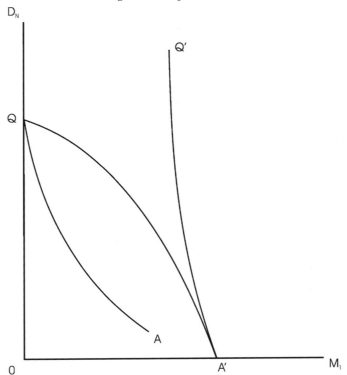

locus remains the same as in Figure 3.5a. A favourable movement in the terms of trade is similar to the impact of having technical progress in the importable good. Also note that in Figure 3.5b, the relative price of the non-traded good increases and hence a favourable movement in the terms of trade may produce structural change.

3.2.4. Monopoly power in trade and the possibility of non-convexity of the consumption set

In the previous two sections, we have established the importance of the difference between the production and the consumption possibility set. We now proceed to demonstrate that the presence of monopoly power in trade (large-country case) may cause the consumption possibility set to become non-convex. Recall that when the terms of trade are given from outside, the point of equilibrium is

Figure 3.5.   *(a) Standard case*

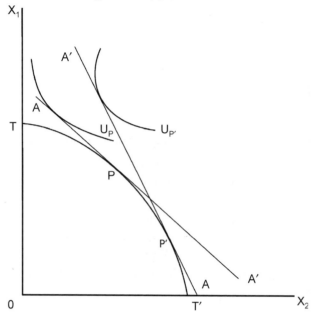

(b) Case of separation between sets

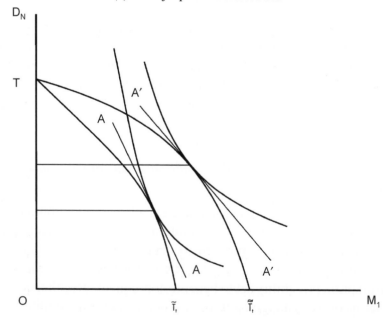

characterized by the following condition:

$$-\frac{dD_1}{dD_N} = \frac{P\,dX_2}{dX_N} \quad \text{or}$$

$$\frac{U_N}{U_1} = \text{DRS} = -\frac{P\,dX_2}{dX_N} = \frac{P}{\text{DRT}} = \frac{\text{FRT}}{\text{DRT}} \tag{3.14}$$

where $-dX_N/dX_2 = \text{DRT}$.

Therefore, $\text{DRS} = \text{FRT}/\text{DRT}$, which states that the slope of the consumption possibility locus equals P divided by the slope of the production possibility locus. Note that this condition is different from that of the standard trade theory, where $\text{DRS} = \text{DRT} = \text{FRT}$ holds for a first best equilibrium. Monopoly power in trade implies that the terms of trade, P, are variable. To show that concavity of the consumption possibility set is not necessarily assured in the case of the dependency model, we use Equation (3.14) and differentiate it totally (after taking logs of both sides). For the small-country case:

$$\frac{d(\text{DRS})}{\text{DRS}} = -\frac{d(\text{DRT})}{\text{DRT}} \tag{3.15a}$$

and concavity is assured. For the large-country case:

$$\frac{d(\text{DRS})}{\text{DRS}} = \frac{d(\text{FRT})}{\text{FRT}} - \frac{d(\text{DRT})}{\text{DRT}} \tag{3.15b}$$

In the large-country case, as is apparent from Equation (3.15b), an additional term arises that relates to a change in FRT. This term can lead to non-concavity of the consumption possibility locus. This model shows the distinction between monopoly power in trade and monopoly in production. The goods X_N and X_2 are produced competitively, yet the country could possess monopoly power in trade leading to a difference between average and marginal terms of trade. Hence, the second-order derivatives of Equation (3.14) will have terms relating to P as shown by Equation (3.15b) and therefore concavity of the production surface does not necessarily establish the concavity of the consumption possibility curve. An illustration is provided in Figure 3.6. The variable terms of trade are given by OAC and the fixed terms of trade by Ot. These lead to consumption possibility curves TM_1^* and TM_1^{**}, respectively. It is clear that TM_1^{**} is not concave to the origin and the consumption set is not convex and the system may be characterized by multiple equilibria as shown

Figure 3.6.   *Non-concavity of the consumption possibility schedule*

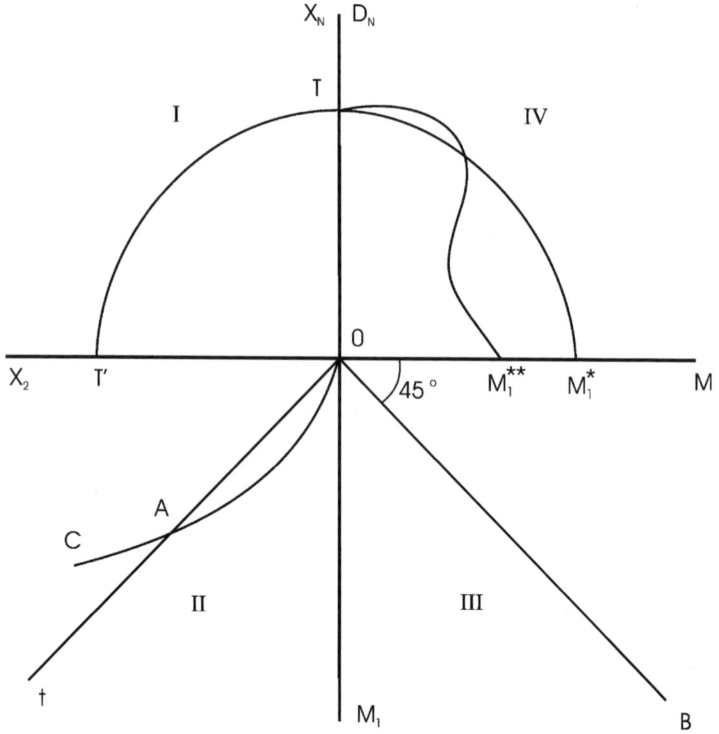

in Figure 3.7. This is an important result as the dependency model can be generalized to the n good case. Many countries produce specialized export products that are not consumed domestically and sometimes rejected export items are sold on the domestic market – many instances of this phenomenon can be found in India and other developing countries.

3.3. Tourism and monopoly power in trade

We are now in a position to introduce tourism in the dependency model. After introducing tourism in the model, we will establish two important results. First, we show that the presence of tourist consumption of non-traded goods and services creates monopoly power in trade, which implies that the equilibrium is characterized by $DRS = DRT \neq FRT$ (or in this model $DRS \neq FRT/DRT$). Given this inequality, free trade in tourism is not the optimal policy. Second, and more importantly, there is no presumption in

Figure 3.7.   *Multiple equilibrium*

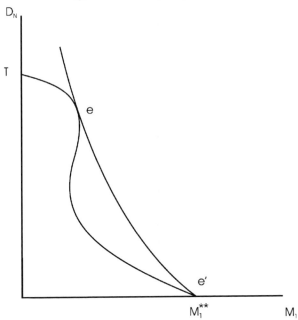

such a model that a demand shift (tourism boom) will necessarily raise the relative price of the non-traded good as it depends on the movement of the offer curve which is not captured by partial equilibrium diagrams – a type of analyses often used in the literature on tourism and trade. It is well known from the work of Bhagwati and Johnson (1960) and later Kemp (1969) that demand shifts of offer curves can take many forms. Hence, it is possible to demonstrate that the relative price of non-traded goods *may* fall as a consequence of a tourism boom and that such a fall may be immiserizing.

We begin by specifying a demand function for the consumption of non-traded goods and services by tourists; let this be denoted by D_{NT}. Hence, market clearing in the non-traded goods sector requires that

$$D_N + D_{NT} = X_N \tag{3.16}$$

It will be assumed that D_{NT} is a function of P_N and a shift factor μ. Let the relation between the production of the exportable good, X_2

and X_N be denoted by

$$X_2 = g(X_N), \qquad g' < 0, \ g'' < 0 \tag{3.17}$$

This is the equation for the transformation surface, which is shown in quadrant I of Figure 3.1.

The market clearing equations for the exportable good and the non-traded goods sector with tourists are

$$PX_2 = M_1 \tag{3.18}$$

$$D_{NT} = (X_N - D_N) = \psi(M_1) \tag{3.19}$$

The derivative $\psi(M_1)$ defines the foreign rate of transformation, which is the slope of the offer curve relating to the exports of tourism and imports of M_1. This is different from the exports of X_2 against M_1 (Equation (3.18)) where the small-country assumption has been made. The average and marginal terms of trade are different. In the small-country case the terms of trade, P, are given from outside. However, P_N is endogenously determined and monopoly power in trade arises as a result of tourism.

The maximization problem of this economy in the presence of tourists is given below[1]

$$
\begin{aligned}
G = D_N^\alpha + M_1^\beta - \lambda_1[g(X_N) - X_2] - \lambda_2[PX_2 - M_1] \\
- \lambda_3[(X_N - D_N) - \psi(M_1)]
\end{aligned}
\tag{3.20}
$$

where λ_i $(i = 1, 2)$ denote the undetermined Lagrange multipliers. Differentiating G with respect to the endogenous variables of the system D_N, M_1, X_N, X_2 and M_1 leads to the following conditions:

$$\frac{\partial G}{\partial D_N} = \alpha D_N^{\alpha-1} + \lambda_3 = 0 \tag{3.21}$$

$$\frac{\partial G}{\partial M_1} = \beta M_1^{\beta-1} + \lambda_2 + \lambda_3 \psi(M_1) = 0 \tag{3.22}$$

---

[1] This technique is borrowed from Bhagwati *et al.* (1998).

$$\frac{\partial G}{\partial X_N} = -\lambda_1 g'(X_N) - \lambda_3 = 0 \tag{3.23}$$

$$\frac{\partial G}{\partial X_2} = \lambda_1 - P\lambda_2 = 0 \tag{3.24}$$

It is clear from Equations (3.20) and (3.21) that

$$\text{DRS} = \frac{U_N}{U_1} = \frac{\lambda_3}{\lambda_2 + \lambda_3 \psi(M_1)} \tag{3.25}$$

where $\psi(M_1)$ is the slope of the offer curve in the space D_{NT} and M_1 and is defined as $(\text{FRT})'$. By differentiating Equation (3.16), we obtain:

$$g'(X_N) = \frac{1}{\text{DRT}} \tag{3.26}$$

By appropriate substitution and manipulation it follows that

$$\text{DRS} = \frac{1}{\text{DRT}/\text{FRT} + (\text{FRT})'} \tag{3.27}$$

Note that when $\psi(M_1) = 0$, that is, the country is also small in the tourism sector, then the expression in Equation (3.27) reduces to DRS = FRT/DRT as obtained earlier in Equation (3.14). Free trade in the presence of monopoly power in tourism is not the optimal policy.

We now proceed to show an example where tourism raises domestic welfare. The four-quadrant diagram is adapted in Figure 3.8 to represent an equilibrium in the presence of tourism. In quadrant I the production possibility curve TT' is shown which translates into the consumption possibility locus $T\tilde{T}$ based on the assumption that $P = 1$ (quadrant 4). That is, $T\tilde{T}$ is an exact replica of TT'. The consumption availability locus in the presence of tourists is given by $T^O A'' \tilde{T}$. This locus lies partially inside the other locus; the proof is given in Appendix A3. On this locus, equilibrium occurs at point A'' and welfare is shown by the indifference curve U_O. Note that AA'' of imports are obtained by exporting the non-traded good $A'A$ (i.e. by sale to tourists) and OD of imports are obtained by exporting OC of X_2. Total imports are $OD + AA''$ and the domestic

Figure 3.8. Welfare-increasing growth

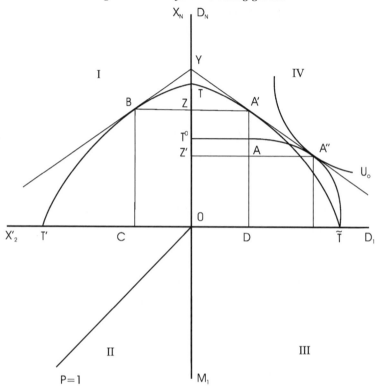

consumption of the non-traded good is *DA*. Production occurs at point *B* where *OC* of X_2 and *OZ* of non-traded good X_N are produced. It is clear that total exports consist of ZZ' of X_N (to tourists) and *OC* of X_2 (a commodity export). National income equilibrium, which is the equality of expenditure and value added, is shown by point *Y*, from which equilibria (P_N/P_2) and (P_N/P_1) are drawn.

3.4. A tourism boom and its consequences

In this section we consider the impact of a boom in tourism on the relative price of good X_N (the non-traded good). The demand shift (or tourism boom) is introduced in the following manner:

$$\zeta(M_1) = X_2 + \frac{P_N D_{NT}(P_N/\mu)}{\mu} \tag{3.28}$$

Note that given the assumption that P equals 1, it follows that the consumption possibility locus as defined by Equation (A3.20) is identical with the production possibility locus defined by Equation (A3.16). If $P \neq 1$ then the consumption possibility locus and production possibility locus will differ by P as it would equal:

$$D_N^2 + \left(\frac{M_1}{P}\right)^2 = 1 \tag{A3.21}$$

The Lagrangian for the maximization problem above (provided a value for P is already given) is

$$G = 2D_N^{1/2} + 4M_1^{1/2} - \lambda[D_N^2 + M_1^2 - 1]$$

From this we obtain the following first-order conditions:

$$\frac{\partial G}{\partial D_N} = D_N^{-1/2} - 2\lambda D_N = 0 \tag{A3.22}$$

$$\frac{\partial G}{\partial M_1} = 2M_1^{-1/2} - 2\lambda M_1 = 0 \tag{A3.23}$$

$$\frac{\partial G}{\partial \lambda} = -D_N^2 - M_1^2 + 1 = 0 \tag{A3.24}$$

Solving Equations (A3.22)–(A3.24), we obtain the optimal values of D_N and M_1:

$$D_N^* = \frac{1}{\sqrt{1 + 2^{4/3}}} \tag{A3.25}$$

$$M_1^* = \frac{2^{2/3}}{\sqrt{1 + 2^{4/3}}} \tag{A3.26}$$

By using the first-order conditions of utility maximization, it follows that the endogenously determined value of the relative price P_N is as given below

$$P_N^* = \left(\frac{1}{2}\right)^{2/3} \tag{A3.27}$$

and the level of utility at the free trade level is $2D_N^{1/2} + 4M_1^{1/2} = 2$. Since $2 > 1$, it follows that free trade is better than no trade.

We now consider the case where tourist consumption of the non-traded good is added and denoted by D_{NT}. The utility function in Equation (A3.17) is used but the constraint is now different as we need to include the tourist demand function. Assume that D_{NT} takes the following form:

$$D_{NT} = a - bP_N \tag{A3.28}$$

The constraint set out in Equation (A3.20) now becomes

$$(D_N + D_{NT})^2 + (M_1 - P_N D_{NT})^2 = 1 \tag{A3.29}$$

Substituting Equation (A3.28) into Equation (A3.29) yields

$$(D_N + a - bP_N)^2 + (M_1 - P_N(a - bP_N))^2 = 1 \tag{A3.30}$$

The representative consumer problem now becomes

Max. $U = 2D_N^{1/2} + 4M_1^{1/2}$

subject to:

$$(D_N + a - bP_N)^2 + (M_1 - P_N(a - bP_N))^2 = 1$$

The Lagrangian for the maximization problem above is

$$G = 2D_N^{1/2} + 4M_1^{1/2} - \lambda[(D_N + a - bP_N)^2$$
$$+ (M_1 - P_N(a - bP_N))^2 - 1]$$

The value of P_N is taken as given for this maximization problem. A social planner can optimize with respect to P_N also.

From this we obtain the following first-order conditions:

$$\frac{\partial G}{\partial D_N} = D_N^{-1/2} - 2\lambda(D_N + a - bP_N) = 0 \tag{A3.31}$$

$$\frac{\partial G}{\partial M_1} = 2M_1^{-1/2} - 2\lambda(M_1 - (a - bP_N)P_N) = 0 \tag{A3.32}$$

$$\frac{\partial G}{\partial \lambda} = -(D_{NT} + a - bP_N)^2 - (M_1 - (a - bP_N)P_N)^2 + 1 = 0 \tag{A3.33}$$

Solving Equations (A3.31)–(A3.33) we obtain the optimal values of

D_N and M_1:

$$D_N^* = \frac{2P_N}{\sqrt{4P_N^2+1}} - a + bP_N \qquad (A3.34)$$

$$M_1^* = \frac{1}{2P_N\sqrt{4P_N^2+1}} + (a - bP_N)P_N \qquad (A3.35)$$

Substituting Equations (A3.34) and (A3.35) into the utility function (A3.17) yields

$$U = 2\left[\frac{2P_N}{\sqrt{4P_N^2+1}} - a + bP_N\right]^{1/2}$$

$$+ 4\left[\frac{1}{2P_N\sqrt{4P_N^2+1}} + (a - bP_N)P_N\right]^{1/2} \qquad (A3.36)$$

For a suitably chosen value of P_N, this U may be below 2, the autarky level of welfare. Thus, the introduction of tourist consumption may decrease utility. Another method of checking this result is by solving for the critical value of P_N. This is obtained by setting the utility level at the free trade level and that, with free trade and tourism to equal each other, then solving for P_N.

References

Bhagwati, J.N. and H.G. Hohnson (1960). "Notes on some controversies in the theory of international trade", *Economics Journal*, Vol. 70, pp. 74–93.

Bhagwati, J.N., T.N. Srinivasan and A. Panagariya (1998), *Lectures on International Economics*, Cambridge, MA: MIT Press.

Copeland, B.R. (1991), "Tourism, welfare and de-industrialization in a small open economy", *Economica*, Vol. 58, pp. 515–529.

Hazari, B.R. and J.-J. Nowak (2003), "Tourism, taxes and immiserization: a trade theoretic analysis", *Pacific Economic Review*, Vol. 8, pp. 279–288.

Kemp, M.C. (1969) *The Pure Theory of International Trade*, Englewood Cliff, NJ: Prentice Hall.

Komiya, R. (1967), "Non-traded goods and the pure theory of international trade", *International Economic Review*, Vol. 8(June), pp. 132–152.

CHAPTER 4

Tourism, Taxes and Immiserization in a Two-Country Trade Model

4.1. Introduction

In Chapter 3, tourism was introduced by allowing the movement of consumers into a country to consume non-traded goods and services. However, the phenomena of tourism was not explained, that is, it was not shown how in a two-country model, tourism arises and how an equilibrium is established. In this chapter, by setting up a very simple two-country model of trade, tourism is generated as an endogenous variable. In fact, it provides a theory of consumer movement based on differentiated non-traded goods and services which the sovereign nationals wish to consume in a different country. The chapter is in the spirit of traditional trade theory concerning the patterns of trade, for example, in the Ricardian model differences in technology explain trade; in the Heckschler–Ohlin model differences in factor endowment explain trade. In this chapter tourism is explained by appealing to the existence of differentiated non-traded goods and services that are consumed by tourists as such goods and services cannot be transported across national boundaries – in fact cannot be found within their national boundaries. A large number of examples of differentiated products that can only be consumed by movement of consumers can be given. A few have been provided in the previous chapters, for example, the Taj Mahal in India, the Sistine Chapel in Rome, Notre Dame in Paris and so on. These are examples of man-made monuments. However, tourists are also attracted by endowments of nature, for example, the Grand Canyon in the USA.

4.2. A two-country model of tourism

We begin our analysis by considering a two-country general equilibrium model consisting of a home and a foreign country.[1] The foreign country variables are denoted by an asterisk (*). The home country produces and consumes two goods: X_M and X_N. Let the aggregate utility function of the home country be given by

$$U = U[D_M, D_N]$$ (4.1)

where U denotes aggregate utility, D_M the consumption of good X_M and D_N that of good X_N. Comments already made about the utility function in Chapter 2 apply to this function. From utility maximization and the assumption of an interior equilibrium, it follows that

$$\frac{U_N}{U_M} = P, \quad \text{where } P = \frac{P_N}{P_M}$$ (4.2)

It is assumed that the non-traded good X_N captures the features of all the non-traded goods and services provided in the host country, for example, all the natural and man-made attractions, hotels, galleries, monuments and other services. This good is assumed to be not available in the foreign country; hence, if the foreign country consumers wish to consume this good on a temporary basis, they must become tourists. In the tradition of the HO model, $X_N > X_N^* = O$. Since X_N cannot be transported, only consumer movement would allow foreign nationals to consume X_N in the home country.

The aggregate utility function of the foreign country is given by

$$U^* = U^*(D_M^*, D_N^*)$$ (4.3)

where U^* denotes aggregate utility and D_i^* $(i = M, N)$ the consumption of goods X_M and X_N. It is assumed that the foreign country only produces good X_M^*, hence, in order to consume D_N^* its residents must travel to the home country which is assumed to produce two goods, X_M and X_N. It would be fairly simple to produce another non-traded good in the foreign country and assume that it is

---

[1] The model may be generalized to produce more goods and other countries without losing the main thrust of this chapter.

significantly differentiated from that in the home country. One could then build a theory of two-way tourism, however, we only consider one-way tourism.

Since the consumers in the foreign country wish to consume D_N, market clearing in the home country requires that

$$D_N + D_N^* = X_N \tag{4.4}$$

where X_N denotes the output of the non-traded good. Later in this chapter an explicit derivation of D_N^* is provided. Market clearing for the good X_M requires that

$$D_M = X_M + M \tag{4.5}$$

where M denotes imports and X_M the output of this good.

For analytical simplicity it is assumed that both goods are produced only with the help of labour. This assumption can be relaxed without any loss of generality. The neoclassical production functions in the home country are given below

$$X_M = F_M(L_M) \tag{4.6}$$

$$X_N = F_N(L_N) \tag{4.7}$$

and with the restrictions that $F_j' > 0$ and $F_j'' < 0$ for $(j = M, N)$. These denote the first and second derivatives of the functions in Equations (4.6) and (4.7).

We assume that both goods are produced, hence, at the point of interior equilibrium, profit maximization ensures that

$$w = F_M' = PF_N' \tag{4.8}$$

where the wage rate, w, equals the value of the marginal product of labour in each sector.

As wages are assumed to be perfectly flexible, the inelastically supplied labour force, $\bar{L}$, is fully employed:

$$L_M + L_N = \bar{L} \tag{4.9}$$

Finally, the balance of payments equilibrium requires that

$$D_M + P_N D_N = X_M + P_N X_N \tag{4.10}$$

or

$$P_N D_N^* = M$$

This completes the specification of the model for the home country.

In the foreign country by assuming utility maximization and an interior equilibrium, the consumer maximizes utility when the following condition is satisfied:

$$\frac{U_N^*}{U_M^*} = P \qquad (4.11)$$

Note that P in Equation (4.11) represents a relative price at the free trade equilibrium. This equilibrium involves movement of people who consume the non-traded goods and services to arrive at the free trade price. It is important to emphasize that in the foreign country there is only a corner solution in autarky and in a two-country environment this solution cannot sustain itself.[2] However, the home country produces and consumes both goods at autarky.

The equations for the foreign country are given below:

$$D_M^* = X_M^* - M \qquad (4.12)$$

Equation (4.12) states that domestic consumption of good X_M equals output minus exports.

$$X_M^* = F_M^*(\bar{L}^*), \quad F_M^{*\prime} > 0, \quad F_M^{*\prime\prime} < 0 \qquad (4.13)$$

and

$$w^* = F_M^{*\prime} \qquad (4.14)$$

Equation (4.13) shows that output of X_M^* is produced by labour only and labour is fully employed. This requires that wages are flexible, hence, in Equation (4.14) w^* denotes the full employment wage rate.

This completes the specification of the model for the foreign country.

---

[2] To have a corner solution, the marginal rate of substitution must have a finite value; otherwise, there are multiple equilibria and the level of welfare is undetermined.

4.3. Results

4.3.1. Derivation of the offer curve, optimal tariff and problems of taxation

We first derive a trading equilibrium for both countries and demonstrate that an optimal tariff on tourism is necessary to obtain a first-best solution for the home country.[3] This framework is then utilized to show the effects of production and demand shifts on the foreign offer curve and home welfare, respectively. As the model is fairly simple, it is presented in terms of geometry. In Figure 4.1 the autarky equilibrium in the home country is shown by point e. Given our assumptions regarding the production structure of this model, we obtain the production possibility curve TT' as shown in Figure 4.1. The home consumers maximize utility subject to this production possibility curve to arrive at autarky equilibrium at point e, where the social indifference curve U_O is tangential to the transformation locus. The self-sufficiency price ratio is given by the slope of the line AA'. The home offer curve is shown as eH, assuming that the non-traded good is consumed by tourists. The foreign country can only face relative prices that are given by the slope of the line AA' and those that are represented by slopes greater than AA', i.e. to the right of AA' as they are only interested in consuming the good X_N. by becoming tourists in the home country. The foreign country has no production of X_N. If X_N is treated as an endowment of nature, for example, the Twelve Apostles on the Great Ocean Road, then there would be no production of X_N. However, there would be production of the infrastructure to enable tourists and domestic residents to consume this good. The tourists would perhaps pay for transportation but not for the cost of building the infrastructure and hence, may be a free-rider of the public good that support the consumption of the natural endowment.

Let us now consider the foreign country. It is most important to note that the offer curve for this country depends on the autarky demand and supply structure of the home country, which gives rise to an autarky price ratio given by the slope of line AA'. Unlike the traditional model, the feasible part of the foreign country offer curve

---

[3] It is assumed that there is no retaliation.

Figure 4.1. Autarky equilibrium and home offer curve

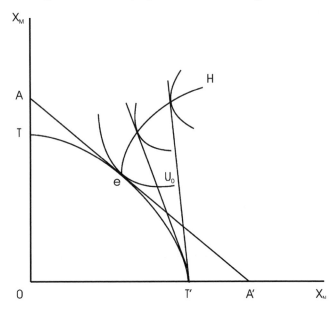

cannot be generated from the knowledge of its own economy, as is shown for the home country in Figure 4.1. In Figure 4.2(a) the full-employment output in the foreign country is shown by $\bar{X}_M^*$. This output is transformed in Figure 4.2(b) into the straight line $\bar{X}_M^* A^*$ in the consumption space (D_N^*, D_M^*). The autarky solution in the foreign country is given by point $\bar{X}_M^*$ and the level of welfare by the social indifference curve U_A'. Prices represented by slopes that are less than $\bar{X}_M^* A'$ (flatter) are not relevant as they are not feasible in the home country. Thus, the foreign offer curve must originate at $\bar{X}_M^*$ and end on the line $\bar{X}_M^* A'$. The relevant price range for trade to occur is between the autarky foreign price ratio, as shown by the slope of $\bar{X}_M^* \beta$ and $\bar{X}_M^* A'$. As we assume that there is free movement of tourists from the foreign to the home country, it follows that the tourists can also consume X_N at the autarky prices of the tourist-receiving country. This would only occur in a fix-price model. Let the home country autarky price be shown by the slope of the price line $\bar{X}_M^* \beta$ which equals AA' in Figure 4.1. If transport costs are incorporated in the model, then the range $\bar{X}_M^* \beta$ and $\bar{X}_M^* A'$ becomes smaller – hence, transport costs reduce the choice set (core) in which mutually advantageous trade can take place. Sufficiently high transport costs will lead to zero trade and the lens area $\bar{X}_M^* \beta e'$ will not exist. At this

Figure 4.2. *(a) Full employment equilibrium in the foreign country*

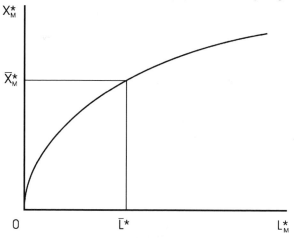

(b) Foreign offer curve

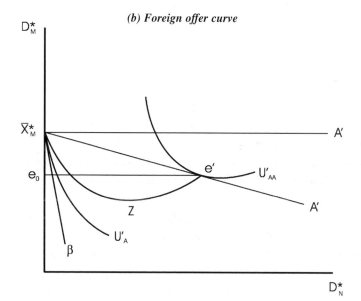

price ratio the tourists demand $e_o e'$ of the non-traded good, making the equilibrium e in Figure 4.1 non-sustainable. By taking parametric changes from this autarky price (specifically, increases in the relative price of X_N), the offer curve of the foreign country is derived as shown by $\bar{X}_M^* Z e'$. By using all of this information, we obtain the free trade equilibrium with tourists in Figure 4.3. In this diagram $\bar{X}_M^* H$ is the home offer curve and $\bar{X}_M^* F$ the foreign offer curve. The free trade equilibrium is given by point e_F and the free

Figure 4.3.   Free trade equilibrium with tourists

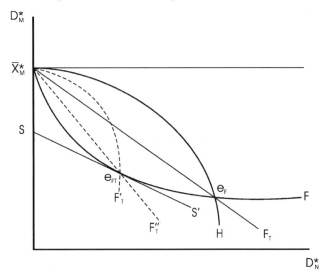

trade terms of trade by the slope of the line $\bar{X}_M^* F_T$. This is obviously sub-optimal for the home country, which imposes a tax (tariff) on tourists to maximize its welfare, as shown by the point e_{FT}, where the terms of trade are given by the slope of $\bar{X}_M^* F_T''$ and the price for the domestic consumers by the slope of SS'. As shown by this model, the lesson seems to be: always tax the tourist. When the non-traded good consumed by the tourists is not differentiated, as is the case in beach-related tourism in the Mediterranean countries, then there would be no monopoly power in trade.

Having established that in the presence of differentiated goods the tourists should always be taxed, it is clear that for the home country DRS = DRT ≠ FRT, hence, the need for an optimal tariff. This is an important finding, for several reasons. First, countries that are small in merchandise trade are not necessarily small in tourist trade. For example, in a small open economy like Fiji, the local residents pay a different hotel rate from foreign tourists. Even in developed countries with large market economies, tourists often pay more for taxis and other services. Some economists may be inclined to attribute this to asymmetric information, but it may also be viewed as monopoly power in trade of non-traded goods and services.

Second, how do we impose an optimal tariff? Tourism is a commodity that comes not through the customs but through human beings. These individuals consume several non-traded goods and services. Some may visit galleries or museums, while others may visit only beaches and resorts. Hence, the need for differential taxation for exploiting the monopoly power in trade or a visa fee that reflects a mapping of all taxes into one tax. Such visa fees may be inequitable. India is a good example of differential taxation. There are separate entry tickets for local residents and tourists to view the Taj Mahal. There is a different charge at hotels for locals and tourists – hence, the commodities are differentially taxed. Moreover, India also has a very high visa fee compared to other countries. While it is not difficult to show that an optimal tariff is required because of monopoly power in trade in tourism, it is not easy to establish and design an optimal tax system for tourists, as they consume many non-traded goods and services. This chapter only establishes the need for taxing tourists, and then discusses the problems inherent in designing an optimal tax system on tourist consumption. If equity considerations are also brought in, then one has to consider whether tourists from poor countries should be taxed the same as those from rich countries. Visa fees for different nationalities can be dissimilar for political reasons but they can also be different on grounds of equity in tourism. These are all open issues for research.

4.3.2. Tourist boom and home immiserization

This section reproduces the result obtained in the previous chapters that an increase in tourist demand may lower home-country welfare. In a celebrated paper Bhagwati and Johnson (1960) demonstrated that demand shifts can be analysed in several ways. These shifts were formalized by Kemp (1969).[4] A particular type of demand shift is used in Figure 4.4 will result in a deterioration in the terms of trade, and then it is possible for the home country to be immiserized from a tourist boom (assuming that an optimal tariff is not in place). This result is illustrated in Figure 4.4, where the free trade equilibrium (without an optimal tariff) is shown by point e. At this point, the offer curves $\bar{X}_M^* H$ and $\bar{X}_M^* F$ intersect. The home welfare is shown by the trade indifference curve U_H. The increase in tourist demand is shown by the shift in the offer curve as represented by

---

[4] See Kemp (1969) for a detailed discussion of demand shifts.

Figure 4.4. Immiserizing growth with tourism

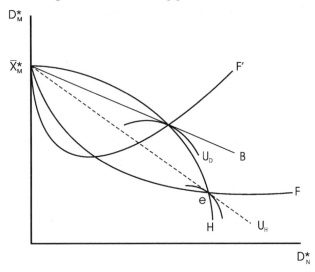

$\bar{X}_M^* F'$. The terms of trade deteriorate as a result of tourism boom. These are shown by the slope of the line $\bar{X}_M^* B$. Welfare of the home country falls, as shown by the trade indifferences curve U_D. This reveals a new application of the Bhagwati (1971) immiserizing growth theorem and reinforces the need for an optimal tariff policy.

It is easy to establish that free trade is not the optimal policy in this model. By differentiating Equation (4.10) totally we obtain:

$$dD_M + P_N\,dD_N + D_N\,dP_N = dX_M + P_N\,dX_N + X_N\,dP_N$$

From the utility function we know that

$$\frac{dU}{U_M} = dD_M + P_N\,dD_N = dI$$

where dI denotes change in real income. Hence,

$$dI = dX_M + P_N\,dX_N + (X_N - D_N)dP_N$$

We know that $dX_M + P_N\,dX_N = 0$, hence,

$$\frac{dU}{U_M} = dI = D_{NT}\,dP_N \neq 0$$

First best equilibrium requires that $dU/U_M = 0$. This is only possible if $dP_N = 0$ which is not the case in our model. It is the expression $D_{NT} dP_N$ that gives rise to monopoly power in trade.

4.3.3. Technical progress (expansion in the tourism sector) and welfare (home country)

In many countries that are reliant upon tourism, a great deal of effort and resources are devoted to expanding the tourism sector, for example, increasing the supply of hotel rooms, beds and so on. This is a favourite theme with many applied researchers on tourism. In this section we consider the terms of trade and welfare consequences of such expansion. Let θ denote an expansion factor, hence, Equation (4.7) is now amended to read:

$$X_N = \theta F_N(L_N) \tag{4.15}$$

We first establish a sign for the movement in output. At constant prices we obtain:

$$\frac{dX_N}{d\theta} = F_N(L_N) - \frac{\theta w}{\varDelta} > 0 \tag{4.16}$$

$$\frac{dX_M}{d\theta} = \frac{F_M w}{\varDelta} < 0 \tag{4.17}$$

where $\varDelta = \theta P_N F_N'' + F_M'' < 0$.

It is clear that at constant prices, technical progress raises the output of the non-traded goods sector (tourism sector) and lowers the output of the importable sector X_M.

A natural question to ask is what happens to the terms of trade as a result of the expansion in the output of the non-traded goods sector. This can be derived from the balance of payments equation. This equation states that

$$P_N D_{NT}(P_N) - M\left(\frac{1}{P_N}, \theta\right) = 0 \tag{4.18}$$

where P_N is the relative price of the exportable goods and θ the expansion factor. By differentiating Equation (4.18) totally and using the equilibrium condition that $M = P_N D_{NT}$, we obtain:

$$\frac{dP_N}{d\theta} = \frac{\partial M / \partial \theta}{[\varepsilon - \varepsilon^* + 1]D_{NT}} \tag{4.19}$$

where $(\varepsilon - \varepsilon^* + 1) < 0$ from the Marshall–Lerner stability condition. Given this stability condition, the sign of $dP_N/d\theta$ depends on $\partial M/\partial \theta$, i.e. the change in imports as a result of the expansion in the tourism sector. A more explicit expression for $\partial M/\partial \theta$ can be derived by using the excess demand equation:

$$M = D_M\left(\frac{1}{P_N}, I\right) - X_M \tag{4.20}$$

where I indicates national income in terms of P_N. By differentiating Equation (4.20) with respect to θ at constant prices, we obtain:

$$\frac{\partial M}{\partial \theta} = m\frac{\partial I}{\partial \theta} - \frac{\partial X_M}{\partial \theta} \tag{4.21}$$

At current prices, $\partial I/\partial \theta$ equals X_N, hence,

$$\frac{\partial M}{\partial \theta} = mX_N - \frac{\partial X_M}{\partial \theta} > 0 \tag{4.22}$$

It follows that

$$\frac{dP_N}{d\theta} = \frac{\partial M / \partial \theta}{[\varepsilon - \varepsilon^* + 1]D_{NT}} < 0 \tag{4.23}$$

That is, the tertiary terms of trade necessarily deteriorate as a result of expansion in the tourism sector.

The intuition behind the above result is easily brought out with the help of Figure 4.5. The original production possibility curve is shown by *TT* in Figure 4.5. Production equilibrium occurs at *P* and consumption equilibrium at *e* where, due to monopoly power in trade, average and marginal terms of trade are not equal to each other. Expansion of the non-traded goods sector results in shifting the locus from *TT* to *TT'*. Consumption at constant prices must take place at *C*, production at *P'* while the trading equilibrium is shown to be at *e'* which cannot be an equilibrium position. The terms of trade must deteriorate as the supply of non-traded goods is greater than the demand for these goods – hence, the result in Equation (4.23).

Figure 4.5. *Determination of tertiary terms of trade*

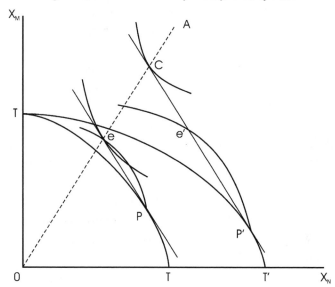

It is fairly easy to show that such expansion can be immiserizing. This is shown in Figure 4.6 without commentary. An important message of this exercise is to show that in the presence of uncorrected monopoly power in trade, an expansion of the tourism

Figure 4.6. *Immiserizing growth*

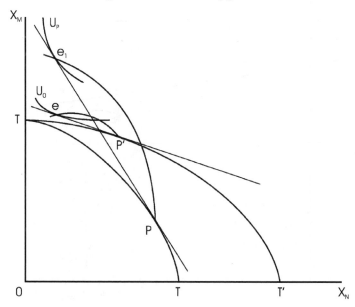

industry is not necessarily welfare improving. This is a very important result for policy makers and tourism specialists who carry out empirical work without any sound theoretical foundation and ignore the possibility of supply side immiserization via tourism.

Finally, we consider the effect of an expansion in the foreign country on terms of trade and home country welfare. It is clear that such expansion in this model is necessarily welfare raising for the home country. This is demonstrated in Figure 4.7. The initial equilibrium is shown by points: P for production in the home country; PH the home offer curve and PF the foreign offer curve; U_H welfare level in the home country. Expansion in the foreign country leads to an improvement in the terms of trade. The home offer curve is now denoted by $P'H$; the foreign offer curve by $P'F'$ and the terms of trade by $P't$. Home welfare has increased as shown by movement of the indifferent curve from U_H to U'_H. World growth

Figure 4.7.   Welfare-increasing growth

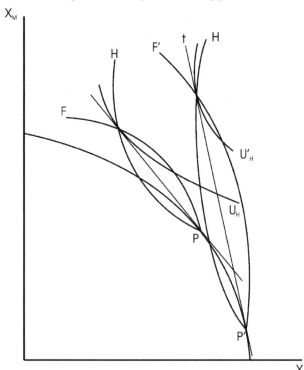

is beneficial for the home country if it leads to expansion in tourism and an improvement in the tertiary terms of trade.

4.4. Conclusion

This chapter clearly demonstrates how monopoly power in trade arises in models of tourism. It establishes the need for an optimal tax on tourists. More importantly, it shows how home-country conditions affect the foreign offer curve and the feasible region for gains from trade. Finally, it shows how immiserization can occur from tourism both from the demand and supply side – hence, the need for following optimal policies in tourism-expanding countries. This chapter also establishes how world growth may lead to welfare improvements via expansion in tourism and improvement in tertiary terms of trade.

References

Bhagwati, J.N. (1971), "The generalized theory of distortions and welfare", in: J.N. Bhagwati and R.W. Jones, editors, *Trade, Balance of Payments and Growth: Papers in International Economics in Honor of Charles P. Kindleberger*, Chapter 12, Amsterdam: North-Holland.

Bhagwati, J.N. and H.G. Johnson (1960), "Notes on some controversies in the theory of international trade", *Economic Journal*, Vol. 70, pp. 74–93.

Kemp, M.C. (1969), *The Pure Theory of International Trade and Investment*, Englewood Cliffs, NJ: Prentice Hall.

CHAPTER 5

Price Discrimination, Tourism and Welfare

5.1. Introduction

In the previous two chapters we have analyzed and justified the existence of monopoly power in trade in the tourism sector. Chapter 3 introduced tourism in the dependency model while in Chapter 4 we set up a two-country model to generate tourism and monopoly power in trade endogenously.[1] On the basis of this two-country model, we established a relation between the core and the possible existence of transport costs. In all this analysis it was assumed that the goods were produced in a competitive framework. The distortion analyzed in those chapters resulted in the following inequality DRS = DRT ≠ FRT.

We now drop the assumption of monopoly power in trade and replace it by monopoly in production. For analytical simplicity we do not wish to deal with a model with two distortions – hence the assumption that there is no monopoly power in trade. In a later chapter in the book we deal with the case of three distortions. Monopolistic production of non-traded goods and services both with domestic and/or foreign ownership of capital is a widely prevalent phenomenon in most countries. Typical examples of this are hotels (chains like The Hilton, The Sheraton, Le Meridien and so on). Moreover, tourism also involves the use of infrastructure, like road and rail network, telecommunication and air routes which generally operate under increasing returns to scale and may also be monopolized either in private or public ownership. Later in this book the prevalence of

---

[1] This chapter represents a generalization of the trade and monopoly model of Cassing (1977).

increasing returns to scale is fully explored. Hence, given our assumption of monopoly it is also possible to analyze increasing returns to scale in the provision of goods for tourists. This chapter uses the framework of monopoly production and explores the consequences of an increase in tourism on the welfare of the domestic residents and the relative price of the non-traded good.

The economy under consideration produces three goods: an exportable, an importable and a non-traded good. The non-traded good is produced by a monopolist. It is consumed by domestic residents and tourists who have demand curves with different elasticities. It is assumed that the monopolist practices price discrimination between domestic consumers and tourists which is a reality in many countries where tourists pay more than local consumers for many services, for example, hotels.[2] In this chapter we establish that under certain conditions an increase in tourism raises resident welfare. Welfare increases provided that the crowding out effect of tourism expansion is outweighed by the favourable movement in the relative price and output of the non-traded good consumed by the tourists. The term crowding out has been borrowed from macro-economics, however, here it is used in a different manner from macroeconomics. The chapter also demonstrates that the welfare effect of an improvement in the terms of trade has three effects: (i) a traditional terms-of-trade effect, (ii) a terms-of-trade effect from the change in the relative price of non-traded goods consumed by tourists and (iii) a volume effect arising from trade of the non-traded goods. The effects (i) and (ii) always raise resident welfare while effect (iii) may have a positive or negative impact. Hence, the change in resident welfare cannot be assigned a unique sign. Importantly the model identifies variables that are significant for applied work on tourism and welfare.

5.2. The model

We assume that three goods: X_1, X_2, and X_N are produced in the economy where X_i ($i = 1, 2$) are the internationally traded goods and

---

[2] This is a well-known practice in many countries, for example, Fiji, Thailand, India and Malaysia. Other examples of price discrimination in this industry are 'corporate rates'.

X_N the non-traded good. This non-traded good, X_N, is consumed by local residents and tourists.

Commodities X_1, X_2 are produced with the help of capital and labour. The good X_N uses labour, capital and a specific factor, S, in production. The neoclassical production functions for these goods are given below:

$$X_1 = F_1[K_1, L_1] \tag{5.1}$$

$$X_2 = F_2[K_2, L_2] \tag{5.2}$$

$$X_N = F_N[K_N, L_N, \bar{S}] = L_N^\alpha K_N^\beta \bar{S}^{1-\alpha-\beta} = AL_N^\alpha K_N^\beta \tag{5.3}$$

where $A = \bar{S}^{1-\alpha-\beta}$ and $\alpha + \beta < 1$, hence, in the production of X_N, there are decreasing returns to scale with respect to L_N and K_N.

The terms K_i, $L_i = [i = 1, 2, N]$, respectively, denote the allocation of capital and labour to the respective sectors and $\bar{S}$ the specific factor used in the production of the non-traded good, N. The specific factor, $\bar{S}$, captures features such as a hotel that has a view of the harbour and such a view attracts tourists. This is typical of the location of several hotels in Hong Kong. For analytical convenience it is assumed that X_N is produced with decreasing returns to scale and Cobb–Douglas type production function.

We shall assume that all factors are fully employed so in the input coefficient notation the resource constraints are

$$a_{L1}X_1 + a_{L2}X_2 + a_{LN}X_N = \bar{L} \tag{5.4}$$

$$a_{K1}X_1 + a_{K2}X_2 + a_{KN}X_N = \bar{K} \tag{5.5}$$

$$a_{SN}X_N = \bar{S} \tag{5.6}$$

where a_{ij}s represent variable input coefficients. Assuming that commodities X_1, X_2 are produced under competitive conditions the unit cost equations for these goods are given below:

$$a_{L1}w + a_{K1}r = P \tag{5.7}$$

$$a_{L2}w + a_{K2}r = 1 \tag{5.8}$$

where w, and r denote the wage rate and rental on capital, respectively, in a small open economy and the terms of trade, P, are given exogenously. Given P, w and r are determined from Equations (5.7) and (5.8). This is the general equilibrium aspect of this model.

Using this information the pricing of commodity X_N is undertaken in a partial equilibrium framework. This two-stage recursive pricing procedure allows the model to blend features of partial and general equilibrium.

Two agents consume the non-traded good X_N at different prices. The solution for these equilibrium prices for the non-traded good, X_N, is shown below. This good is produced by a monopolist and its pricing system can be separated from the rest of the system provided the terms of trade P are given and the utility function is quasi-linear. There exist two types of consumers for this product: residents and tourists. The specific inverse demand functions for these agents are given below:

$$P_N = a - bD_N + cP \tag{5.9}$$

$$P_{NT} = d - eD_{NT} \tag{5.10}$$

where D_N denotes the demand for the non-traded good by domestic residents and D_{NT} by tourists. The relative price of the non-traded good consumed by domestic residents depends on P, the terms of trade, while the non-traded good consumed by tourists does not depend on the terms of trade. This is the case as we have assumed that the tourists do not consume the other two goods. As it is assumed that these agents have separate demand functions with different elasticities, the monopolist must charge different prices to the two groups to maximize profits. Hence, there is price discrimination in the model. The terms D_N and D_{NT} denote demands in the two markets in which the monopolist sells. Note that these demand functions do not directly depend on income due to quasi-linearity of the utility function. This assumption is necessary for closing a general equilibrium model with monopoly.[3]

The total cost function (TC) for the monopolist is given below:

$$\text{TC} = ZX_N^2 \tag{5.11}$$

where Z is an increasing function of w. The term X_N^2 is based on the simplifying assumption that the coefficients $\alpha + \beta = 0.5$ in Equation (5.3). Other values for α and β can be used, however, it

---

[3] See Batra (1975) and Cassing (1977) for elaboration of this point.

is easy to derive results with this specification. The cost function is increasing in output due to the presence of a specific factor $\bar{S}$ in the production of X_N. By using the assumption of profit maximization the following solutions for the equilibrium values for D_N^*, D_{NT}^*, P_N^*, P_{NT}^* are obtained:

$$D_N^* = \frac{ae + (a - d)Z}{D} + \frac{(ec + cZ)}{D}P \qquad (5.12)$$

$$D_{NT}^* = \frac{bd + (d - a)Z}{D} - \frac{cZP}{D} \qquad (5.13)$$

$$P_N^* = a - b\left(\frac{ae + (a - d)Z}{D}\right) - \frac{b(ec + cZ)}{D}P + cP \qquad (5.14)$$

$$P_{NT}^* = d - e\left(\frac{bd + (d - a)Z}{D}\right) + e\left(\frac{cZ}{D}\right)P \qquad (5.15)$$

$$X_N^* = D_N^* + D_{NT}^* \qquad (5.16)$$

where $D = 2(be + (b + e)Z)$ and D_N^* and D_{NT}^* denote the equilibrium values of output in domestic resident and tourist markets for the non-traded good. We will assume throughout this chapter that

$$P_{NT}^* > P_N^* \qquad (5.17)$$

which requires that

$$d - \frac{e}{D}(bd + AZ - cZP) > a - \frac{b}{D}(ae + AZ - b(ec + cZ)P) + cP$$

where $A = (d - a)$.

It is assumed that the tourists always pay more than the local residents and this is illustrated in Figure 5.1. In this figure the left-hand quadrant shows the domestic demand curve D_N and the domestic marginal revenue curve MR. In the right-hand quadrant the tourist demand curve D_{NT} and its associated marginal revenue curve MR_T are drawn. The aggregate marginal revenue curve is drawn as $BAMR$. Profit maximization equilibrium is obtained at the point of equality between the aggregate marginal revenue and the marginal cost curves which occurs at point e. This results in equilibrium prices P_N^* for the domestic residents; P_{NT}^* for tourists; D_N^* represents the output level for the domestic market and D_{NT}^* for the tourists. This completes the discussions of output and price determination in

Figure 5.1.   Domestic and tourist market

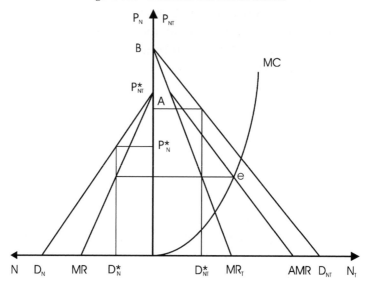

Figure 5.1.   Domestic and tourist market

the monopolized sector of the economy. Note that the terms of trade appear in Equations (5.14) and (5.15), clearly highlighting the interface between the partial and general equilibrium nature of the analysis.

Market clearing in the non-traded goods sector requires that

$$D_N + D_{NT} = X_N \tag{5.18}$$

Equation (5.18) shows that the output of X_N is consumed by local residents and tourists.

The balance-of-payments constraint requires that

$$PE_1 + P_{NT}D_{NT} = M \tag{5.19}$$

where the value of exports equals the value of imports.

5.3. Results

5.3.1. Terms of trade, output changes and resident welfare

In this section, we analyze the consequences of an improvement in the terms of trade for monopoly output and resident welfare. This section utilizes the interaction between the general equilibrium structure of the traded goods sector and the monopolized non-traded good sector, thus highlighting how partial and general equilibrium analysis can be combined. It is exceedingly important to do this to avoid slipping back into the tradition of Marshall and moving trade theory into a setting of a partial equilibrium framework. To derive these results the impact of an improvement in the terms of trade on factor rewards must be examined first. By differentiating Equations (5.7) and (5.8) we solve for $\hat{w}$ and $\hat{r}$ as follows:

$$\hat{w} = \frac{\theta_{K2}}{|\theta|} \hat{P} > 0 \tag{5.20}$$

$$\hat{r} = \frac{-\theta_{L2}}{|\theta|} \hat{P} < 0 \tag{5.21}$$

where θ_{ij} $(i = K, L)$ $(j = 1, 2)$ are the distributive factor shares and $|\theta| = \theta_{L1}\theta_{L2}(k_2 - k_1)$ where k_i $(i = 1, 2)$ denotes the physical factor intensity, i.e. the capital–labour ratio. It is assumed that $k_2 - k_1 > 0$, i.e. the importable good is capital intensive. Hence, an improvement in the terms of trade raises the wage rate and reduces the return to land (in line with the Stolper–Samuelson theorem).

We now proceed to examine the implications of a change in the terms of trade for the discriminating monopolist. The market for the non-traded good, X_N, is influenced via two channels: (a) from the terms-of-trade effect through the demand function and (b) via the cost function. These two effects are illustrated in Figure 5.2. An improvement in the terms of trade (see Equation (5.11)) shifts the resident demand curve from BD_N to $B'D'_N$ and the respective marginal revenue curves from MR to MR'. As a result of this, the aggregate marginal revenue curve AMR shifts to AMR'. Given our intensity conditions, an improvement in the terms of trade raises the wage rate, hence the MC curve shifts to OMC'. It is this shift in the MC curve that highlights the link between partial and general equilibrium. In the case shown in Figure 5.2, both $\hat{P}_{NT}$ and $\hat{P}_N$ rise while $\hat{D}_{NT}$ falls and $\hat{D}_N$ rises. We can summarize these results in the form of Proposition 5.1.

Proposition 5.1. *An improvement in the terms of trade (an increase in P) necessarily raises the relative price of the non-traded good (consumed by both residents and tourists) provided $k_2 > k_1$. An increase in the relative price of the non-traded good consumed by the tourists represents an improvement in the tertiary terms of trade.*

Figure 5.2. Growth and tourism

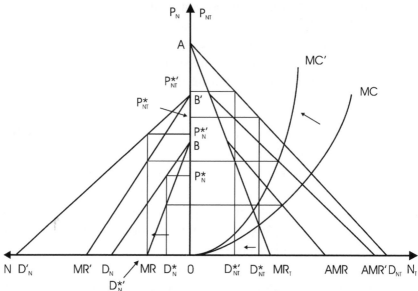

The above proposition shows that an improvement in the terms of trade (P) also results in an improvement in the tertiary terms of trade. Structural adjustment is along the traditional lines. However, an *important* and interesting feature of the model is the impact of a change in P on P_{NT}. Since P_{NT} is the relative price which is paid by tourists it represents an increase in the relative price of exports, hence, an additional favourable movement in the terms of trade, referred to in this book as a tertiary terms of trade.

Finally, we explore the relationship between the terms of trade and resident welfare. By utilizing the national income equation and properties of the transformation surface, we obtain

$$\hat{I} = \frac{PE_1}{I}\hat{P} + \frac{D_{NT}P_{NT}}{I}\hat{P}_{NT} + \frac{D_N}{(\varepsilon_{DN}-1)I}\hat{D}_N + \frac{D_{NT}}{(\epsilon_{DNT}-1)I}\hat{D}_{NT} \quad (5.22)$$

This expression has three effects:

(a) The traditional terms-of-trade effect captured by the term

$$\frac{PE_1}{I}\hat{P} > 0.$$

(b) A tertiary terms-of-trade effect captured by

$$\frac{D_{NT} P_{NT}}{I} \hat{P}_{NT}$$

which is also positive for the factor intensities assumed in our model.

(c) Two volume effects arising from the distortion in the product markets caused by the presence of a discriminating monopolist in the production of non-traded good. It is clear that $\hat{D}_{NT} < 0$ while $\hat{D}_N \lesseqgtr 0$ for the intensities assumed. These expressions reflect the non-tangency between the transformation and price surfaces. This is in line with results on the effect of a change in terms-of-trade and welfare discussed in the trade and distortion literature (see Hazari (1978)).

It is evident that resident welfare cannot be given a unique sign. Resident welfare increases provided price effects are greater than the volume effects of the presence of monopoly in production. Thus, in the presence of tourism with monopoly production, the Krueger–Sonnenschein result on the relation between terms of trade and welfare does not hold.

5.3.2. Increase in tourist demand, output changes and resident welfare

In this section, we examine the consequences of an increase in demand for tourism and its impact on outputs and resident welfare. The shift in the tourist demand function is captured by θ_1 and θ_2 as shown below:

$$P_{NT} = \theta_1 d - \theta_2 e D_{NT} \tag{5.23}$$

Note that θ_1 changes the intercept of the linear demand curve and θ_2 the slope. The new mathematical expressions for the equilibrium values of P_N, P_{NT}, D_N, D_{NT} are as follows.

$$D_N^{'*} = \frac{a\theta_2 e + A'}{D'} + \frac{(e\theta_2 c + cZ)}{D'} P \tag{5.24}$$

$$D_{NT}^{'*} = \frac{b\theta_1 d + A'Z}{D'} + \frac{cZP}{D'} \tag{5.25}$$

$$P_N^{'*} = a - b\left(\frac{a\theta_2 e - A'Z}{D'}\right) - \left(\frac{b(\theta_2 ec + cZ)}{D'}\right)P + cP \qquad (5.26)$$

$$P_{NT}^{'*} = \theta_1 d - \theta_2 e\left(\frac{b\theta_1 d + A'Z}{D'}\right) + \frac{\theta_2 cZ}{D'}P \qquad (5.27)$$

where $D' = 2(b\theta_1 d + (b + \theta_2 e)Z)$ and $A' = (\theta_1 d - a)$.

Comparing the above equilibrium values for prices and demands of the post-tourism boom with corresponding equilibrium values of the pre-tourist boom (Equations (5.12)–(5.15)), the movement in the equilibrium values of prices and demands depends on the values of the coefficients of the demand and marginal cost curves and the values of θ_1 and θ_2. We illustrate the following case:

$$P_{NT}^{'*} > P_{NT}^* \text{ provided } \theta_1 d - \frac{\theta_2 e}{D'}(b\theta_1 d + A'Z - \theta_2 cZP)$$

$$> d - \frac{e}{D}(bd + AZ) - cZP \qquad (5.28)$$

$$P_{NT}^{'*} > P_N^* \text{ provided } a - \frac{b}{D'}(a\theta_2 e - A'Z + b(\theta_2 ec + cZ)P)$$

$$+ cP > a - \frac{b}{D}(ae + AZ + b(ec + cZ)P) + cP \qquad (5.29)$$

$$D_{NT}^{'*} > D_{NT}^* \text{ provided } \frac{1}{D'}(b\theta_1 d + A'Z - cZP)$$

$$> \frac{1}{D}(bd - AZ - cZP) \qquad (5.30)$$

$$D_N^{'*} < D_N^* \text{ provided } \frac{1}{D'}(a\theta_2 e - A'Z + (e\theta_2 c + cZ)P)$$

$$< \frac{1}{D}(ae + AZ + (ec + cZ)P) \qquad (5.31)$$

Figure 5.3 illustrates the above case where the foreign demand curve shifts such that its intercept is greater than the old one (as shown by points A and A' where $A' > A$) and is flatter. This result in a new aggregate marginal revenue curve $A'AMR'$ which intersects the marginal cost curve at e' providing us with the

Figure 5.3. Terms of trade and non-traded goods

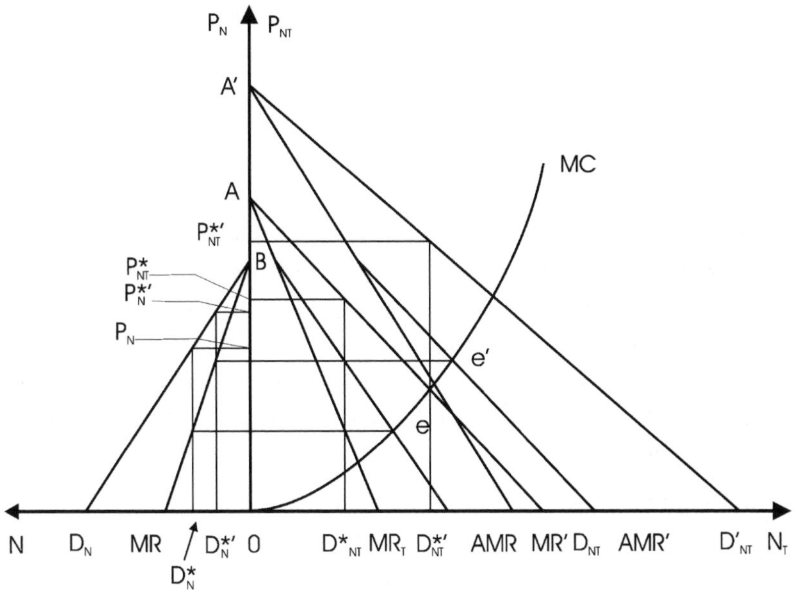

equilibrium values, which are compared with the pre-shift values as shown in the diagram.

We now proceed to examine the impact of an increase in tourist demand on domestic welfare. By utilizing the national income equation and the properties of the transformation surface we obtain the following expression:

$$\hat{I} = \alpha_T \left[\frac{\hat{D}_{NT} + (\varepsilon_{DN} - 1)\hat{P}_{NT}}{(\varepsilon_{DN} - 1)} \right] + \frac{\alpha_2}{(\varepsilon_D - 1)} \hat{D}_N \qquad (5.32)$$

where

$\alpha_T = P_{NT}X_{NT}/I =$ share of non-traded good (produced for tourists) in total income.

$\alpha = P_N X_N/I =$ share of non-traded good (produced for residents) in total income.

$\varepsilon_{DNT} =$ price elasticity of demand for the non-traded good consumed by tourists.

$\varepsilon_{DN} =$ price elasticity of demand for the non-traded good consumed by residents.

We first comment on expressions in Equations (5.28)–(5.31). As is obvious from these expressions, output of the monopolist rises in the market selling this good to the tourists and falls in the market where it is sold to the domestic consumers. Thus, on one side of the market, monopoly power is falling due to the exogenous increase in demand while on the other side it is increasing – one side of the market moves towards competitive outputs while the other moves further away from the competitive output. The residents consume less of this good as they are 'crowded out' by tourists.

The effect on resident welfare is captured in Equation (5.32) by the terms already used in Equation (5.24)–(5.31). The first square bracketed term captures the output and price effects on welfare (as shown in Figure 5.3) and are both positive. The second term captures the 'crowding out' effect on the residents' consumption of the non-traded good (as shown in Figure 5.3) which in this case is negative. It is this 'crowding out' or an increase in the monopoly distortion which may lower domestic welfare. Note that the economy always gains from a tourist generated terms-of-trade effect as shown by $P_{NT}^{'*} > P_{NT}^{*}$. The resident welfare will only fall provided the two positive effects are outweighed by the 'crowding out' effect.

5.4. Increasing returns to scale

In our discussion so far we have assumed that the monopolist faces increasing marginal cost. Tourists not only consume private but also a host of public and quasi-public goods. Hence, it is not unrealistic to assume that the production of good, X_N, may be characterized by increasing returns to scale.

We consider two scenarios in the case of increasing returns to scale. First is the case where the output of the non-traded good is positive irrespective of tourist demand. Second is the case where tourist demand allows the output of the non-traded good to be produced. The solutions are shown geometrically and then related to the mathematics that has already been presented.

In Figure 5.4 the AD^d curve shows the domestic demand for the non-traded good. In the absence of tourist demand the equilibrium output will be at X_N^d and the monopoly price at P_N^d. The aggregate

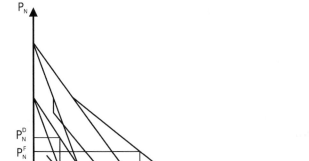

Figure 5.4. *Increasing returns and equilibrium*

demand consisting of domestic and tourist demand is given by the demand curve AD^{d+F} and the marginal revenue curve MR^{d+F}. In the absence of price discrimination this gives rise to an equilibrium output of X_N^{d+F} and price of P_N^F.

Monopoly output increases due to additional demand while the equilibrium price falls from P_N^d to P_N^F. In this case welfare outcomes depend again on the movements of $\hat{P}_N$ and $\hat{X}_N$. Due to increasing returns to scale, price falls and output increases. Figure 5.5 depicts an interesting case. In this case domestic demand is not sufficient for this industry to operate. Given the downward sloping marginal cost curve, domestic marginal revenue is always less than marginal cost, so there is no equilibrium and this good is not produced. However, foreign demand may bring this industry into existence as the foreign marginal revenue curve may intersect the marginal cost curve, resulting in equilibrium in this market. In fact the equilibrium would be attained at the point where aggregate marginal revenue equals marginal cost and in this case both domestic and foreign consumers can consume this good since it is now profitable to produce it. That is, prior to the tourist demand, the only goods entering the resident utility function were

Figure 5.5. **Increasing returns and no do domestic market**

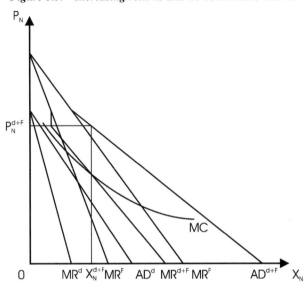

goods X_1 and X_2.[4] Post-tourists, we have a third good entering the resident utility function, X_N. We are, therefore, unable to draw any welfare conclusions between the two situations.

5.5. Conclusion

This chapter analyzes the role of tourism in a trade model which has aspects of general and partial equilibrium. To our knowledge, this represents the first attempt at incorporating a discriminating monopolist who is able to charge different prices to tourists and residents. This discriminatory pricing policy exploits the implicit gains from trade from tourism. The chapter also shows how a movement in the terms of trade leads to a favourable movement in the tertiary terms of trade. We also derive conditions for an increase in resident welfare as a consequence of expansion in tourism.

---

[4] These changes all affect the output levels of X_1 and X_2 due to the general equilibrium properties of the model. These changes are not of interest given the focus of this book, hence their omission.

References

Batra, R.N. (1975), *The Theory of International Trade Under Uncertainty*, New York: Academic Press.

Cassing, J. (1977), "International trade in the presence of pure monopoly in the non-traded goods sector", *The Economic Journal*, Vol. 87, pp. 523–532.

Hazari, B.R. (1978), *The Pure Theory of International Trade and Distortions*, London: Croom Helm.

CHAPTER 6

Tourism, Guest Workers and Resident Immiserization

6.1. Introduction

As stated previously tourism is a growing and important industry in many countries. It provides employment to a large proportion of the domestic labour force as well as to guest workers. A large number of guest workers are visible in many hotels and restaurants in both developed and developing economies. However, to our knowledge, there is no theoretical analysis of the impact of a boom in tourism on the welfare of the residents in the presence of guest workers.[1] The presence of guest workers in the tourism industry adds interesting dimensions to the analysis of the interaction between such an increase in tourism and resident welfare. First, as demonstrated in Chapter 3 tourism generally bestows monopoly power in trade to the host country by converting non-traded goods into tradeable goods with endogenous and flexible prices. If guest workers are employed in tourism or any other industry then they also consume the non-traded goods. This consumption by guest workers also converts non-traded goods into tradables, specifically exportables, hence, again bestowing guest worker generated monopoly power in trade to the home country. We establish that under certain plausible conditions a tourist boom in the presence of guest workers results in the immiserization of the resident population. This result is shown to be a consequence of two effects: (i) a favourable terms-of-trade effect from an increase in tourism and (ii) an unfavourable terms-of-trade effect of guest

---

[1] The impact of tourism boom on domestic welfare without guest workers has been analyzed by several authors. Several papers have appeared in a special issue on tourism and trade in Pacific Economic Review, October, 2003.

workers consumption of non-traded goods and services. If effect (ii) is greater than effect (i) then the host country is immiserized. In the process of establishing the above result we also present other interesting trade theory results, for example, establishing a proper technique for analyzing guest worker consumption by using microeconomic foundations. This technique may also be used for consumption of non-traded goods by other temporary entrants, for example, overseas students and illegal workers.

These results are based on a static model of trade and may not necessarily be valid in a growth model with guest workers. In the static model the optimal policy for avoiding resident immiserization is in line with trade and distortion theory and would be a tax on the consumption of the non-traded goods to raise its price and a subsidy to domestic residents whose welfare matters to the social planner. In a dynamic framework guest workers may add to the productivity in the system. However, even in a dynamic setting the social planner (government) should be aware of possible adverse movement in the terms of trade arising from the consumption of non-traded goods by guest workers.

6.2. A model of tourism with guest workers

To obtain the above results we utilize the interesting and innovative production and consumption structure of the generalized Harris–Todaro model (without the HT migration function and the minimum wage restriction).[2] The economy is divided into two regions: an urban and a coastal region. The urban region produces two goods: an internationally traded good X_1 and a non-traded good, X_N. The coastal region also produces two goods: an internationally traded good, X_2 and X_S, a non-traded good only consumed by tourists and produced in the rural region.[3] Coastal areas provide three S's: sun, sand and sea but its enjoyment requires the production of non-traded goods and services like hotels, parks, transport and so on. In many countries, for example, Fiji, tourists may not be attracted to the urban areas while in

---

[2] See Hazari and Sgro (2001) for a treatment of the generalized Harris–Todaro model.

[3] It is very easy to relax this assumption but its relaxation does not add any new insights or any new results. Hence, for mathematical tractability the demand by domestic residents and guest workers has been ignored in our analysis.

European cities like Rome, Paris, or London, the cities themselves may be the main attraction.

The production functions for the four goods by regions are given below:

Urban region:

$$X_1 = F_1[K_1, L_1] \tag{6.1}$$

$$X_N = F_N[K_N, L_N] \tag{6.2}$$

Coastal region:

$$X_2 = F_2[T_2, L_2] \tag{6.3}$$

$$X_S = F_S[T_S, \bar{L}_{SG}] \tag{6.4}$$

Some comments are in order on the use of factors in the production of these goods. Urban output is produced by labour (domestic) and urban capital which is mobile within the urban region but is not used in the coastal area: the terms K_1, L_1, K_N, L_N denote the factor allocations to the sectors X_1 and X_N. The coastal region uses land, labour and guest workers. Both rural sectors use land: T_2 by the agricultural sector and T_S by the coastal tourism sector. However, sector X_S uses guest workers admitted on a quota basis and denoted by $\bar{L}_{SG}$. Four goods are produced with four factors of production satisfying the requirement of equality between goods and factors. Note that the model represents a mix of mobility of factors and specificity: $\bar{L}_{SG}$ specific to the tourism sector, land and capital mobile between two sectors and domestic labour mobile among three sectors and across regions.

On the demand side of our model, we postulate that there exist two utility functions: one for domestic residents and the other for guest workers. There may be several plausible reasons for justifying this assumption including differences in culture and tastes. It is assumed that the resident utility function is given by

$$U^R = U^R[D_1^R, D_2^R, D_N^R] \tag{6.5}$$

where D_1^R, D_2^R and D_N^R denote the consumption of goods X_1, X_2 and X_N, respectively, by residents. This function is maximized subject to the budget constraint that

$$D_1^R + PD_2^R + P_N D_N^R = X_1 + PX_2 + P_N X_N + P_S X_S - w_G \bar{L}_{SG}$$
$$= wL + rK + \Pi T \qquad (6.6)$$

which states that domestic expenditure equals net national product. The price of good X_1 has been taken as a numeraire. The P_is denote relative commodity prices and w_G the wage received by the guest workers.

The guest worker utility function is defined as

$$U^G = U^G[D_1^G, D_2^G, D_N^G] \qquad (6.7)$$

where D_i^G $(i = 1, 2, N)$ denote the consumption of goods X_i $(i = 1, 2, N)$ by the guest workers. They maximize the utility function U^G subject to the budget constraint that

$$D_1^G + PD_2^G + P_N D_N^G = w_G \bar{L}_{SG} \qquad (6.8)$$

Note that there are two maximization problems in this system with different utility functions and budget constraints. The utility functions of residents and guest workers are assumed to be quasi-concave and possess both behavioural and welfare significance.

Market clearing requires that the following constraints are satisfied:

$$D_N^R + D_N^G = X_N \qquad (6.9)$$

$$D_{ST} = X_S \qquad (6.10)$$

The demand for the non-traded good ($D_N^R + D_N^G$) equals the supply of the non-traded good, X_N. Equation (6.10) shows that the demand for D_{ST} equals its supply, X_S. This good is consumed only by the tourists. The price structure of the model is given below:

Urban region:

$$a_{L1}w + a_{K1}r = P_N \qquad (6.11)$$

$$a_{LN}w + a_{KN}r = 1 \qquad (6.12)$$

Coastal region:

$$a_{LG}w_G + a_{TS}\Pi = P_S \qquad (6.13)$$

$$a_{L2}w + a_{T2}\Pi = P \tag{6.14}$$

where

Π = rent on land
P_N = the relative price of the non-traded good
P = the international terms of trade
P_S = the relative price of good X_S which is solely consumed by tourists.

Finally the full employment conditions are given below:

$$a_{LN}X_N + a_{L1}X_1 + a_{L2}X_2 = \bar{L} \tag{6.15}$$

$$a_{KN}X_N + a_{K1}X_1 = \bar{K} \tag{6.16}$$

$$a_{T2}X_2 + a_{TS}X_S = \bar{T} \tag{6.17}$$

$$a_{LG}X_S = \bar{L}_{SG} \tag{6.18}$$

The right-hand side of the above equations denote the inelastic supply of the factors of production. This completes the specification of the model. This provides a system of 26 unknowns: $X_1, K_1, L_1, X_N, K_N, L_N, X_2, T_2, L_2, X_S, T_S, U^R, D_1^R, D_2^R, D_N^R, P_N, w_G, U^G, D_1^G, D_2^G, D_N^G, D_S^G, w, r, \Pi$ and P_S in 26 equations. The equations for determining the a_{ij}s have been omitted.

6.3. Results

We begin by obtaining expressions for the change in the income of residents and guest workers. By differentiating totally Equations (6.6) and (6.8) and using the utility function in Equations (6.5) and (6.7) to define change in real income we obtain

$$\hat{I}^R - \theta'_{NG}\hat{P}_N + \theta'_G\hat{w}_G = \theta_S\hat{P}_S \tag{6.19}$$

$$\hat{I}^G + \theta_{NG}\hat{P}_N - \theta_G\hat{w}_G = 0 \tag{6.20}$$

where

$$\theta'_{NG} = \frac{P_N D_N^G}{I^R}$$

$$\theta_{NG} = \frac{P_N D_N^R}{I^G}$$

$$\theta'_G = \frac{w_G \bar{L}_{SG}}{I^G}$$

$$\theta_S = \frac{X_S}{I^R}$$

where $\hat{I}^R$ and $\hat{I}^G$ denote changes in real income for resident and guest workers.

It is important to point out at this stage that the change in resident income depends on the consumption by guest workers and their wage rate. The consumption of the non-traded good by guest workers transforms this good into a traded good leading to a terms-of-trade effect. Thus in this model there are two terms-of-trade effects: one via P_S (tertiary) and the other via P_N (non-standard). If both effects are positive then domestic residents always gain from an increase in tourism.

By differentiating Equations (6.11)–(6.14) and solving we obtain

$$\hat{w} = -\frac{\theta_{K1}\hat{P}_N}{|\theta|^U} \tag{6.21}$$

$$\hat{r} = \frac{\theta_{L1}\hat{P}_N}{|\theta|^U} \tag{6.22}$$

$$\hat{\Pi} = \frac{\theta_{L2}}{\theta_{T2}} \frac{\theta_{K1}}{|\theta|^U} \hat{P}_N \tag{6.23}$$

$$\hat{P}_S = \theta_{LG}\hat{w}_G + \frac{\theta_{TS}\theta_{L2}}{\theta_{T2}} \frac{\theta_{K1}}{|\theta|^U} \hat{P}_N \tag{6.24}$$

where $|\theta|^U = \theta_{L1}\theta_{LN}(k_N - k_1)$.

First, note that we have used P_N as a parameter to solve for w, r and Π. Since P_N is an endogenous variable a solution for this variable will be obtained later in the chapter. Equation (6.24) gives a relation between w_G, P_N and P_S. While the changes in w and r are in line with the Stolper–Samuelson theorem, this is not the case for rental on land which depends on urban factor intensities $|\theta|^U$. The following proposition follows from Equation (6.23).

Proposition 6.1. *An increase in the relative price of the urban non-traded good raises the rental on coastal land for $k_N - k_1 > 0$. A decrease in the relative price of the urban non-traded good lowers the rental on coastal land for $k_N - k_1 < 0$.*

The above proposition clearly shows the links between the coastal and urban price structures. An increase in the price of the urban non-traded good raises the rental on land when the non-traded good is capital intensive and lowers it when it is labour intensive. The result is illustrated in Figure 6.1. The unit cost functions for P_2 and ($P_1 = 1$) are given for a small open economy as shown in Figure 6.1. note that $P = (P_2/P_1)$ Let us assume that there is a given level of P_N as shown by the curve passing through e_0. This is an equilibrium point with wage, w_0, rental on capital r_0 and rental on land Π_0. The diagram clearly shows the dependence of the coastal rent on urban variables and this dependence arises due to labour mobility across regions and sectors.

An explanation for Equation (6.24) is developed by adding another quadrant to Figure 6.1 as is shown in Figure 6.2. Let us assume that P_S has been obtained from the demand and supply equation for this market. This P_S is shown in the Π and w_G space by the cost function P_S. Let us assume that P_N is also given, then we obtain the equilibrium values of r^*, Π^*, w^* and w_G^* for all our

Figure 6.1.   Equilibrium factor prices 1

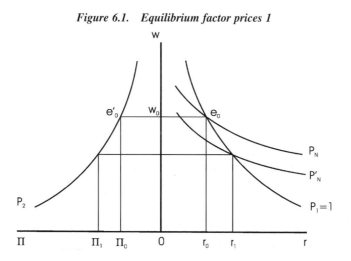

Figure 6.2. Equilibrium factor prices 2

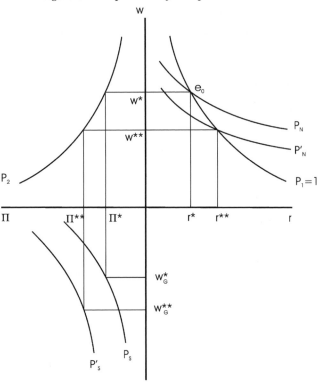

variables. Now suppose that P_S increases as shown by P_S' and P_N falls to P_N'. It then follows that r^* rises to r^{**}, Π^* to Π^{**}, w_G from w_G^* to w_G^{**} and w falls from w^* to w^{**} illustrating all the mechanisms that are involved in Equations (6.21)–(6.24) (on the assumption that P_N falls). An increase in P_S lowers the wage of domestic workers. These workers would oppose tourism as it adversely affects their wages.

We now proceed to use the rest of the model to obtain solutions for the variables P_N, w_G, I^G and I^R. From Equation (6.12) it is easy to establish that a boom in tourism raises P_S, i.e. $\hat{P}_S$ is positive. Given this information we differentiate Equation (6.9) totally to obtain

$$A\hat{P}_N + \alpha \hat{I}^R + \alpha' \hat{I}^G = \varepsilon_{NS}\hat{P}_S \qquad (6.25)$$

where

$$A = \left[\frac{P_N}{X_N} \left(\frac{\partial D_N^R}{\partial P_N} + \frac{\partial D_N^G}{\partial P_N} \right) - \frac{P_N}{X_N} \frac{\partial X_N}{\partial P_N} \right] < 0$$

$$\alpha = \frac{I^R}{X_N} \frac{\partial D_N^R}{\partial I^R} > 0$$

$$\alpha' = \frac{I^G}{X_N} \frac{\partial D_N^G}{\partial I^G} > 0$$

$$\varepsilon_{NS} = \frac{P_S}{X_N} \frac{\partial X_N}{\partial P_S}$$

With this expression we obtain a system of four equations in four unknowns as given below:

$$\begin{pmatrix} 0 & 1 & -\theta_{NG}' & \theta_G \\ 1 & 0 & \theta_{NG} & \theta_G \\ 0 & 0 & \dfrac{Z}{|\theta|^U} & \theta_{LG} \\ \alpha' & \alpha & A & 0 \end{pmatrix} \begin{pmatrix} \hat{I}^G \\ \hat{I}^R \\ \hat{P}_N \\ \hat{w}_G \end{pmatrix} = \begin{pmatrix} \theta_S \hat{P}_S \\ 0 \\ \hat{P}_S \\ \varepsilon_{NS} \hat{P}_S \end{pmatrix} \qquad (6.26)$$

where

$$Z = \frac{\theta_{TS} \theta_{L2} \theta_{K1}}{\theta_{T2}} > 0$$

The above system is solved to obtain the following solution for the two important variables in the system

$$\hat{P}_N = \frac{\theta_{LG} \varepsilon_{NS} - \alpha' \theta_G}{D} \hat{P}_S \qquad (6.27)$$

$$\hat{I}^R = \theta_S \hat{P}_S + \theta_{NG}' \hat{P}_N - \theta_{LG} \hat{w}_G \qquad (6.28)$$

where

$$D = \theta_{LG}(A + \alpha\theta'_{NG} - \alpha'\theta_{NG}) + \frac{Z}{|\theta|^U}(\alpha\theta'_G - \alpha'\theta_G)$$

Due to the stability conditions, the term D will be negative.

From Equation (6.26) we can solve for $\hat{w}_G$ as shown below:

$$\hat{w}_G = \frac{1}{\theta_{LG}}\hat{P}_S - \frac{Z}{|\theta|^U\theta_{LG}}\hat{P}_N \qquad (6.29)$$

By substituting from Equation (6.29) into Equation (6.28) and some manipulation we obtain

$$\hat{I}^R = \left[\frac{\theta_S Z}{|\theta|^U} + \theta'_{NG}\right]\hat{P}_N \qquad (6.30)$$

Note that the direct terms-of-trade effect of P_S on I^R is always equal to the effect of P_S on w_G, hence, they cancel each other out. The only change that affects I^R is through a change in P_N. This is captured directly through the terms-of-trade effect, θ'_{NG}, in Equation (6.30) and indirectly through a change in w_G, wage bill paid to guest workers. This is shown by $(\theta_S Z/|\theta|^U)$ in Equation (6.30). The following propositions are based on Equations (6.27) and (6.30).

Proposition 6.2. *The relative price of the urban non-traded good falls (rises) as a consequence of an increase in tourism if and only if*

$$\theta_{LG}\varepsilon_{NS} - \alpha'\theta_G > 0 \, (< 0)$$

Proposition 6.3. *Resident welfare falls (increases) as a consequence of a tourist boom in the coastal region provided that P_N falls and*

$$\theta'_{NG} + \frac{Z\theta_S}{|\theta|^U} > 0$$

Proposition 6.4. *Resident welfare falls (increases) as a consequence of a tourist boom in the coastal region provided that*

P_N rises and

$$\theta'_{NG} + \frac{Z\theta_S}{|\theta|^U} > 0$$

Propositions 6.2 and 6.3 clearly show that for the case in which $\hat{P}_N$ is negative, as a result of an increase in coastal tourism, this could immiserize the resident population. A few remarks are in order regarding the inequalities in Propositions 6.2 and 6.3.

Remarks on Equation (6.27). An increase in the relative price of P_S results in an increase in X_S, hence, more land is required by this sector. To meet this demand, the agricultural sector releases land and employment decreases in the rural areas. As a result, the increase in the supply of labour to the urban region gives rise to a Rybczynski effect, therefore, X_N increases provided it is labour intensive ($|\theta|^U < 0$ and then $\varepsilon_{NS} > 0$; see Appendix A6). If the supply effect is greater than the change in demand, the price of the urban non-traded good falls ($\hat{P}_N < 0$), i.e. $\theta_{LG}\varepsilon_{NS} - \theta_G\alpha' > 0$.

Remarks on Equation (6.30). Note that $\hat{I}^R$ depends on the sign of both $|\theta|^U$ and P_N. We distinguish between two cases of immiserization:

Case 1: $|\theta|^U < 0$, $\hat{P}_N < 0$ positive bracketed term
Case 2: $|\theta|^U < 0$, $\hat{P}_N > 0$, negative bracketed term.

In this latter case there is a terms-of-trade improvement from guest workers but the rise in the relative price of P_N also leads to an increase in w_G which increases the wage bill paid to guest workers. It is clear from the above discussion that an adverse movement in the terms of trade in the market for good X_N may be a cause of immiserization. It is also clear that even if there is an increase in P_N, I^R may still be negative. Let us explain Case 1 where P_N falls. Let us start with the top part of Figure 6.3. The box 0_sACB shows the availability of land and guest workers in the coastal region – guest workers by the distance 0_SA and land by the distance 0_SB. Guest workers are only used by the tourism industry, hence, its output must be on the line AC so that it fully employs all the guest workers. Let this output be denoted by the isoquant $\tilde{X}_S$. The supply of land available for use by sector X_2 is the distance $A'C$, hence, it must also

Figure 6.3.   *Coastal and urban production*
Coastal Box And Production

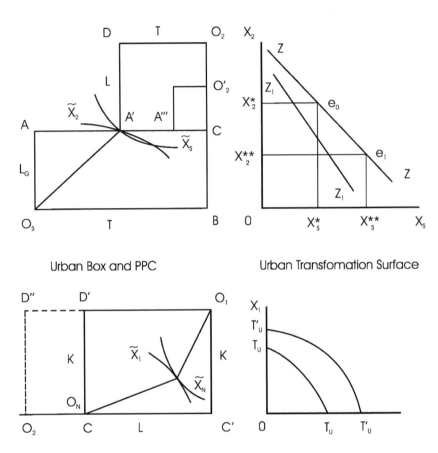

Urban Box and PPC   Urban Transfomation Surface

attain equilibrium at point A'. Suppose it uses 0_2C of domestic labour with $A'C$ of land to generate output level $\tilde{X}_2$. It is *important* to note that at point A' the slopes of the isoquants will not be equal because they represent different factor price ratios: w_G/Π for X_S and w/Π for X_2. In our model, since guest workers are specific to the coastal region, and are skilled workers, we shall assume that $w_G > w$. This gives rise to the rural output boxes $0X_2^*e_0X_S^*$ and $0X_2^{**}e_1X_S^{**}$. Now consider the urban region. The total supply of labour to the economy equals the distance $0_2C'$ of which 0_2C is absorbed by the coastal region. The urban region has CC' of labour and CD' of capital that it can use to produce X_N and X_1. Let the equilibrium outputs be denoted by $\tilde{X}_N$ and $\tilde{X}_1$ at equilibrium. The transformation surface for this region is given by $T_U T_U$ and the factor box by $CD'0_1C'$. It is clear that the two regions are linked with each other via the boxes and movements in labour.

Now suppose that there is a tourism boom that raises the output of X_S as shown by A''' in the box on the top part of Figure 6.3. This implies that output of X_2 must contract as land available to this sector has fallen and P is fixed. In the extreme case sector X_S could produce at C wiping out sector 2 completely (a case of coastal de-industrialization of the region). As X_2 contracts it releases labour for use in the urban region and now only uses $C0'_2$ of labour and CA''' of land to produce output of X_2. The coastal transformation box changes as shown in the top panel. The coastal region is losing income in the diagram. The urban area has more supply of the labour force, hence, its box expands to $C'0_2D''0_1$ which is larger than $CD'0_1C'$, hence, the urban production possibility curve moves from $T_U T_U$ to $T'_U T'_U$ with the Rybczynski production bias shifting the supply curve of good X_N to the right as shown in Figure 6.4. The supply curve shifts from S_N to S'_N. A change in P_S induces both a demand and a supply shift in the X_N market leading to the possibility of a rise or a fall in the relative price P_N. In Figure 6.4 the case of a fall in P_N is depicted. A fall in the relative price of P_N

Figure 6.4.   *Equilibrium in the urban non-traded sector*

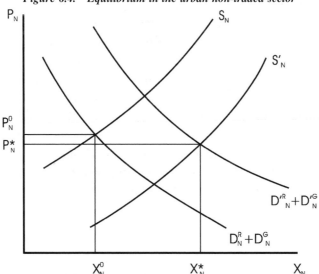

represents a terms of trade loss from the consumption of guest workers.

Remarks for Policy. In the discussion above we have demonstrated how resident immerization could occur as a consequence of a boom in tourism in the presence of guest workers. The mechanism for this process is 2-fold: (i) the presence of monopoly power in trade and (ii) the possibility of an adverse movement in the terms of trade (arising from the consumption of non-traded goods by guest workers) outweighing the gains from expansion in tourism (Case 1), (iii) a favourable movement in the terms of trade but a corresponding and greater increase in the wage bill paid to workers (Case 2). Thus resident immiserization arises due to a distortion in the system. For Case 1 the policy prescription for avoiding immiserization is a tax on the consumption of non-traded goods and a subsidy for the domestic residents whose welfare matters.[4] The tax on consumption of the non-traded good would raise its price, hence, removing the adverse terms-of-trade effect. Tax revenue distributed to residents will restore or raise their welfare. A tax on the non-traded good raises its price reversing the adverse movement in the terms of trade (the tax should be at least as large as to restore the price which prevailed before the tourism boom occurred) and the tax revenue should be given to domestic residents.

In Case 1 the decline in P_N has a negative terms-of-trade effect on I^R arising from the monopoly power in trade for good X_N, but it also has a positive effect on I^R because it lowers the wage bill paid to guest workers. The optimal policy should remove the distortion and the negative terms-of-trade effect without affecting the positive effect (through w_G). Therefore, after the imposition of the export tax, $\hat{I}^R$ should not be equal to 0 but to some positive amount (corresponding to the gain due to the decline of w_G). Note that the domestic residents consume three goods; hence, this policy should not be confused with the revenue being collected and being simply transferred to residents. Moreover, guest workers would not be compensated.

---

[4] The proof of this result is available from the authors.

We now proceed to derive the optimal export tax

$$P_N(1 + t) = P_N^*$$

or

$$P_N T = P_N^*$$

where $T = (1 + t)$ and P_N is the price of non-traded goods for residents and P_N^* the price of X_N for guest workers.

Equations (6.21)–(6.24) now become

$$\hat{w} = -\frac{\theta_{KM}(\hat{P}_N^* - \hat{T})}{|\theta|^{\mathrm{U}}} \tag{6.31}$$

$$\hat{\alpha} = \frac{\theta_{LM}}{|\theta|^{\mathrm{U}}}(\hat{P}_N^* - \hat{T}) \tag{6.32}$$

$$\hat{\Pi} = \frac{Z}{|\theta|^{\mathrm{U}}}(\hat{P}_N^* - \hat{T}) \tag{6.33}$$

$$\hat{w}_G = \frac{1}{\theta_{LG}}(\hat{P}_N^* - \hat{T}) \tag{6.34}$$

while Equation (6.27) is replaced by

$$A\hat{P}_N^* + (A' - A)\hat{T} + \alpha\hat{I}^{\mathrm{R}} + \alpha'\hat{I}^{\mathrm{G}} = \varepsilon_{NS}\hat{P}_S \tag{6.35}$$

with

$$A = \frac{P_N}{X_N}\left(\frac{\partial D_N^{\mathrm{R}}}{\partial P_N} - \frac{\partial X_N}{\partial P_N}\right) + \frac{P_N^*}{X_N}\frac{\partial D_N^{\mathrm{G}}}{\partial P_N^*} < 0$$

$$A' = \frac{P_N^*}{X_N}\frac{\partial D_N^{\mathrm{G}}}{\partial P_N^{\mathrm{G}}} < 0$$

$$A - A' = \frac{P_N}{X_N}\left(\frac{\partial D_N^{\mathrm{R}}}{\partial P_N} - \frac{\partial X_N}{\partial P_N}\right) < 0$$

The expressions for $\hat{I}^R$ and $\hat{I}^G$ are

$$\hat{I}^R = \theta_S \hat{P}_S - \theta'_G \hat{w}_G + \theta'_{NG} \hat{P}^*_N + \theta_{tN} \hat{D}^G_N \tag{6.36}$$

$$\hat{I}^G = \theta_G \hat{w} - \theta_{NG} \hat{P}^*_N \tag{6.37}$$

with

$$\theta_{tN} = \frac{(P^*_N - P_N)D^G_N}{I^R} = \frac{(T - 1/T)P^*_N D^G_N}{I^R}$$

Let us set the initial export tax to zero, therefore, $t = 0$ implies that $T = 1$ so that $\theta_{tN} = 0$. Hence, the new system of equations, using Equations (6.27), (6.31), (6.36) and (6.37), is

$$\begin{pmatrix} 0 & 1 & -\theta'_{NG} & \theta'_G \\ 1 & 0 & \theta_{NG} & -\theta_G \\ 0 & 0 & \dfrac{Z}{|\theta|^U} & \theta_{LG} \\ \alpha' & \alpha & A & 0 \end{pmatrix} \begin{pmatrix} \hat{I}^G \\ \hat{I}^R \\ \hat{P}^*_N \\ \hat{w}_G \end{pmatrix}$$

$$= \begin{pmatrix} \theta_S \hat{P}_S \\ 0 \\ \hat{P}_S + \dfrac{Z}{|\theta|^U}\hat{T} \\ \varepsilon_{NS}\hat{P}_S + (A - A')\hat{T} \end{pmatrix} \tag{6.38}$$

From which we can obtain

$$\hat{I}^R = \frac{1}{D}\left\{[\theta_{LG}\varepsilon_{NS} - \theta_G\alpha']\left(\theta'_{BG} + \frac{Z\theta_S}{|\theta|^U}\right)\hat{P}_S \right.$$
$$\left. + \theta_{LG}\left[-A'\frac{Z\theta_S}{|\theta|^U} + \theta'_{NG}(A - A')\right]\hat{T}\right\} \tag{6.39}$$

For Case 1, $|\theta|^U < 0$, $\theta_{LG}\varepsilon_{NS} - \theta_G\alpha' > 0$, $\theta_{NG} + Z\theta_S/|\theta|^U > 0$ which implies that $\hat{P}_N < 0$. The export tax should only be used to remove the loss rising from the adverse movement in the terms-of-trade, that is

$$\frac{1}{D}[\theta_{LG}\varepsilon_{NS} - \theta_G\alpha']\theta'_{NG}\hat{P}_S \; (< 0)$$

Therefore, $\hat{T}$ has to be set such that

$$\frac{1}{D}\left\{\theta_{LG}\left[-A'\frac{Z\theta_S}{|\theta|^U}+\theta'_{NG}(A-A')\right]\hat{T}-[\theta_{LG}\varepsilon_{NS}-\theta_G\alpha']\theta_{NG}\hat{P}_S\right\}=0$$

which gives us the optimal value of T:

$$\hat{T}=\frac{[\varepsilon_{NS}-\alpha'\theta'_S]\theta'_{NG}}{A'\dfrac{Z\theta_S}{|\theta|^U}+\theta'_{NG}(A'-A)}\hat{P}_S>0 \quad \text{with } \theta'_S=\frac{P_SX_S}{I^G} \tag{6.40}$$

The imposition of this export tax results in the following expression for the change in resident income.

$$\hat{I}^R=\frac{1}{D}[\theta_{LG}\varepsilon_{NS}-\alpha'\theta_G]\frac{Z\theta_S}{|\theta|^U}\hat{P}_S$$

which is positive.

In Case 2 the policy measure will be different because there is a terms-of-trade improvement ($\hat{P}_N>0$) and an increase in the wage bill (larger than the terms-of-trade gain). Here the optimal policy should be a tax on the guest workers wage rate w_G and a transfer payment to domestic residents. This implies that

$$P_ND_N^G+P_MD_M^G+D_A^G=\bar{L}_{SG}\hat{w}_G(1-t) \tag{6.41}$$

$$P_ND_N^R+P_MD_M^R+D_A^R=(P_NX_N+P_MX_M+P_SX_S+X_A)$$
$$-\bar{L}_{SG}\hat{w}_G(1-t) \tag{6.42}$$

and

$$\hat{I}^R=\theta_S\hat{P}_S+\theta'_{NG}\hat{P}_N-\theta'_G\hat{w}_G+\theta'_{tG}\hat{t} \tag{6.43}$$

$$\hat{I}^G=\theta_G\hat{w}_G-\theta_{NG}\hat{P}_N-\theta_{tG}\hat{t} \tag{6.44}$$

with

$$\theta'_G=\frac{\bar{L}_{SG}(1-t)w_G}{I^R}, \qquad \theta_G=\frac{\bar{L}_{SG}(1-t)w_G}{I^G},$$

$$\theta'_{tG}=\frac{\bar{L}_{SG}w_Gt}{I^R} \qquad \theta_{tG}=\frac{\bar{L}_{SG}w_Gt}{I^G}$$

The new system is Equations (6.27), (6.31), (6.42) and (6.43) and is as follows:

$$
\begin{pmatrix}
0 & 1 & -\theta'_{NG} & \theta'_G \\
1 & 0 & \theta_{NG} & -\theta_G \\
0 & 0 & \dfrac{Z}{|\theta|^U} & \theta_{LG} \\
\alpha' & \alpha & A & 0
\end{pmatrix}
\begin{pmatrix}
\hat{I}^G \\
\hat{I}^R \\
\hat{P}^*_N \\
\hat{w}_G
\end{pmatrix}
=
\begin{pmatrix}
\theta_S \hat{P}_S + \theta'_{tG}\hat{t} \\
-\theta_{tG}\hat{t} \\
\hat{P}_S \\
\varepsilon_{NS}\hat{P}_S
\end{pmatrix}
\tag{6.45}
$$

In this new system, Equation (6.45), by setting initially $t = 0$, we obtain the same results as for Case 1.

6.4. Conclusion

A large number of countries (both developed and third world) promote tourism and also use guest workers in the tourism industry. In general, tourism brings benefits to many countries by earning much needed foreign exchange, promoting the development of the infrastructure and possibly acting as an engine of growth.[5] In this chapter we have shown that under plausible conditions, tourism with guest workers may be immiserizing. This is due to the fact that the consumption by tourists as well as guest workers of non-traded goods creates monopoly power in trade. Such monopoly power in trade may lead to a favourable as well as an unfavourable movement in the two terms of trade identified in this chapter. If the movement in the latter terms of trade is larger than the former then it is possible that residents may be immiserized as a result of a boom in tourism. This chapter has added a new mechanism for possible immiserization and also suggested optimal policy for avoiding resident immiserization.

Appendix A6. Derivations

All the terms are defined in the main text. Hence, they will not be repeated here. The residents have the following utility function:

$$
U^R = U^R[D^R_N, D^R_2, D^R_1]
\tag{A6.1}
$$

---

[5] See the important work of Sinclair and Stabler (1997) for the benefits of tourism.

which they maximize subject to a budget constraint

$$P_N D_N^R + P D_2^R + D_1^R = P_N X_N + P X_2 + P_S X_S - w_G \bar{L}_G \qquad \text{(A6.2)}$$

The guest workers have the utility function

$$U^G = U^G[D_N^G, D_2^G, D_1^G] \qquad \text{(A6.3)}$$

This is maximized subject to the constraint

$$P_N D_N^G + P D_2^G + D_1^G = w_G \bar{L}_G \qquad \text{(A6.4)}$$

The balance equations are

$$D_N^R + D_N^G = X_N \qquad \text{(A6.5)}$$

$$X_S = D_{ST} \qquad \text{(A6.6)}$$

$$D_2^R + D_2^G = X_2 - E \qquad \text{(A6.7)}$$

$$D_1^R + D_1^G = X_1 + M \qquad \text{(A6.8)}$$

From Equation (A6.1)

$$\frac{\mathrm{d}U^R}{P_2} = P_N \,\mathrm{d}D_N^R + P \,\mathrm{d}D_2^R + \mathrm{d}D_1^R = \mathrm{d}I^R \qquad \text{(A6.9)}$$

This is the definition of a change in real income with P_1 as numeraire.

From Equation (A6.2)

$$P_N \,\mathrm{d}D_N^R + P \,\mathrm{d}D_2^R + \mathrm{d}D_1^R + D_1^R \,\mathrm{d}P_N$$

$$= P_N \,\mathrm{d}X_N + P \,\mathrm{d}X_2 + P_S \,\mathrm{d}X_S + X_S \,\mathrm{d}P_S - \bar{L}_G \,\mathrm{d}w_G + X_N \,\mathrm{d}P_N$$

$$\mathrm{d}I^R = (X_N - D_N^R)\mathrm{d}P_N + X_S \,\mathrm{d}P_S - \bar{L}_G \,\mathrm{d}w_G$$

$$\therefore, \qquad \hat{I}^R = \theta_{NG}' \hat{P}_N + \theta_S \hat{P}_S - \theta_G \hat{w}_G$$

Or

$$\hat{I}^R - \theta_{NG}' \hat{P}_N + \theta_G \hat{w}_G = \theta_S \hat{P}_S \qquad \text{(A6.10)}$$

A similar operation for guest workers yields

$$\hat{I}^G + \theta_{NG} \hat{P}_N - \hat{w}_G = 0 \qquad \because \quad \frac{w \bar{L}^G}{I^R} = 1 \qquad \text{(A6.11)}$$

Pricing equations for the coastal region:

$$a_{LG}w_G + a_{TS}\Pi = P_S \tag{A6.12}$$

$$a_{T2}\Pi + a_{L2}w = P \tag{A6.13}$$

Pricing equations for the urban region:

$$a_{LN}w + a_{KN}r = P_N \tag{A6.14}$$

$$a_{L1}w + a_{K1}r = 1 \tag{A6.15}$$

From Equations (A6.14) and (A6.15) by total differentiation yields the solution

$$\hat{w} = -\frac{\theta_{K1}\hat{P}_N}{|\theta|^U} \tag{A6.16}$$

$$\hat{r} = \frac{\theta_{L1}}{|\theta|^U}\hat{P}_N \tag{A6.17}$$

where

$$|\theta|^U = 1/(\theta_{L1}\theta_{LN}(k_N - k_1))$$

In the coastal region from Equation (A6.12) it follows on differentiation

$$\theta_{T2}\hat{\Pi} + \theta_{L2}\hat{w} = 0$$

Hence, by substitution for $\hat{w}$ from Equation (A6.16)

$$\hat{\Pi} = \frac{\theta_{L2}}{\theta_{T2}}\frac{\theta_{K1}}{|\theta|^U}\hat{P}_N \tag{A6.18}$$

From Equation (A6.12)

$$\theta_{LG}\hat{w}_G + \theta_{TS}\hat{\Pi} = \hat{P}_S \tag{A6.19}$$

Hence,

$$\theta_{LG}\hat{w}_G + \frac{\theta_{TS}\theta_{L2}}{\theta_{T2}}\frac{\theta_{K1}}{|\theta|^U}\hat{P}_N = \hat{P}_S \tag{A6.20}$$

The change in $\hat{P}_S$ is obtained from the balance equation (A6.6).

$$\frac{\partial D_{ST}}{\partial P_S} \mathrm{d}P_S + \frac{\partial D_{ST}}{\partial \Delta} \mathrm{d}\Delta = \frac{\mathrm{d}X_S}{\mathrm{d}P_S} \mathrm{d}P_S$$

$$\left(\frac{\partial D_{ST}}{\partial P_S} - \frac{\mathrm{d}X_S}{\mathrm{d}P_S} \right) \mathrm{d}P_S = -(\partial D_{ST}/\partial \Delta)\mathrm{d}\Delta$$

$$\mathrm{d}P_S = -\left(\frac{\partial D_{ST}/\partial \Delta}{\dfrac{\partial D_{ST}}{\partial P_S} - \dfrac{\mathrm{d}X_S}{\mathrm{d}P_S}} \right) \mathrm{d}\Delta$$

$$\therefore, \hat{P}_S = B\hat{\Delta} \qquad B > 0 \text{ hence, } \hat{P}_S > 0.$$

where $\mathrm{d}\Delta$ represents a shift parameter.

From the balance Equation (A6.5) we obtain

$$A\hat{P}_N + \alpha\hat{I}^R + \alpha'\hat{I}^G = \varepsilon_{NS}\hat{P}_S \tag{A6.21}$$

where

$$\varepsilon_{NS} = \frac{P_S}{X_N} \frac{\partial X_N}{\partial P_S}$$

$$A < 0 \text{ and equals } \left[\frac{\partial D_N^R}{\partial P_N} + \frac{\partial D_N^G}{\partial P_N} - \frac{\partial X_N}{\partial P_N} \right] \frac{P_N}{X_N}$$

$$\alpha = \frac{I^R}{X_N} \frac{\partial D_N^R}{\partial I^R}, \qquad \alpha' = \frac{I^G}{X_N} \frac{\partial D_N^G}{\partial I^G}$$

Hence, we obtain the system below

$$\begin{pmatrix} 0 & 1 & -\theta'_{NG} & \theta_G \\ 1 & 0 & \theta_{NG} & -1 \\ 0 & 0 & Z\hat{P}_N & \theta_G \\ \alpha' & \alpha & A & 0 \end{pmatrix} \begin{pmatrix} \hat{I}^G \\ \hat{I}^R \\ \hat{P}_N \\ \hat{w}_G \end{pmatrix} = \begin{pmatrix} \theta_S\hat{P}_S \\ 0 \\ \hat{P}_S \\ \varepsilon_{NS}\hat{P}_S \end{pmatrix} \tag{A6.22}$$

The determinant of the left-hand side

$$D = [A\theta_{LG} + \alpha\theta_{LG}\theta'_{NG} + \alpha'\theta_{NG}\theta_{LG}] + \frac{[\alpha\theta_{LG} + \alpha']}{|\theta|'^U}$$

For stability of the system D will be assumed to be negative irrespective of factor intensities $k_N - k_1 > 0 \ (< 0)$.

$$\hat{P}_N = \frac{\theta_{LG}[\varepsilon_{NS} + \alpha(1 - \theta_S)] - \alpha'}{D}$$

$\hat{P}_N > 0 \ (< 0)$ because $\varepsilon_{NS} > 0 \ (< 0)$. Hence, for $\hat{P}_N < 0$ we require that $\varepsilon_{NS} > 0$ and $\theta_{LG}[\varepsilon_{NS} + \alpha(1 - \theta_S)] - \alpha' > 0$.

From Equation (A6.22)

$$\hat{I}^R = \theta_S \hat{P}_S - \theta_G \hat{w}_G + \theta'_{NG} \hat{P}_N$$

We know that $\theta_S \hat{P}_S - \theta_G \hat{w}_G > 0$ but $\theta'_{NG} \hat{P}_N > 0 \ (< 0)$. If it outweighs the first two terms immiserizing tourist boom is obtained.

Proof that $\varepsilon_{NS} > 0 \ (< 0)$.

Differentiation of the full employment conditions (6.15)–(6.18) gives us

$$\lambda_{LN} \hat{X}_N + \lambda_{L1} \hat{X}_1 + \lambda_{L2} \hat{X}_2 = -\lambda_{LN} \hat{a}_{LN} - \lambda_{L1} \hat{a}_{L1} - \lambda_{L2} \hat{a}_{L2} \quad \text{(A6.23)}$$

$$\lambda_{KN} \hat{X}_N + \lambda_{K1} \hat{X}_1 = -\lambda_{KN} \hat{a}_{KN} - \lambda_{K1} \hat{a}_{K1} \quad \text{(A6.24)}$$

$$\lambda_{T2} \hat{X}_2 + \lambda_{TS} \hat{X}_S = -\lambda_{T2} \hat{a}_{T2} - \lambda_{TS} \hat{a}_{TS} \quad \text{(A6.25)}$$

$$\hat{X}_S = -\hat{a}_{LG} \quad \text{(A6.26)}$$

By using the definition of the a_{ij}s in terms of factor elasticities (σ_j) we obtain

$$\lambda_{LN} \hat{X}_N + \lambda_{L1} \hat{X}_1 + \lambda_{L2} \hat{X}_2 = E(\hat{w} - \hat{r}) + F(\hat{w} - \hat{\Pi}) \quad \text{(A6.27)}$$

$$\lambda_{KN} \hat{X}_N + \lambda_{K1} \hat{X}_1 = G(\hat{r} - \hat{w}) \quad \text{(A6.28)}$$

$$\lambda_{T2} \hat{X}_2 + \lambda_{TS} \hat{X}_S = H(\hat{\Pi} - \hat{w}) + I(\hat{\Pi} - \hat{w}_G) \quad \text{(A6.29)}$$

$$\hat{X}_S = J(\hat{w}_G - \hat{\Pi}) \quad \text{(A6.30)}$$

where

$$E = \lambda_{LN} \sigma_N \theta_{KN} + \lambda_{L1} \sigma_1 \theta_{K1} > 0$$

$$F = \lambda_{L2} \sigma_2 \theta_{T2} > 0$$

$$G = \lambda_{KN} \sigma_N \theta_{LN} + \lambda_{K1} \sigma_1 \theta_{L1} > 0$$

$$H = \lambda_{T2}\sigma_2\theta_{L2} > 0$$

$$I = \lambda_{TS}\sigma_S\theta_{LG} > 0$$

$$J = \sigma_S\theta_{TS} > 0$$

After using Equations (A6.23)–(A6.26), we obtain in a matrix form

$$
\begin{pmatrix}
\lambda_{LN} & \lambda_{L1} & \lambda_{L2} & 0 \\
\lambda_{KN} & \lambda_{K1} & 0 & 0 \\
0 & 0 & \lambda_{T2} & \lambda_{TS} \\
0 & 0 & 0 & 1
\end{pmatrix}
\begin{pmatrix}
\hat{X}_N \\
\hat{X}_1 \\
\hat{X}_2 \\
\hat{X}_S
\end{pmatrix}
=
\begin{pmatrix}
\Delta \\
\Psi \\
\Omega \\
\Sigma
\end{pmatrix}
\qquad \text{(A6.31)}
$$

where

$$\Delta = -\frac{(E + \theta_{K1}F)}{|\theta|^{U}}\hat{P}_{NS}, \qquad \Psi = \frac{G\hat{P}_N}{|\theta|^{U}},$$

$$\Omega = \frac{\hat{P}_N}{|\theta|^{U}}\left(\theta_{K1}H + \frac{\theta_{L2}\theta_{K1}}{\theta_{T2}\theta_{LG}}I\right) - \frac{\hat{P}_S}{\theta_{LG}}I$$

$$\Sigma = -\frac{J}{|\theta|^{U}}\left(\frac{\theta_{L2}\theta_{K1}}{\theta_{T2}\theta_{LG}}\right)\hat{P}_N + \frac{J}{\theta_{LG}}\hat{P}_S$$

whose resolution gives us (after some rearrangement):

$$\varepsilon_{NS} = \frac{\hat{X}_N}{\hat{P}_N} = -\frac{\lambda_{L2}\lambda_{K1}\lambda_{TS}}{\lambda_{T2}\theta_{LG}}\frac{\sigma_S}{|\lambda|^{U}} \qquad \text{(A6.32)}$$

where

$$|\lambda|^{U} = \lambda_{LN}\lambda_{L1}\left(\frac{\lambda_{KN}}{\lambda_{LN}} - \frac{\lambda_{K1}}{\lambda_{L1}}\right)$$

$|\lambda|^{U}$ and $|\theta|^{U}$ have the same sign.

A rise in P_S increases X_S which requires more land. The agricultural sector releases land and labour. Therefore, the supply of labour in the urban region increases which gives rise to a Rybczynski effect: X_N expands if it is labour intensive ($|\lambda|^{U} < 0$) and contracts if it is capital intensive ($|\lambda|^{U} > 0$).

Appendix B6. An alternative model[6]

B6.1. Introduction

The purpose of this section is to present a variant of the model discussed in the main text. The reason for this is to emphasize that the rather surprising result that tourism with guest workers may be immiserizing carries over to other models of trade, that is, the immiserization result need not be model specific. The structure of the model is different, however, the notation of the chapter is maintained as far as possible. In this section, the urban region has the same production structure while the coastal region now employs domestic labour and guest workers in both sectors (X_2 and X_S). The factor land is no longer used in the coastal region but guest workers are mobile between the two sectors in the coastal region.

B6.2. The model

The economy produces four goods: two in the urban area, X_1 and X_N and two in the rural area, X_2 and X_S. These goods are produced with the following neo-classical production functions

Urban region

$$X_1 = F_1(K_1, L_1) \tag{B6.1}$$

$$X_N = F_N(K_N, L_N) \tag{B6.2}$$

Coastal regions

$$X_2 = F_2(L_2, L_2^G) \tag{B6.3}$$

$$X_S = F_S(L_S, L_S^G) \tag{B6.4}$$

where L_i ($i = 1, 2, N, S$), K_i ($i = 1, N$), L_i^G ($i = 2, S$) denotes the allocation of domestic labour, domestic capital and guest labour to the production of output X_i ($i = 1, 2, N, S$), respectively. Commodities X_1 and X_2 are traded internationally, X_N is the urban non-traded good and X_S is produced and consumed *solely* by the tourists. This assumption can be relaxed without any loss of generality of the

---

[6] J.-J. Nowak has substantially contributed to this appendix.

results. The commodity X_S is also a non-traded good produced solely for consumption by tourists who move in order to consume it.

Assuming that all factor prices are flexible it follows that the factors are fully employed, hence,

$$a_{L1}X_1 + a_{L2}X_2 + a_{LS}X_S + a_{LN}X_N = \bar{L} \tag{B6.5}$$

$$a_{K1}X_1 + a_{KN}X_N = \bar{K} \tag{B6.6}$$

$$a_{G2}X_2 + a_{GS}X_S = \bar{L}_G \tag{B6.7}$$

The a_{ij}s represent the variable input coefficients where $\bar{L}$ and $\bar{K}$ represent the inelastic supply of labour and capital; and $\bar{L}_G$ the quota (government imposed) determined supply of guest workers. Note that domestic labour is fully mobile across regions and sectors, domestic capital is only mobile within the urban region and guest workers are only mobile within the rural area.

The pricing equations of this model are

Urban region:

$$a_{LN}w + a_{KN}r = P_N \tag{B6.8}$$

$$a_{L1}w + a_{K1}r = P \tag{B6.9}$$

Coastal region:

$$a_{L2}w + a_{G2}w_G = 1 \tag{B6.10}$$

$$a_{LS}w + a_{GS}w_G = P_S \tag{B6.11}$$

The terms of trade, P, are given from outside.

The relative price of the non-traded good X_S is determined by market clearing condition that

$$D_{ST}(P_S, \tilde{\Delta}) = X_S \tag{B6.12}$$

where D_{ST} denotes tourist demand for this good. It is assumed that this is a function of P_S and a shift parameter $\tilde{\Delta}$ which will be used to represent a boom in tourism.

The non-traded good X_N is consumed by both domestic residents and guest workers, hence,

$$D_N^R + D_N^G = X_N \tag{B6.13}$$

Figure B6.1.   (a) Demand and supply

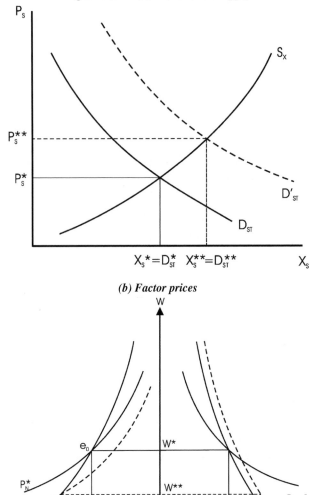

(b) Factor prices

where D_N^R and D_N^G denote the consumption of good X_N by domestic residents and guest workers.

The above model is depicted in Figures B6.1 and B6.2. These diagrams have been drawn for illustrative purposes only and depict the equilibrium outcomes of the model both in the price and quantity spaces. We commence with the price quantity space first.

Figure B6.2.   Equilibrium outputs

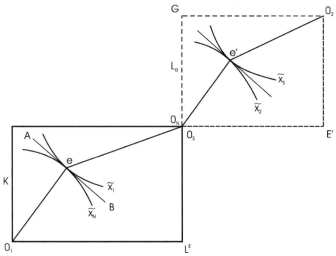

In the top panel of Figure B6.1 we depict the supply curve for good, X_S, which is solely consumed by the tourists. The demand curve D_S and supply curve S_X provide the equilibrium quantity of the output of X_S produced and its price – shown by P_S^* and X_S^* in the panel. The price of the rural or agricultural good is given exogenously and is used as a numeraire. The intersection of the iso-price curves at point e_0 in the lower panel determines the two wage rates in the coastal region: the wage of the guest workers w_G^* and of domestic workers w^*. Once w is determined r can be determined from the iso-price curve for the manufactured good P_1 as shown by the point r^* in Figure B6.1. The relative price of the urban non-traded good P_N must adjust passively from supply side economics such that it intersects the P_1 curve at point e_0 to validate the existing rental on capital r^* and the wage rate w^*. The pricing side of this model highlights the procedure for determining all the price variables in a tourism dependent economy. From the price space we know the equilibrium values for P_S, X_S, D_{ST}, w, w_G, P_N and r – hence, a solution for all the price variables.

   The price solutions can then be used to determine all the remaining physical variables. Let us start from the top part of Figure B6.2. The equilibrium output of X_S is determined in Figure B6.1 and is shown by the isoquant $\tilde{X}_S$ in Figure B6.2.

The distance $O_S G$ is the government determined supply of guest workers and GO_A the supply of domestic workers to the coastal region. The coastal equilibrium is denoted by point e' showing the equilibrium levels of output for sector A and S. By using similar logic the equilibrium in the urban area can be derived and is depicted in the lower box. The economy is in full employment equilibrium and the equilibrium values for the physical variables: X_N, X_1, X_2, X_S, urban employment and coastal employment can all be read from the box.

To complete the model we finally write the national income equation

$$(D_N^R + D_N^G)P_N + (D_2^R + D_2^G) + (D_1^R + D_1^G)P_1$$

$$= P_N X_N + P_1 X_1 + X_2 + P_S X_S \qquad (B6.14)$$

where the left-hand side of this equation shows total expenditure and the right-hand side total output. The terms: D_N^R, D_N^G, D_2^R, D_2^G, D_1^R and D_1^G denote the consumption of goods X_2, X_1 and X_N by domestic residents and guest workers. The budget constraint for guest workers is given by the following equation:

$$P_N D_N^G + P_1 D_1^G + D_2^G = w_G \bar{L}_G \qquad (B6.15)$$

This completes the specification of the model.

B6.3. Results

As in the main text, our interest is in establishing a relation between a tourist boom and resident welfare. To arrive at this result we have to obtain some key relationships. We proceed to obtain these now. By differentiating Equation (B6.12) totally we obtain the impact of a tourist boom on the relative price of good X_S. This is shown below:

$$\hat{P}_S = \frac{\varepsilon \hat{\Delta}}{A}, \qquad \hat{\Delta} > 0 \qquad (B6.16)$$

where

$$A = \left[\frac{P_S}{D_S} \frac{\partial D_S}{\partial P_S} - \frac{P_S}{X_S} \frac{\partial X_S}{\partial P_S} \right] < 0$$

Term A is negative since $\partial D_S / \partial P_S < 0$ and $\partial X_S / \partial P_S > 0$. The term $\varepsilon = (P_S / D_S)(\partial D_S / \partial P_S) < 0$, hence, the relative price of tourism good, X_S, rises. Thus, this entire system is driven from a change in the relative price of the tourism good X_S.

By differentiating Equations (B6.8)–(B6.11) and solving we obtain

$$\hat{w} = -\frac{\theta_{G2}}{|\theta|^C}\hat{P}_S \tag{B6.17}$$

$$\hat{w}_G = \frac{\theta_{L2}}{|\theta|^C}\hat{P}_S \tag{B6.18}$$

$$\hat{r} = \frac{\theta_{LM}\theta_{G2}}{\theta_{KM}|\theta|^C}\hat{P}_S \tag{B6.19}$$

$$\hat{P}_N = \frac{|\theta|^U}{|\theta|^C}\frac{\theta_{L2}}{\theta_{K1}}\hat{P}_S \tag{B6.20}$$

where

$$|\theta|^C = \theta_{L2}\theta_{LS}[l_{GS} - l_{G2}]$$

$$|\theta|^U = \theta_{L1}\theta_{LN}[k_N - k_1]$$

We will assume that $l_{GS} - l_{G2} > 0$, that is that the tourism sector, X_S, is more guest worker intensive than the agricultural sector. Furthermore, we will assume that $(k_N - k_1) < 0$ implying that the urban manufacturing sector is more capital intensive than the urban services sector. The following proposition follows from Equations (B6.16)–(B6.19).

Proposition A6.1. *A tourist boom that raises the relative price of good X_S results in an increase in the wages of the guest workers and a fall in the wages of domestic workers given our intensity condition. The rental on capital increases and the relative price of the non-traded good P_N falls (again on our factor intensity assumption).*

The above proposition is illustrated with the help of Figure B6.1. A tourist boom raises the relative price of good X_S from P_S^* to P_S^{**} (assuming that X_S does not shift or shifts in such a way that P_S still rises). This increase in P_S moves the iso-price curve from P_S^* to P_S^{**} in the right panel of the bottom diagram raising w_G and lowering w. Since P_M is fixed r must rise and it increases from r^* to r^{**}. This

Tourism, Trade and National Welfare

requires that P_N must fall as shown by the movement of the iso-price curve from P_N^* to P_N^{**}. Some observations are in order. An increase in P_S is generated by a boom in tourism. However, the price rise can also be created by a tariff or other fiscal devices. This increase in P_S transmits itself into four markets: the market for guest workers; the market for domestic labour; the rental market and the non-traded good market. The movement in the guest and domestic worker wages is governed by physical intensities in the same manner as in the Stolper–Samuelson theorem. However, the movement in the rental on capital ($\hat{r}$) is not a function of urban capital intensities but of coastal intensities. This is so because this model is driven from the coastal regions, which in turn is driven by tourists. Since P_M is fixed the urban non-traded good market has to adjust to accommodate changes in w and r and its relative price, P_N, (for the given factor intensities) must fall. It is *important* to note that the movement in this price depends on both coastal and urban intensities.

We now proceed to examine the impact of an increase in tourism on welfare. By totally differentiating the national income equation we obtain

$$dD_2^R + P_1\,dD_1^R + P_N\,dD_N^R = (P_N\,dX_N + P_1\,dX_1 + dX_2) + X_S\,dP_S$$
$$- dD_2^G - dD_1^G - P_N\,dD_N^G$$

(B6.21)

The bracketed term on the right-hand side of Equation (B6.21) equals zero due to the tangency condition while the left-hand side provides an expression for the change in real income of domestic residents (I^R). Hence,

$$dI^R = X_S\,dP_S - dD_2^G - P_1\,dD_1^G - P_N\,dD_N^G$$

(B6.22)

We now establish that the terms on the right-hand side of Equation (B6.22) (with the exception of $X_S\,dP_S$) denote the effect of a change in the consumption of goods, X_2, X_1 and X_N by guest workers on the welfare of the domestic residents. We know that the consumption by guest workers exhausts their income, hence,

$$D_2^G + P_1 D_1^G + P_N D_N^G = w_G \bar{L}_G$$

(B6.23)

By differentiating Equation (B6.23) it is easily established that

$$\bar{L}_G \, dw_G = P_N \, dD_N^G + P_1 \, dD_1^G + dD_2^G + D_N^G \, dP_N \tag{B6.24}$$

By substituting expressions from Equation (B6.24) into Equation (B6.22) and writing it in the hat notation we obtain

$$\hat{I}^R = \theta_{DS}\hat{P}_S + \theta_{DG}\hat{P}_N - \theta_G\hat{w}_G = \left[\frac{\theta_{NG}|\theta|^U}{\theta_{KI}} - \delta_{LC} \right]\frac{\theta_{G2}}{|\theta|^C}\hat{P}_S \tag{B6.25}$$

where

$\theta_{DS} = D_N^G P_N / I^R$ Share of guest workers consumption in resident income

$\theta_{DS} = P_S D_S / I^R$ Proportion of tourist demand in resident income

$\delta_{LC} = (L_2 + L_S)^W / I^R$ Share of domestic workers in coastal regions in resident income

$\theta_{DG} = P_N D_N^G / I^R$ Proportion of guest worker demand for the non-traded good in resident income

$\theta_G = w_G \bar{L}_G / I^R$ Proportion of guest worker income in resident income

Some comments are in order on Equation (B6.25). Resident welfare depends on three effects: a traditional terms-of-trade effect from the boom in tourism ($\theta_{DS}\hat{P}_S$); a terms-of-trade effect from the consumption of the urban non-traded good by guest workers ($\theta_{DU}\hat{P}_N$) (this is so because guest worker consumption of the non-traded good transforms it into an exportable good); and an effect from the change in the guest worker wage rate ($\theta_G\hat{w}_G$). We have already established that $\hat{P}_S > 0$; $\hat{w}_G > 0$ for $|\theta|^C > 0$. and $\hat{P}_N < 0$ for $|\theta|^U < 0$ and $|\theta|^C > 0$. The alternative form of writing Equation (B6.25) provides another way of examining resident immiserization.

Proposition B6.2. *A tourist boom immiserizes domestic residents provided that*

$$\theta_{DS}\hat{P}_S + \theta_{DG}\hat{P}_N - \theta_G\hat{w}_G < 0 \qquad \text{or}$$

$$(\theta_{NG}|\theta|^U / \theta_{K1} - \delta_{LC})(\theta_{G2}/|\theta|^C) < 0$$

If $|\theta|^C > 0$ and $|\theta|^U < 0$ then it follows that $\hat{r}^R/\hat{P}_S < 0$. In this case $\hat{w}G/\hat{P}_S > 0$ which creates a loss for domestic residents as the real wage of guest workers increases. An additional loss occurs from the fact that $|\theta|^U < 0$ implies that $\hat{P}_N/\hat{P}_S < 0$, that is, the terms of trade were against domestic residents. Hence, from these two sources of losses the residents get immiserized as a result of a boom in tourism. In a model with no monopoly power in trade and guest workers the relative price of non-traded goods will not change, hence, $\hat{P}_N = 0$. It is trivial to prove that $\theta_{DS}\hat{P}_S - \theta_G\hat{w}_G > 0$. Our results again show that changes in relative prices of non-traded goods consumed by guest workers could have adverse terms-of-trade effects and under certain conditions could lower resident welfare.

B6.4. *Derivation of the results to Appendix B6*

From Equations (B6.8)–(B6.11) we obtain

$$\theta_{LN}\hat{w} + \theta_{KN}\hat{r} = \hat{P}_N \tag{B6.1$'$}$$

$$\theta_{L1}\hat{w} + \theta_{K1}\hat{r} = 0 \tag{B6.2$'$}$$

$$\theta_{LR}\hat{w} + \theta_{G2}\hat{w}_G = 0 \tag{B6.3$'$}$$

$$\theta_{LS}\hat{w} + \theta_{GS}\hat{w}_G = \hat{P}_S \tag{B6.4$'$}$$

$$\hat{w} = \frac{\theta_{G2}}{|\theta|^C}\hat{P}_S \tag{B6.5$'$}$$

$$\hat{w}_G = \frac{\theta_{L1}}{|\theta|^C}\hat{P}_S \tag{B6.6$'$}$$

where

$$|\theta|^C = \theta_{L2}\theta_{GS} - \theta_{LS}\theta_{G2} = \theta_{L2}\theta_{LS}(l_{GS} - l_{G2}) \tag{B6.7$'$}$$

$$\hat{r} = \frac{\theta_{L1}}{\theta_{K1}}\hat{w} = +\frac{\theta_{L1}\theta_{G2}}{\theta_{K1}|\theta|^C}\hat{P}_S \tag{B6.8$'$}$$

$$\hat{P}^N = \frac{|\theta|^U}{|\theta|^C}\frac{\theta_{L2}}{\theta_{K1}}\hat{P}_S \tag{B6.9$'$}$$

if $|\theta|^C > 0$ then

$$\frac{\hat{w}}{\hat{P}_S} < 0 \qquad \text{and} \qquad \frac{\hat{w}_G}{\hat{P}_S} > 0$$

moreover,

$$\frac{\hat{r}}{\hat{P}_S} > 0 \qquad \text{and} \qquad \frac{\hat{P}_N}{\hat{P}_S} < 0$$

if sector N is labour-intensive $(|\theta|)^U < 0$.

$$I^R = P_N X_N + P_1 X_1 + X_2 + P_S X_S$$

$$= (D_N^G + D_N^R)P_N + (D_2^G + D_2^R) + (D_1^G + D_1^R)P_1$$

$$= w\bar{L} + r\bar{K} + w_G \bar{L}_G \qquad\qquad\qquad (B6.1')$$

$$w_G \bar{L}_G = P_N D_N^G + P_1 D_1^G + D_2^G \qquad\qquad (B6.11')$$

$$\bar{L}_G \, dw_G = (P_N \, dD_N^G + P_1 \, dD_1^G + dD_2^G) + D_N^G \, dP_N \qquad (B6.12')$$

$$dD_2^R + P_1 \, dD_1^R + P_N \, dD_N^R$$

$$= (P_N \, dX_N + P_1 \, dX_1 + dX_2 + P_S \, dX_S) + X_S \, dP_S$$

$$- dD_2^G - P_M \, dD_1^G - P_N \, dD_N^G - X_S \, dP_S + dP_N D_N^G$$

$$- \bar{L}_G \, dw_G \qquad\qquad\qquad\qquad\qquad (B6.13')$$

$$\hat{I}_R = \left(\frac{X_S P_S}{I^R}\right)\hat{P}_S + \left(\frac{P_N D_N^G}{I^R}\right)\hat{P}_N - \left(\frac{\bar{L}_G w_G}{I^R}\right)\hat{w}_G \qquad (B6.14')$$

or

$$\hat{I}^R = \left(X_S P_S + P_N D_N^G \frac{|\theta|^U}{|\theta|^C}\frac{\theta_{GA}}{\theta_{K1}} - \bar{L}_G w_G \frac{\theta_{L2}}{|\theta|^C}\right)\frac{\hat{P}_S}{I^R} \qquad (B6.15')$$

or

$$\hat{I}^R = \left(\frac{\upsilon_{NG}|\theta|^U}{\theta_{K1}} - \delta_{LC}\right)\frac{\theta_{G2}}{|\theta|^C}\hat{P}_S$$

with

$$v_{NG} = \frac{D_N^G P_N}{I^R}$$

$$\delta_{LC} = \frac{(L_2 + L_S)w}{I^R} \qquad\qquad (B6.16')$$

References

Hazari, B.R. and P. Sgro (2001), *Migration, Unemployment and Trade*, Norwell, MA: Kluwer.

Sinclair, M.T. and M.J. Stabler (1997), *The Economics of Tourism*, London: Routledge.

CHAPTER 7

Tourism, Illegal Migrants and Resident Welfare

7.1. Introduction

This chapter examines the impact of the shift in demand for tourism in the presence of illegal migrants. Illegal migrants are defined as those individuals who are gainfully employed and enter and/or remain in a country without gaining permission to work from the government, or migration authorities. Many countries receive illegal migrants who work in the services sector and these services are mainly consumed by tourists and domestic residents. Developed and developing countries (Singapore, Malaysia, India and so on) provide legal entry only to those workers whose abilities they need and these may be treated as guest workers. For less qualified and unskilled workers, entry is illegal and India, France, Italy and other European countries are all recipients of illegal workers. In India these illegal workers come mainly from Bangladesh, while in European countries they come from Africa, Bangladesh, India, Sri Lanka and so on. Countries are reluctant to accept immigrants as they are concerned about the possible negative externalities associated with a large inflow of illegal foreign workers. In spite of this fear, not only does illegal migration occur, but more importantly, in many countries it is not policed.[1] In other countries, although there is a threat of being deported, such threats are extraordinarily difficult to administer; for example, in India it is difficult to distinguish between a Bangladeshi

---

[1] Djajic (1997) analyzed illegal migration. He found that illegal workers were employed in the informal (underground) sector where it was difficult to enforce legislation. Hazari and Sgro (2000) analyzed the consequences of illegal migration with policing costs in a model of growth.

and a local Indian resident. Detection may not be a problem in the case of, for example, France, where their physical features may reveal whether or not a person is a migrant. Further investigation may then show whether the person is a legal or an illegal migrant. Throughout this chapter we shall assume that, although the threat of punishments exists, the policing of illegal migrants is not rigorously imposed. We provide a rationale for not policing illegal migration by linking it to the tourism industry.

The model used in this chapter is an extension of the general equilibrium models of tourism in previous chapters. First, the market clearing equation for the non-traded good now consists of three elements: resident consumption, illegal migrant's consumption and tourist consumption which in turn is a function of their income and prices. Second, a utility function and a maximization constraint for illegal migrants have been introduced into the model. Finally, the resident income is properly adjusted to incorporate the consumption by illegal workers.

7.2. The model

Assume that an economy produces three goods X_1, X_2 and X_N. The production functions for these goods are given below:

$$X_1 = F_1[K_1, L_1, L_{S1}] \tag{7.1}$$

$$X_2 = F_2[K_2, L_2, L_{S2}] \tag{7.2}$$

$$X_N = F_N[K_N, L_N + L_{NA}] \tag{7.3}$$

X_1 and X_2 as in earlier chapters are internationally traded goods and are produced with only domestic labour (skilled L_{Si} and unskilled L_i, $i = 1, 2$), and capital (K_i, $i = 1, 2, N$). It is assumed that X_2 is the capital intensive, and that X_1 is the labour intensive good. The non-traded good, X_N, is produced with capital, domestic labour and illegal migrants denoted by L_{NA}. It is important to note that illegal migrants are employed only in the non-traded good sector, that is, they are sector specific, and are assumed to be perfect substitutes for unskilled domestic labor. Note that an implicit assumption of this model is that unskilled illegal migrants are only tolerated in the non-traded goods and services sector. It is this feature of the model that allows us to ignore the policing of these migrants. In France, it is reported that many unskilled illegal migrants work in smaller hotel establishments. These illegal workers are willing to work for a wage less than that of the local workers. This may also be true in other countries. These unskilled illegal migrants help to maintain and/or lower and relative price of the non-traded goods that the tourists consume, thereby helping tourism by making high-wage countries competitive in the world tourism market. High-wage countries become competitive because, by using cheap illegal migrants, they can lower the prices of goods consumed by tourists. Again, as in previous chapters, the above production functions are assumed to satisfy neoclassical properties.

The migration function for the illegal migrants is given by:[2]

$$L_{NA} = f\left[\frac{E}{\bar{L}} U(\alpha\bar{w}) - U(\bar{w}_A) \right] \tag{7.4}$$

where f is an increasing function of the difference between the utility received from the wage in the country of migration $U(\alpha\bar{w})$, and the utility received from the wage in the country of origin $U(\bar{w}_A)$. The term α represents the degree to which illegal migrants are exploited in the country of migration, and it is assumed to be positive but less than one. It is assumed that for illegal migrants the threat of being punished is captured by the term α. This exploitation is visible in terms of the lower wage that illegal migrants receive compared with the wage received by domestic workers. The term $E/\bar{L}$ represents the probability of gaining employment where E denotes the actual level of employment so that $E = L_1 + L_2 + L_N$ and $\bar{L}$ the total inelastic supply of labour. When there is unemployment, that is, $E/\bar{L} < 1$, illegal migrants are discouraged from migrating as the probability of gaining employment on arrival is very small.

It is assumed that there exists an exogenously given and binding minimum real wage within the economy denoted by $\bar{w}$ that results in general unemployment of unskilled labour. This should be distinguished from urban unemployment introduced in Chapter 8. The unemployment introduced here is in the tradition of Brecher (1974). Skilled labour receives an equilibrium wage rate equal to w_S, where w_S is greater than $\bar{w}$. The rental paid on capital is denoted by r.

---

[2] This migration function was first introduced by Chesney *et al.* (1999).

The price equations are given below:

$$a_{L1}\bar{w} + a_{LS1}w_S + a_{K1}r = P \tag{7.5}$$

$$a_{L2}\bar{w} + a_{LS2}w_S + a_{K2}r = 1 \tag{7.6}$$

$$a_{LN}\bar{w} + a_{LNA}\alpha\bar{w} + a_{KN}r = P_N \tag{7.7}$$

where a_{ij} represents the variable input coefficients.

It is assumed that skilled labor is also inelastic in its supply. The model may be extended to include the transformation of unskilled to skilled workers. As this is not the focus of this work, this process has been ignored. The factor endowment conditions for this economy are given by:

$$a_{K1}X_1 + a_{K2}X_2 + a_{KN}X_N = \bar{K} \tag{7.8}$$

$$a_{L1}X_1 + a_{L2}X_2 + a_{LN}X_N = E \leq \bar{L} \tag{7.9}$$

$$a_{LS1}X_1 + a_{LS2}X_2 = \bar{L}_S \tag{7.10}$$

$$a_{LNA}X_N = L_{NA} \tag{7.11}$$

Domestic unskilled labour is partly unemployed as shown by Equation (7.9) while illegal migrants are fully employed (Equation (7.11)) as their wage is fully flexible and endogenously determined.

Market clearing in the non-traded goods sector requires that:

$$D_N^R[P, P_N, I^R] + D_N^I[P, P_N, I^I] + D_N^T[P_N, \beta] = X_N \tag{7.12}$$

Residents (D_N^R), illegal migrants (D_N^I) and tourists (D_N^T) consume the non-traded good X_N. In this model the non-traded good is converted into a tradable commodity via consumption by tourists and illegal migrants. The economy now has three different agents: domestic residents, illegal workers and tourists. Illegal migrants demand for the non-traded good is a function of the price of the non-traded good P_N, the price of traded goods P, and illegal migrant income. Tourist demand for the non-traded good is a function of the price of the non-traded good P_N, and β which represents a shift factor.

It is assumed that residents and illegal migrants may differ in their tastes and preferences, therefore, they may not maximize the same utility functions as residents. The resident utility function is given by:

$$U^R = U^R[D_1^R, D_2^R, D_N^R] \tag{7.13}$$

where D_1^R, D_2^R, D_N^R denotes the consumption of the goods X_1, X_2 and X_N. The utility function of illegal migrants is given by:

$$U^I = U^I[D_1^I, D_2^I, D_N^I] \tag{7.14}$$

where D_1^I, D_2^I, D_N^I denote the consumption of goods X_1, X_2 and X_N by illegal migrants in the host country. Illegal migrants maximize their utility subject to the following constraint:

$$PD_1^I + D_2^I + P_N D_N^I = \alpha \bar{w} L_{NA} \tag{7.15}$$

As remarked earlier, the wage received by illegal migrants is determined endogenously within the model, hence, α is determined within the model.

7.3. Results

It is appropriate now to examine the impact of an increase in tourism on the welfare of the residents in the presence of illegal migrants. Totally differentiating Equation (7.15) and using Equation (7.11) the following expression for the change in the income of illegal migrants is obtained:

$$\hat{I}^I = \hat{L}_{NA} + \hat{\alpha} - \theta_{NI} \hat{P}_N \tag{7.16}$$

where

$$\theta_{NI} = \frac{D_N^I P_N}{I^I}.$$

The change in illegal migrant income (utility) depends on the change in the number of illegal migrants employed, the change in the degree of exploitation of the illegal workers and the change in the relative price of the non-traded good.

By differentiating the national income equation and using the resident utility function, the following expression for the change in resident income is obtained:

$$\hat{I}^R - \theta_{LR}\hat{E} + A'\hat{P}_N + \theta_{LNA}\hat{\alpha} = -\theta_{NT}\varepsilon_\beta\hat{\beta} \tag{7.17}$$

where

$$A' = \theta_{NT}\varepsilon_{PN}^{T} + \theta_{IR}, \qquad \hat{I}^{R} = \frac{dI^{R}}{I^{R}}, \qquad \theta_{LE} = \frac{wE}{I^{R}},$$

$$\theta_{IR} = \frac{D_{N}^{I}}{I^{R}}, \qquad \theta_{NT} = \frac{P_{N}D_{N}^{T}}{I^{R}}, \qquad \theta_{LNA} = \frac{\bar{w}\alpha L_{NA}}{I^{R}}$$

A change in resident income (welfare) is dependent upon the rate of domestic employment, the degree to which illegal migrants are exploited, a terms of trade effect emerging from tourist and illegal migrant consumption of non-traded goods, and the impact that a tourist boom has on the economy.

The change in the price of non-traded goods is a function of the degree to which illegal migrants are exploited and is given below as:

$$\theta_{LNA}\hat{\alpha} = \hat{P}_{N} \tag{7.18}$$

Note that the remaining prices are fixed due to the assumption of a small open economy.

To obtain an expression for the change in the flow of illegal migrants as a consequence of a boom in tourism, we differentiate Equation (7.4) to obtain:

$$\hat{L}_{NA}L_{NA} = Z\hat{E} + Z'\hat{\alpha} \tag{7.19}$$

where

$$Z = \frac{E}{\bar{L}}U(\bar{w}\alpha)f', \qquad Z' = \alpha\frac{E}{\bar{L}}U'(\bar{w}_{A})$$

and are both positive.

The change in the labour allocation of illegal migrants (which is the same as the inflow or outflow of the illegal migrants) to the non-traded good sector is a function of total domestic employment and the degree of exploitation. Both effects are weighted by the marginal utility the illegal migrants receive from their wage when employed in the non-traded good sector.

Totally differentiating the employment conditions given by Equations (7.8)–(7.11) we obtain:

$$\lambda_{K1}\hat{X}_{1} + \lambda_{K2}\hat{X}_{2} + \lambda_{KN}\hat{X}_{N} = 0 \tag{7.20}$$

$$\lambda_{L1}\hat{X}_1 + \lambda_{L2}\hat{X}_2 + \lambda_{LN}\hat{X}_N = \hat{E} \tag{7.21}$$

$$\lambda_{LS1}\hat{X}_1 + \lambda_{LS2}\hat{X}_2 = 0 \tag{7.22}$$

$$\hat{X}_N + \hat{a}_{LNA} = \hat{L}_{NA} \tag{7.23}$$

where λ_{ij} represents the factor shares.

By differentiating the market clearing Equation (7.12) for the non-traded good we obtain:

$$A\hat{P}_N + \eta_{RN}\hat{I}^R + \eta_{LNA}\hat{I}^I - \varphi_{LNA}L_{NA}\hat{L}_{NA} = \varphi_{TN}\hat{\beta} \tag{7.24}$$

where

$$A = \left[\frac{\partial D_N^R}{\partial P_N} + \frac{\partial D_N^I}{\partial P_N} + \frac{\partial D_N^T}{\partial P_N} - \frac{\partial X_N}{\partial P_N} \right] < 0$$

From the stability condition

$$\eta_{RN} = \left[\frac{I^R}{N} \frac{\partial D_N^R}{\partial I^R} \right] > 0$$

$= $ Resident income elasticity for the non-traded good,

$$\eta_{LNA} = \left[\frac{I^I}{N} \frac{\partial D_N^I}{\partial I^I} \right] > 0$$

$= $ Illegal migrant income elasticity for the non-traded good,

$$\varphi_{LNA} = \left[\frac{L_{NA}}{N} \frac{\partial X_N}{\partial L_{NA}} \right], \qquad \varphi_{TN} = \left[\frac{\beta}{N} \frac{\partial D_N^T}{\partial \beta} \right]$$

Although the above is a system of nine equations in nine unknowns, we solve the system by using subsets. The first three variables that will be solved are $\hat{X}_1$, $\hat{X}_2$ and $\hat{L}_{NA}$ in terms of $\hat{E}$ by differentiating Equations (7.19)–(7.22) we obtain:

$$\begin{pmatrix} \lambda_{K1} & \lambda_{K2} & \lambda_{KN} \\ \pi_{L1} & \lambda_{L2} & \lambda_{LN} \\ \lambda_{LS1} & \lambda_{LS2} & 0 \end{pmatrix} \begin{pmatrix} \hat{X}_1 \\ \hat{X}_2 \\ \hat{L}_{NA} \end{pmatrix} = \begin{pmatrix} 0 \\ \hat{E} \\ 0 \end{pmatrix}$$

The solutions for these variables in terms of $\hat{E}$ are

$$\hat{X}_1 = \frac{\lambda_{LS2}\lambda_{KN}}{D}\hat{E} \tag{7.25}$$

$$\hat{X}_2 = -\frac{\lambda_{LSI}\lambda_{KN}}{D}\hat{E} \tag{7.26}$$

$$\hat{L}_{NA} = -\frac{\lambda_{LS2}\lambda_{LS1}(k_{1S} - k_{2S})}{D}\hat{E} \tag{7.27}$$

where $D = \lambda_{LSX}[\lambda_{LN}\lambda_{LY}(k_2 - k_N)] - \lambda_{LSY}[\lambda_{LX}\lambda_{LN}(k_1 - k_N)]$

Assuming that $k_i - k_N > 0$, for $i = 1, 2$ and the first term is greater than the second term implies that $D > 0$. Hence, it is clear from Equations (7.25) and (7.26) that $\hat{X}_2$ is falling in E and $\hat{X}_1$ is rising in E. This is like a Rybczynski effect of a decrease in unemployment, which is the same as an increase in employment. From Equation (7.27), $\hat{L}_{NA}$ and $\hat{E}$ are also positively related with each other, provided $k_{2S} - k_{1S} > 0$. We also know from Equation (7.18) that $\hat{\alpha} = \hat{P}_N/\theta_{LNA}$.

By using the above equations, and substituting we obtain

$$\begin{pmatrix} 0 & 1 & \theta'_{LNA}B/D & \theta_{NT} \\ \eta_{RN} & \eta_{IN} & \varphi_{LNA}B/D & A \\ 0 & 0 & (-Z + L_{NA})B/D & -Z'/\theta_{LNA} \\ 1 & 0 & -\theta_{LE} & C \end{pmatrix}\begin{pmatrix} \hat{I}^R \\ \hat{I}^I \\ \hat{E} \\ \hat{P}_N \end{pmatrix} = \begin{pmatrix} 0 \\ -\varepsilon_\beta\hat{\beta} \\ 0 \\ -\theta_{NT}\varepsilon_\beta\hat{\beta} \end{pmatrix} \tag{7.28}$$

where $B = \lambda_{LS2}\lambda_{LS1}(k_{1S} - k_{2S})$.

From the above system the following solutions are obtained:

$$\hat{P}_N = \frac{Z + L_{NA}\dfrac{B}{D}\varepsilon_\beta[-\gamma + 1]}{D'}\hat{\beta} \tag{7.29}$$

$$\hat{E} = \frac{(-Z'/\delta_{LNA})\varepsilon_\beta\hat{\beta}[-\gamma + 1]}{D'}\hat{\beta} \tag{7.30}$$

From Equation (7.15)

$$\hat{I}^I = \hat{L}_{NA} + \hat{\alpha} - \theta_{NI}\hat{P}_N$$

Substituting for $\hat{\alpha}$ from Equation (7.18), the above equation can be simplified to

$$\hat{I}^{\mathrm{I}} = \hat{L}_{NA} + \left(\frac{1}{\theta_{LNA}} - \theta_{NI} \right) \hat{P}_N \tag{7.31}$$

Note that both θ_{LNA} and θ_{NI} are less than one, therefore, the bracketed term is always positive.

From Equation (7.19) $\hat{L}_{NA} > 0$ for $\hat{E} > 0$ and $\hat{P}_N > 0$, therefore, the welfare and income of the illegal migrants increases ($\hat{I}^{\mathrm{I}} > 0$) as a consequence of an increase in tourism.

From Equation (7.24)

$$\eta_{RN}\hat{I}^{\mathrm{R}} = \varphi_{TN}\hat{B} - A\hat{P}_N - \eta_{LNA}\hat{I}^{\mathrm{I}} + \varphi_{LNA}L_{NA}\hat{L}_{NA}$$

Solving for $\hat{L}_{NA}$ from Equation (7.19) and using Equation (7.18), this expression simplifies to

$$\eta_{RI}\hat{I}^{\mathrm{R}} = \varphi_{TN}\hat{B} - A\hat{P}_N - \eta_{LNA}\hat{I}^{\mathrm{I}} + \varphi_{LNA}Z\hat{E}$$

$$+ \varphi_{LNA}L_{NA}Z' \frac{\hat{P}_N}{\theta_{LNA}} \tag{7.32}$$

Note that

$$D' = Z + L_{NA}\frac{B}{D}(Z'/\delta_{LNA})\left[\eta_{RN}(C - \theta_{LE}) - \left(\varphi_{LNA}\frac{B}{D} + A \right) \right.$$

$$\left. + \eta_{LNA}\left(\theta_{LNA}\frac{B}{D} + \theta_{NT} \right) \right] > 0$$

The stability conditions in the non-traded good market ensure that the bracketed term is negative (regardless of factor intensities) $B < 0$ for $k_{2S} > k_{1S}$, therefore, $D' > 0$. The change in the relative price of the non-traded good is as follows:

$$\hat{P}_N = \frac{Z + L_{NA}\dfrac{B}{D}\varepsilon_\beta[-\gamma + 1]}{D'} \hat{\beta}$$

The relative price of the non-traded good *necessarily* rises as a consequence of a boom in tourism. This result shows that the presence of illegal migrants combined with a tourist boom has a positive effect on the tertiary terms-of-trade. This demand shift is different to that considered in chapter three of this book.

The change in domestic employment is given as

$$\hat{E} = \frac{(-Z'/\delta_{LNA})\varepsilon_\beta\hat{\beta}[-\gamma+1]}{D'}\hat{\beta}$$

Note also that $\hat{E} > 0$. Therefore, a tourist boom has a positive effect on both domestic employment and the tertiary terms-of-trade. This result runs against the often commonly held view in many countries that illegal migrants replace domestic workers in occupations. In this model the opposite is the case and illegal migrants help reduce domestic unemployment.

The change in illegal migrant income is given by Equation (7.31) while that for resident income by Equation (7.32). As a result of a tourist boom, all the terms on the right hand side of Equation (7.32) are positive, therefore, as stated earlier, illegal migrant income rises. This is due to the positivity of both the employment effect ($\hat{L}_{NA} > 0$) and the tertiary terms of trade ($\hat{P}_N > 0$). For resident income the result is ambiguous. The change in resident income consists of five effects: tourism boom effect ($\hat{\beta}$), standard tertiary terms-of-trade effect $\hat{P}_N$, illegal migrant income effect ($\hat{I}^l$), employment effect ($\hat{E}$) and a tertiary terms-of-trade effect of illegal migration ($L_{NA}\hat{P}_N$). Four effects are positive and the only negative effect comes from the increase in the income of illegal migrants. Since illegal migrant income rises, resident income may increase or decrease.

7.4. Conclusion

In a distortionary framework, a tourist boom in the presence of illegal migrants may lower resident welfare. This possibility occurs because of the increase in illegal migrant income that results from the tourist boom. However, the tertiary terms-of-trade improve and domestic resident employment also increases. Illegal migrants do not necessarily take jobs from local residents.

References

Brecher, R.A. (1974), "Minimum wage rates and the pure theory of international trade", *The Quarterly Journal of Economics*, Vol. 88, pp. 98–116.

Chesney, M., B.R. Hazari and P.M. Sgro (1999), "Immigration, unemployment and welfare", *International Economic Journal*, Vol. 13, pp. 59–74.

Djajic, S. (1997), "Illegal immigration and resource allocation", *International Economic Review*, Vol. 38, pp. 97–117.

Hazari, B.R. and P.M. Sgro (2000), "Illegal migration, border enforcement and growth", *Review of Development Economics*, Vol. 4, pp. 258–267.

CHAPTER 8

Tourism in the Generalized Harris–Todaro Model and Regional Immiserization

8.1. Introduction

In the last seven chapters we have been concerned with incorporating and analyzing tourism and its consequences in the framework of a general equilibrium model of trade with full employment. This framework is now extended and used for analyzing tourism in a regional setting with urban unemployment. In particular this chapter analyzes the consequences of tourism in rural and urban areas on regional incomes, welfare and urban unemployment using a generalized Harris–Todaro model (GHT).[1] We begin by depicting the GHT model in terms of the following boxes:

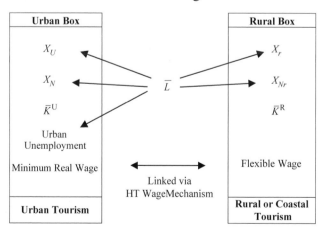

The urban region produces two goods: an internationally traded good X_U and a non-traded good X_N; while the rural region also

---

[1] A detailed treatment of the GHT model is available in Hazari and Sgro (2001).

produces two goods, an internationally traded rural good, X_r, and a rural non-traded good, X_{Nr}. Capital is assumed to be region specific and not mobile between regions. It is denoted by $\bar{K}^U$ and $\bar{K}^R$. Note that the region specific capital is mobile within the region, that is, it can be used in X_U and X_N in the urban region, and in X_r and X_{Nr} in the rural region. However, labour is perfectly mobile and moves across regions via the Harris–Todaro (HT) migration function. In the urban region there exists employed and unemployed labour, while in the rural region due to wage flexibility, labour is fully employed. Several versions of the HT model can be derived as a subset of the GHT model depicted in the two boxes, for example, the Corden–Findlay version of the model can be derived by setting X_N and X_{Nr} to equal zero and assuming that capital is mobile between the two regions. The original HT model can be derived by setting X_N and X_{Nr} equal to zero.

Tourism can be introduced into the above model in the urban region and/or rural region.[2] This model provides an appropriate framework for analyzing the impact of regional tourism in a general equilibrium setting and is particularly relevant for developing economies that are characterized by HT urban unemployment. A variant of this model can also be applied to developed countries by dropping the assumption of the HT wage mechanism.

The most important result obtained in this general framework is that a tourist boom in the urban region *may* immiserize the rural area. Hence, the welfare interests of rural and urban consumers may be in conflict as a result of tourist expansion in the urban region. Several other interesting results are obtained below and this asymmetrical nature of welfare results is highlighted. This asymmetry arises because of the unique structure of the HT model.[3]

---

[2] Consider, for example, the case of Fiji Islands, where many tourists book holidays only at specific resorts and do not visit the rest of the economy (in our case, the urban region). This applies, for example, in Thailand, where many tourists book holidays to visit Phuket (much popularized after the Bond film) and do not venture further to visit cities like Bangkok. It is also true that the reverse holds; i.e. many tourists visit Bangkok but do not travel to outlying rural areas.

[3] This model is general enough to also capture regional tourism in developed countries where the HT mechanism does not prevail. A model of this type is available in Hazari and Sgro (1996) and has been extended for analyzing tourism by Hazari *et al.* (2003). Note that the consumer has to visit the country in order to become a tourist and consume non-traded goods and services.

8.2. A regional model with tourism

In this section we set up a model that incorporates both urban and rural tourism. The economy in question, as set out in the two boxes, produces four goods: X_U and X_N in the urban and X_r and X_{Nr} in the rural region. The urban goods X_U and X_N are produced with the help of labor and urban-specific capital, while the rural goods X_r and X_{Nr} are produced with the help of labor and rural specific capital. Thus, labor is mobile between both sectors and regions while capital is specific to each region. These commodities are produced with the help of the following neoclassical production functions:

Urban goods

$$X_U = F_U[L_U, K_U] \tag{8.1}$$

$$X_N = F_N[L_N, K_N] \tag{8.2}$$

Rural goods

$$X_r = F_r[L_r, K_r] \tag{8.3}$$

$$X_{Nr} = F_{Nr}[L_{Nr}, K_{Nr}] \tag{8.4}$$

where L_U, K_U and L_N, K_N denote the allocation of labor and urban-specific capital to the production of X_U and X_N. The terms L_r, L_{Nr}, K_r and K_{Nr} represent the allocation of labor and rural-specific capital to the outputs of X_r and X_{Nr}.

In the variable input coefficient notation the resource constraints can be written as follows.

Urban resource constraints

$$a_{LU}X_U + a_{LN}X_N = E^U \tag{8.5}$$

$$a_{KU}X_U + a_{KN}X_N = \bar{K}^U \tag{8.6}$$

Rural resource constraints

$$a_{Lr}X_r + a_{LNr}X_{Nr} = E^R \tag{8.7}$$

$$a_{Kr}X_r + a_{KNr}X_{Nr} = \bar{K}^R \tag{8.8}$$

where a_{ij}s are the variable input coefficients. The terms E^U and E^R denote the aggregate levels of urban and rural employment, and $\bar{K}^U$ and $\bar{K}^R$ the inelastically supplied amounts of region-specific capital in the urban and rural areas. Note that in our model both E^U and E^R are endogenously determined. Due to the presence of urban unemployment, the sum of E^U and E^R does not equal the total supply of labour $\bar{L}$.

In the tradition of the HT model, it is assumed that there exists a binding real minimum wage constraint that prevails in the urban region. At the point of equilibrium it is required that the rural wage equals the expected wage in the urban area. This equilibrium condition is

$$w = w^e = \frac{\bar{w}}{(1 + \lambda)} \tag{8.9}$$

where w represents the rural wage rate, w^e the expected wage rate, $\bar{w}$ the binding urban minimum real wage defined in terms of good X_r and λ the ratio of urban unemployed to employed. Given the definition of λ, we can write the economy-wide constraint for labor as

$$E^U(1 + \lambda) + E^R = \bar{L} \tag{8.10}$$

where $\bar{L}$ represents the inelastic supply of the labor force in the economy. Note that two models can be generated from Equation (8.9): first, the case of a binding uniform minimum real wage which makes $w = \bar{w}$ and results in a Brecher (1974)/Batra and Seth (1977)-type framework; second, a first-best model where there is no binding minimum wage, but two regions with endogenously determined labour allocations of E^U and E^R and $\lambda = 0$. The presence of non-traded goods in the urban region removes the indeterminacy problem present in the Brecher (1974) model.

The unit cost equations for the above system at the point of an interior equilibrium are as follows:

Urban unit cost equations

$$a_{LU}\bar{w} + a_{KU}r = P_U \tag{8.11}$$

$$a_{LN}\bar{w} + a_{KN}r = P_N \tag{8.12}$$

Rural unit cost equations

$$a_{Lr}w + a_{Kr}\Pi = 1 \tag{8.13}$$

$$a_{LNr}w + a_{KNr}\Pi = P_{Nr} \tag{8.14}$$

where r denotes the rental on urban capital, Π the rental on rural capital, P_N the relative price of the urban non-traded good, and P_{Nr} the relative price of the rural non-traded good.

It is appropriate now to introduce tourism and the market clearing equations for the non-traded goods:

$$D_N(P_N, P_U, I^U) + D_{NT}(P_N, \beta) = X_N \tag{8.15}$$

$$D_{Nr}(P_{Nr}, P_U, I^R) + D_{NrT}(P_{Nr}, \alpha) = X_{Nr} \tag{8.16}$$

where D_N and D_{Nr} show the demand for the urban and rural non-traded goods by domestic residents. The terms D_{NT} and D_{NrT} denote the demand for these goods by tourists; the terms I^U and I^R denote urban and rural incomes, respectively. Note that these functions depend only on their own relative price and shift parameter – β for the urban and α for the rural non-traded good. The parameters β and α can capture a large number of variables, for example, changes in taste, foreign income, and so on. Tourists do not consume X_U and X_r.[4] A more sophisticated model would endogenize the choice between D_{NT} and D_{NrT}. This choice framework has not been used in this book.

It is important to note that in Equations (8.15) and (8.16) the demand for the non-traded goods by domestic residents depends on regional income I^U in the urban and I^R in the rural region. This distinction is essential, as the urban consumers do not consume the rural non-traded good while the rural consumers do not consume the urban non-traded good; hence, it is not possible to construct an aggregate utility function which can be translated for welfare purposes into national income I. We now define the following balance equations for each region:

$$P_U D_{UU} + D_{Ur} + P_N D_N = P_U X_U + P_N X_N = \bar{w}E^U + r\bar{K}^U \tag{8.17}$$

---

[4] Similarly, in developed countries many tourists visit Paris but not the countryside of France.

$$P_U D_{rU} + D_{rr} + P_{Nr} D_{Nr} = X_r + P_{Nr} X_{Nr} = w E^R + \Pi \bar{K}^R \qquad (8.18)$$

where D_{UU}, D_{Ur}, D_{rU} and D_{rr} denote the urban and rural consumption of internationally traded goods, respectively. It is evident that an urban consumer consumes three goods: the urban manufactured good, D_{UU}; the rural traded good D_{Ur}; and the urban non-traded good D_N. Similarly, the rural consumer consumes three goods: the urban traded good, D_{rU}; the rural traded good D_{rr}; and the rural non-traded good D_{Nr}. The underlying utility functions for the two regions are

$$U^U = U^U[D_{UU}, D_{Ur}, D_N] \qquad (8.19)$$

$$U^R = U^R[D_{rU}, D_{rr}, D_{Nr}] \qquad (8.20)$$

Several comments are pertinent concerning the above model. First, the urban region in this model behaves exactly like the Heckscher–Ohlin model with a minimum wage à la Brecher (1974) and an urban non-traded good. It is fairly easy to derive the features of this model. Second, the rural region is not in the Heckscher–Ohlin tradition, as its variables cannot be solved without the HT wage mechanism that links urban and rural regions. Finally, by using two utility functions (one for each region), the model is able to shed light on problems in regional economics, in particular potential regional conflict.

8.3. A geometric representation of the model

In this section we provide a geometric representation of the GHT model with tourists. We begin by examining Equation (8.15) which states that

$$D_N(P_N, P_U, I^U) + D_{NT}(P_N, \beta) = X_N$$

The left-hand side of this equation has two components, domestic demand D_N and tourist demand D_{NT}. From the previous equations we know that the urban wage $\bar{w}$ and the international price for the manufacturing good P_U are given, hence, Equations (8.11) and

Figure 8.1.   Urban production box

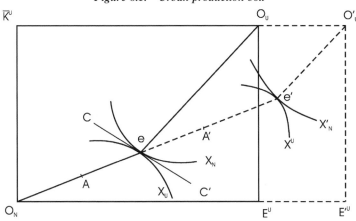

(8.12) provide a solution for the relative price of the non-traded good P_N and the urban rental rate r. For illustrative purposes let us assume that the left-hand side of the equation is known, i.e. I^U along with P_N, P_U and β are known. This then determines the level of X_N. In Figure 8.1 we draw the urban box diagram. In this box $O_N E^U$ represents urban employment and $O_N \bar{K}^U$ urban capital. Equilibrium is attained at point e where the wage–rental ratio $(\bar{w}/r)$ as given by the slope of CC' is tangential to the isoquants for X_U and X_N. The output of X_N is divided into $O_N A$ domestic demand and Ae foreign demand. Thus, tourist demand is represented by Ae.

Recall that the utility function in the urban region is given by

$$U^U = U^U[D_{UU}, D_{Ur}, D_N]$$

The distance $O_N A$ specifies D_N, hence, for a given level of D_N we can draw a social indifference curve in the $[D_{UU}, D_{Ur}]$, space for the urban region. This is shown in Figure 8.2. The slope of the line AB represents the international terms of trade.

Equilibrium is reached at point e and welfare is shown by the social urban indifference curve U^U for a given level of D_N.

In Figure 8.3 we draw the production possibility frontier AB for the urban region. Note that due to the presence of a binding minimum wage, the frontier is linear. Given the terms of trade and the non-tangency property of the model. Equilibrium can be either at e_0 or $e_0{}'$

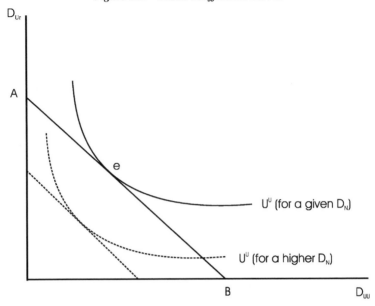

Figure 8.2. Social indifference curves

depending on how the terms of trade given by the slope of this line cuts the production possibility frontier. The equilibrium outputs are X_U^* and X_N^*.

We now proceed to determine λ and the rural equilibrium. In Figure 8.4 we determine the value of λ (as denoted by λ^*). The left-hand vertical side axis represents w_r and the right-hand side vertical axis w_e. The two horizontal axes are represented by OR the rural rental rate and $O'O$ the value of λ. Since P_r is given we can draw the isoprice curve $P_r = 1$. This isoprice curve performs the same function as the VMP curve in the Corden–Neary (1982) model (it is given and fixed). The intersection of this curve with expected wage curve solves for w and λ. Once we know these variables we can solve for Π and P_{Nr}.

The HT curve is drawn from the right hand vertical axis. These curves intersect at point e which determines the optimal value of λ^* and also of Π. Once this information is available then all the rural variables can be solved as is shown in Figures 8.5 and 8.6. In Figure 8.5 we have the Edgeworth–Bowley boxes for the urban and rural regions. Equilibrium in the urban region is represented

Figure 8.3.   Production possibility frontier – urban region

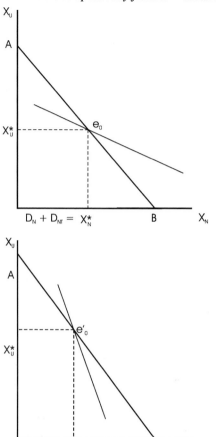

at the point A with unemployment, λ^*, represented by the distance $E^U E / \theta_N E^U$. Rural equilibrium is at the point D. Note that the overall labour constraint from Equation (8.10) is captured by the distance $O_N E^U E E^R$. The utility function for the rural region is given by Equation (8.20) and for a given D_{Nr} we can represent the equilibrium in Figure 8.6 as e'. The slope of the line AB again represents the international terms of trade.

The production possibility frontier for the rural region is drawn as AB in Figure 8.7. The equilibrium occurs at point e_0 where there is a tangency between P_{Nr} and the production possibility frontier.

It is appropriate now to present our results.

Figure 8.4.   Unemployment and rural equilibrium

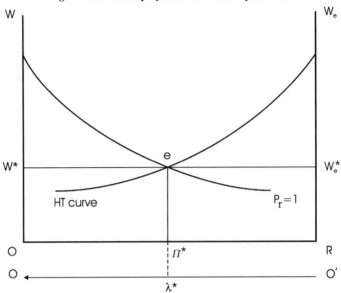

Figure 8.5.   Rural production box

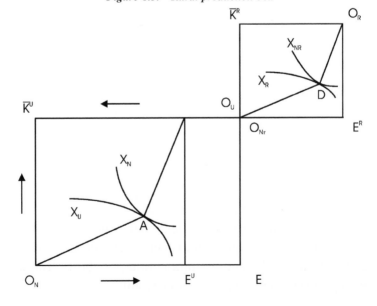

Figure 8.6.   Rural equilibrium

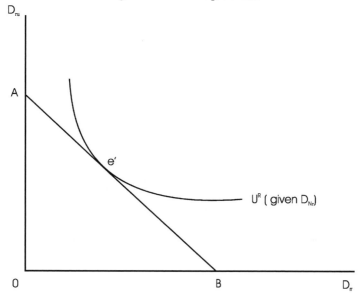

Figure 8.7.   The production possibility frontier – rural region

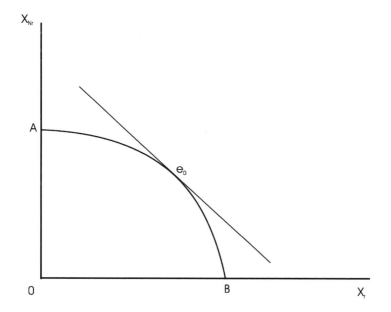

8.4. Results

8.4.1. Urban tourism boom

Consider an economy in which a boom in tourism occurs. This is represented by a shift in parameter β. The effects of this shift on important endogenous variables are obtained from the following system by differentiating Equations (8.5), (8.6), (8.15) and (8.17):

$$\begin{bmatrix} 0 & \lambda_{KU} & \lambda_{KN} & 0 \\ 0 & \lambda_{LU} & \lambda_{LN} & -1 \\ \eta_{IN} & 0 & -1 & 0 \\ 1 & 0 & 0 & -\alpha_{EU} \end{bmatrix} \begin{bmatrix} \hat{I}^U \\ \hat{X}_U \\ \hat{X}_N \\ \hat{E}^U \end{bmatrix} = \begin{bmatrix} 0 \\ 0 \\ -\dfrac{\beta}{X_N}\dfrac{\partial D_{NT}}{\partial \beta}\hat{\beta} \\ 0 \end{bmatrix} \quad (8.21)$$

where the λ_{ij}s represent factor shares, η_{IN} the income elasticity of the urban non-traded good, and α_{EU} the share of wage income in total urban income. The change in real income is defined from the urban utility function as

$$\mathrm{d}I^U = p_U\,\mathrm{d}D_{UU} + \mathrm{d}D_{Ur} + p_N\,\mathrm{d}D_N$$

This follows from the urban utility function (8.19). This change in real income has been converted into proportional terms ($\hat{I}^U$) in Equation (8.21).

The ^ notation as usual denotes proportional change. The solution for urban employment, urban income (welfare) and urban non-traded and traded good outputs is given below:

$$\hat{E}^U = \frac{\left(\dfrac{\beta}{X_N}\dfrac{\partial D_{NT}}{\partial \beta}\right)|\lambda|^U \hat{\beta}}{\Delta^U} \quad (8.22)$$

$$\hat{I}^U = \frac{\alpha_{EU}\left(\dfrac{\beta}{X_N}\dfrac{\partial D_{NT}}{\partial \beta}\right)|\lambda|^U \hat{\beta}}{\Delta^U} \quad (8.23)$$

$$\hat{X}_N = \frac{\lambda_{KU}\left(\dfrac{\beta}{X_N}\dfrac{\partial D_{NT}}{\partial \beta}\right)\hat{\beta}}{\Delta^U} \quad (8.24)$$

$$\hat{X}_U = \frac{-\lambda_{KN}\left(\dfrac{\beta}{X_N}\dfrac{\partial D_{NT}}{\partial \beta}\right)\hat{\beta}}{\Delta^U} \tag{8.25}$$

and

$$|\lambda|^U = \lambda_{KU} - \lambda_{LU} = \lambda_{LN} - \lambda_{KN}$$

$$\Delta^U = \lambda_{KU} - \eta_{IN}\alpha_{EU}|\lambda|^U > 0$$

We can represent the output results by using Figure 8.8. As a result of the increase in urban tourism, the production possibility frontier shifts from AB to $A'B'$. At a given terms of trade, the equilibrium point shifts from e_0 to e_1 with X_N increasing from X_N^* to X_U^{**} ($\hat{X}_N > 0$) while X_U falls from X_U^* to X_U^{**} ($\hat{X}_U < 0$).

From the above solution we obtain the following proposition.

Proposition 8.1. *An increase in urban tourism raises urban welfare and lowers urban unemployment, provided that the urban traded goods sector is relatively more capital-intensive than the urban non-traded goods sector* ($|\lambda|^U > 0$).

Figure 8.8.   Urban tourism and the production possibility frontier

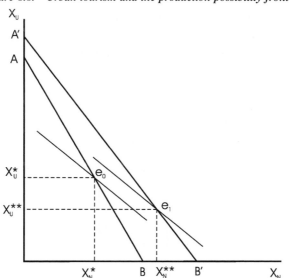

Comments on Proposition 8.1. An increase in tourism at constant prices, raises the demand for the non-traded goods and services, and this increase in demand results in an expansion of the output of the non-traded good to satisfy the equilibrium conditions. Since this sector is labour-intensive it requires more labour to be employed than that used by sector X_U. As output of sector X_U contracts, it releases capital and labour. However, it does not release enough labour to meet the needs of the non-traded goods sector. Hence, extra labour is drawn from the pool of unemployed and urban unemployment falls. The logic behind this output expansion (contraction) is exactly the same as in the Rybczynski theorem. All urban prices are fixed due to the presence of the minimum real wage. The urban region only has quantity effects. The welfare result arises because of the expansion of the tourist-receiving sector which leads to a reduction in urban unemployment (or an expansion of urban employment) and hence, an increase in urban welfare.

In Figure 8.1 the urban box expands and the new level of employment is shown by E'^U. The new tourist demand is shown by $A'e'$ and domestic demand by $O_N A'$. Note that the domestic consumption of non-traded goods has increased, hence, the old welfare level in the $D_{UU} D_{Ur}$ space is now represented by dashed lines in Figure 8.2. Since urban income increases, urban welfare must rise and will be above the solution on the dashed line.

We now proceed to examine the effect of the urban tourist boom on the rural region. By differentiating Equations (8.7)–(8.10), (8.13), (8.14), (8.16) and (8.18), we obtain the following system for the rural region:

$$
\begin{bmatrix}
1 & \dfrac{\theta_{Kr}}{|\theta|^R} & 0 & 0 & 0 \\
\bar{w} & 0 & \lambda w & 0 & 0 \\
0 & 0 & \lambda_{EU} & E^R & 0 \\
0 & A & 0 & -\alpha_{XNr} & \eta_{Nr} \\
0 & -\alpha_{ENr} & 0 & -\alpha_{Er} & 1
\end{bmatrix}
\begin{bmatrix}
\hat{w} \\
\hat{P}_{Nr} \\
\hat{\lambda} \\
\hat{E}^R \\
\hat{I}^R
\end{bmatrix}
=
\begin{bmatrix}
0 \\
0 \\
-(1+\lambda)E^U \hat{E}^U \\
0 \\
0
\end{bmatrix}
\qquad (8.26)
$$

when the term $\hat{I}^R$ is derived in the same manner as $\hat{I}^U$.

The solutions to the above system for unemployment, rural employment, rural income, the price of the rural non-traded good and rural wages, are as follows:

$$\hat{w} = \frac{(1+\lambda)\lambda w E^U \theta_{Kr}(\alpha_{XNr} - \eta_{Nr}\alpha_{Er})\left(\dfrac{\beta}{X_N}\right)\left(\dfrac{\partial D_{NT}}{\partial \beta}\right)}{\Delta^U \Delta^R} \frac{|\lambda|^U}{|\theta|^R}\hat{\beta} \quad (8.27)$$

$$\hat{P}_{Nr} = -\frac{(1+\lambda)\lambda w E^U(\alpha_{XNr} - \eta_{Nr}\alpha_{Er})\left(\dfrac{\beta}{X_N}\right)\left(\dfrac{\partial D_{NT}}{\partial \beta}\right)|\lambda|^U}{\Delta^U \Delta^R}\hat{\beta} \quad (8.28)$$

$$\hat{\lambda} = -\frac{(1+\lambda)w E^U \theta_{Kr}(\alpha_{XNr} - \eta_{Nr}\alpha_{Er})\left(\dfrac{\beta}{X_N}\right)\left(\dfrac{\partial D_{NT}}{\partial \beta}\right)}{\Delta^U \Delta^R}\frac{|\lambda|^U}{|\theta|^R}\hat{\beta} \quad (8.29)$$

$$\hat{E}^R = -\frac{(1+\lambda)\lambda w E^U(A + \eta_{Nr}\alpha_{Er})\left(\dfrac{\beta}{X_N}\right)\left(\dfrac{\partial D_{NT}}{\partial \beta}\right)|\lambda|^U}{\Delta^U \Delta^R}\hat{\beta} \quad (8.30)$$

$$\hat{I}^R = \frac{(1+\lambda)\lambda w E^U(-\alpha_{XNr}\alpha_{ENr} - A\alpha_{Er})\left(\dfrac{\beta}{X_N}\right)\left(\dfrac{\partial D_{NT}}{\partial \beta}\right)|\lambda|^U}{\Delta^U \Delta^R}\hat{\beta}$$

$$(8.31)$$

where

α_{Er} : share of rural labour in rural income

α_{ENr}: share of tourist expenditure in rural income

$$A = p_{Nr}\left[\frac{\partial D_{Nr}}{\partial P_{Nr}} + \frac{\partial D_{NrT}}{\partial P_{Nr}} - \frac{\partial X_{Nr}}{\partial P_{Nr}}\right] < 0$$

$$\alpha_{XNr} = \frac{E^R}{X_{Nr}}\frac{\partial X_{Nr}}{\partial E^R}$$

$\quad$ = the Rybczynski effect in the rural non-traded good

Δ^R: the determinant of the system and is assumed to be negative for stability

$A + \eta_{Nr}\alpha_{Er} < 0$ for stability in the rural non-traded goods market

$\alpha_{XNr} - \eta_{Nr}\alpha_{Er} > 0$

$|\theta|^{R} = \theta_{Lr}\theta_{KNr} - \theta_{LNr}\theta_{Kr}$

From the above equations, the following propositions are derived.

Proposition 8.2. *Urban tourist booms results in an increase in the rural wage rate* ($\hat{w} > 0$), *an increase in the relative price of the rural non-traded good* ($\hat{P}_{Nr} > 0$) *and a decrease in the ratio of urban unemployment to employment* ($\hat{\lambda} < 0$), *provided that the rural non-traded good sector is labour-intensive* ($|\theta|^{R} < 0$).

Proposition 8.3. *An increase in urban tourism decreases rural employment provided that the urban non-traded goods sector is labour-intensive* ($|\lambda|^{U} < 0$).

Proposition 8.4. *An increase in urban tourism lowers (raises) rural welfare provided that Proposition 8.3 holds and the following conditions are satisfied:*

$$|\theta|^{R} < 0 \quad \text{and} \quad -\alpha_{Er}A - \alpha_{ENr}\alpha_{XNr} < 0 \; (> 0) \tag{8.32}$$

Comments on Propositions 8.2–8.4. The most important result we obtain is that, under certain conditions, an increase in urban tourism immiserizes the rural region. The story of rural immiserization is best explained by rewriting the rural income expression in the following form:

$$\hat{I}^{R} = \left[\frac{X_{Nr} - D_{NrT}}{I^{R}} \right]\hat{P}_{Nr} + \alpha_{ER}\hat{E}^{R} \tag{8.33}$$

Equation (8.33) which is rewritten from the matrix on the left-hand side of Equation (8.26) states that the change in rural income depends on a tourism terms-of-trade effect (first expression in Equation (8.33) and a Rybczynski effect the second expression in the same equation. We explain the second term on the right-hand side of Equation (8.33) first. It has been already established that a tourist boom raises urban employment, which lowers λ. Hence, the urban expected wage increases, resulting in more migration from the rural to the urban region. This causes a decline in the quantity of labour available for employment in the rural region. The change in E^R has a rural Rybczynski effect, lowering the output of the labour-intensive good in the rural sector, i.e.X_{Nr}. We can represent this in Figure 8.9 where the Rybczynski effect is captured by the shift of the production possibility frontier from AB to $A'B'$ and the production equilibrium from e_0 to e_1. The Rybczynski line is drawn passing through points e_0 and e_1. As a result of the decrease in X_{Nr}, P_{Nr} increases and by the Stolper–Samuelson theorem w rises. Change in rural welfare is dependent on two effects: the employment effect ($\hat{E}^R$) and the tourism terms-of-trade effect ($\hat{P}_{Nr}$). Figure 8.10 captures the additional effect of an increase in P_{Nr} (the tourism terms of trade) which shifts the production equilibrium to e_2 where the slope of the relative price P_{Nr} is steeper. The employment effect is negative while the terms-of-trade effect is positive; hence, rural welfare depends on the net effect of these positive and negative consequences of urban tourist boom; a result that can be presented in terms of the rural diagrams. In Figures 8.11 and 8.12 we have drawn the now familiar Edgeworth–Bowley boxes for the urban and rural regions. Note that in the case

Figure 8.9. Urban tourist boom and the rural Rybczynski effect

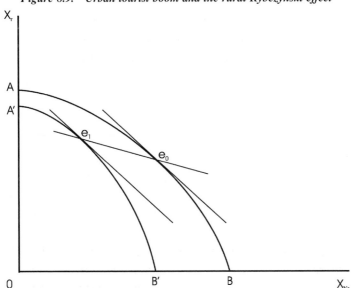

Figure 8.10.   Urban tourist boom and $\hat{P}_{Nr}$

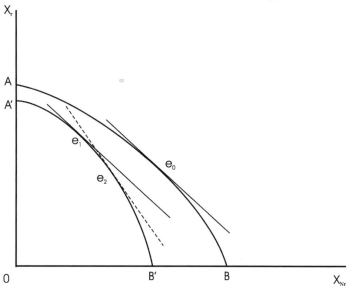

illustrated, rural employment falls from $O_{Nr}E^{R}$ to $O_{Nr}E'^{R}$, while urban employment rises to $O_{N}E'^{U}$, the output of the rural non-traded good falls from $O_{Nr}B$ to $O_{Nr}B'$. Figure 8.12 represents the welfare result for the rural sector.

Figure 8.11.   Urban tourist boom

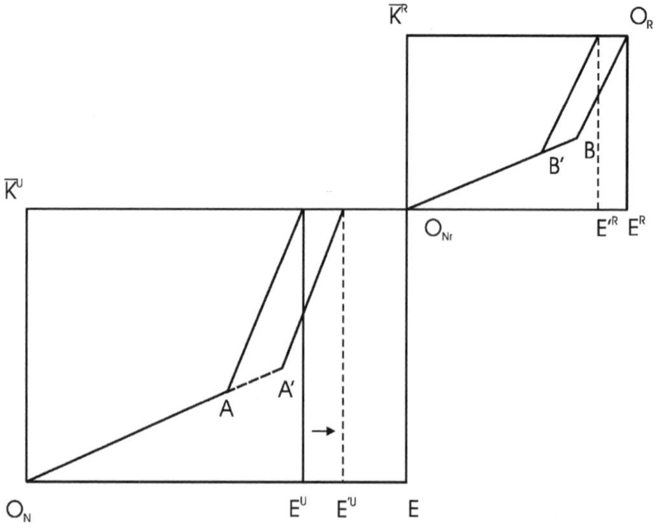

Figure 8.12.   Urban welfare

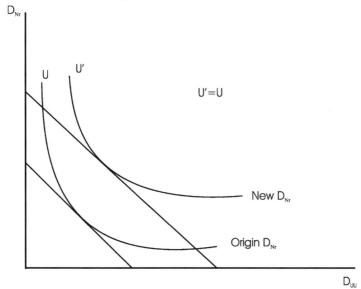

8.4.2. Rural tourist boom

We now proceed to analyze the consequence of an increase in rural tourism on important variables. Compared with the urban tourist boom, the effects of this expansion are simple to analyze. Due to the wage rigidity in the urban sector, a rural tourism increase has no effects on P_N, X_N, P_U, X_U and I^U, it only affects the urban unemployment rate λ. Most of the effects are confined to the rural region alone, as shown below.

By differentiating Equations (8.7)–(8.10), (8.13), (8.14), (8.16) and (8.17), we obtain the following system of equations:

$$
\begin{bmatrix}
1 & \dfrac{\theta_{Kr}}{|\theta^R|} & 0 & 0 & 0 \\
\hat{w} & 0 & \lambda_W & 0 & 0 \\
0 & 0 & \lambda_{EU} & E^R & 0 \\
0 & A & 0 & -\alpha_{XNr} & \eta_{Nr} \\
0 & -\alpha_{ENr} & 0 & -\alpha_{Er} & 1
\end{bmatrix}
\begin{bmatrix}
\hat{w} \\
\hat{P}_{Nr} \\
\hat{\lambda} \\
\hat{E}^R \\
\hat{I}^R
\end{bmatrix}
=
\begin{bmatrix}
0 \\
0 \\
0 \\
-\alpha \dfrac{\partial D_{NrT}}{\partial \alpha}\hat{\alpha} \\
0
\end{bmatrix}
\qquad (8.34)
$$

Solving the above system, we obtain

$$\hat{w} = \frac{\lambda w E^{R} \theta_{Kr} \alpha \left(\dfrac{\partial D_{NrT}}{\partial \alpha} \right)}{\Delta^{R} |\theta|^{R}} \hat{\alpha} \tag{8.35}$$

$$\hat{P}_{Nr} = -\frac{\lambda w E^{R} \alpha \left(\dfrac{\partial D_{NrT}}{\partial \alpha} \right)}{\Delta^{R}} \hat{\alpha} \tag{8.36}$$

$$\hat{\lambda} = -\frac{\alpha E^{R} \bar{w} \theta_{Kr} \left(\dfrac{\partial D_{NrT}}{\partial \alpha} \right)}{\Delta^{R} |\theta|^{R}} \hat{\alpha} \tag{8.37}$$

$$\hat{E}^{R} = \frac{\alpha E^{U} \lambda \bar{w} \theta_{Kr} \left(\dfrac{\partial D_{NrT}}{\partial \alpha} \right)}{\Delta^{R} |\theta|^{R}} \hat{\alpha} \tag{8.38}$$

$$\hat{I}^{R} = \frac{\left(-w E^{R} \alpha_{ENr} + \bar{w} \alpha_{Er} E^{U} \dfrac{\theta_{Kr}}{|\theta|^{R}} \right) \lambda \alpha \left(\dfrac{\partial D_{NrT}}{\partial \alpha} \right)}{\Delta^{R}} \hat{\alpha} \tag{8.39}$$

Proposition 8.5. *An increase in rural tourism necessarily raises the rural wage rate ($\hat{w} > 0$) and the relative price of the rural non-traded good ($\hat{p}_{Nr} > 0$), provided that the rural traded goods sector is more capital-intensive than the rural non-traded goods sector ($|\theta|^{R} < 0$).*

Proposition 8.6. *An increase in rural tourism necessarily increases rural employment ($\hat{E}^{R} > 0$) and decreases urban unemployment (in absolute and relative terms) assuming that $|\theta|^{R} < 0$.*

Proposition 8.7. *An increase in rural tourism necessarily increases both rural and national welfare, provided $|\theta|^{R} < 0$.*

The most interesting result we obtain for the increase in rural tourism is contained in Proposition 8.7, which establishes that, in spite of the presence of a distortion, increased tourism raises both rural and national welfare. An explanation of this result follows. The rural tourist boom increases the relative price of the rural non-traded

Figure 8.13.   Rural tourism boom, Rybczynski effect and $\hat{P}_{Nr}$

good. We can represent the rural tourist boom with the help of Figure 8.13. As a result of the tourist boom, the production possibility frontier shifts from AB to $A'B'$. At constant prices, production equilibrium shifts from e_0 to e_1. There is, however, also an increase in P_{Nr} which is captured by the shift from e_0 to e_2 where the relative price ratio P_{Nr} is steeper than at e_1. Again the Rybczynski line passes through the points e_0 and e_1. This by the Stolper–Samuelson mechanism increases the rural wage rate and lowers the rental on rural capital. This rise in the rural wage rate results in reverse migration, relieving the problem of urban unemployment. This is similar to giving a wage subsidy to the rural sector in the original HT model. An increase in employment provides a gain in rural income, as shown by the first bracketed term in Equation (8.39). This income gain is further reinforced by a rural tourist terms-of-trade effect that arises from an increase in P_{Nr}, as shown by the second term in the first parentheses of Equation (8.39). As a rural tourist boom leaves the welfare of the urban area unchanged, such a boom is necessarily welfare improving for the economy as a whole. No agent has become worse off; hence, rural tourist boom represents a Pareto improvement. This result stands in sharp contrast to the case of urban tourist boom, which may immiserize the rural region.[5] An important policy message of this chapter is that in the HT model economies should promote rural rather than urban tourism and/or at least subsidize the losers when an urban tourism boom occurs.

8.5. Conclusion

This chapter uses the GHT model to examine the consequences of urban and rural tourism on several variables, in particular its consequences for welfare and urban unemployment. It is demonstrated that urban tourism (given certain intensity conditions) always raises urban welfare and lowers urban unemployment. However, it has an ambiguous effect on rural welfare; hence, it is possible for urban tourism to result in immiserizing the rural region. This chapter highlights regional conflict. Rural tourism necessarily raises welfare for the economy as a whole and does not result in regional conflict. Thus, it is important to take into consideration regional interests in all policies that are designed to promote tourism.

Appendix A8. Tourism and regional immiserization

The GHT model with tourism can be easily expressed in terms of modern duality theory and in this section we demonstrate how it can be done. The dual approach is an alternative formulation of the model, which can sometimes simplify the derivation of results. We re-derive some results of this chapter using the dual approach and for this purpose we only introduce those equations that are not in the text. In the case of the urban region, we only require the use of the expenditure and revenue functions as additional equations.

A8.1. Urban region

We begin by introducing the expenditure function for the urban area:

$$e^{U}[P, P_N, \bar{U}^U] = \operatorname{Min} PD_{UU} + D_{Ur} + P_N D_N$$
$$\text{subject to} \quad \bar{U}^U = U^U(D_{UU}, D_{Ur}, D_N) \qquad (A8.1)$$

---

[5] Many examples of regional conflict can be provided, such as Italy and India (between north and south).

The urban expenditure function depends on the terms of trade, P, the relative price of the non-traded good, P_N, and the pre-determined level of urban utility, $\bar{U}^U$, and is derived from a constrained expenditure minimization problem.

The revenue function for the urban region is given by

$$R^U = [P, P_N; \bar{K}^U, E^U] \tag{A8.2}$$

This function depends on the terms of trade, P, the relative price of the non-traded good, P_N, the exogenously given supply of urban capital, $\bar{K}^U$, and the endogenously determined level of urban employment, E^U.

Equilibrium requires that expenditure equals revenue, hence,

$$e^U[P, P_N, \bar{U}^U] = R^U[P, P_N; \bar{K}^U, E^U] \tag{A8.3}$$

From Equation (A8.3) and the fact that tourists also consume this good we can write the market clearing equation for the non-traded goods sector with tourism as

$$e^U_{P_N} + D_{NT}(P_N, \beta) = R^U_{P_N} \tag{A8.4}$$

which states that the domestic demand for non-traded goods ($e^U_{P_N}$), plus tourism demand D_{NT}, equals the supply of this good which is given by $R^U_{P_N}$.

In the GHT model, for a small economy the terms of trade, P, are exogenously given and the relative price of the non-traded good, P_N, is fixed from the assumption of a binding real minimum wage. By differentiating Equations (A8.3) and (A8.4) with respect to the shift factor β, we obtain:

$$\begin{bmatrix} e^U_{P_N \bar{U}^U} & -R^U_{P_N E^U} \\ e^U_{\bar{U}^U} & -R^U_{E^U} \end{bmatrix} \begin{bmatrix} d\bar{U}^U \\ dE^U \end{bmatrix} = \begin{bmatrix} -\dfrac{\partial D_{NT}}{\partial \beta} \\ 0 \end{bmatrix} \tag{A8.5}$$

Solving the above system we obtain

$$d\bar{U}^U = \frac{R^U_{E^U} \dfrac{\partial D_{NT}}{\partial \beta}}{-e^U_{P_N \bar{U}^U} R^U_{E^U} + e^U_{1^U} R^U_{P_N \bar{U}^U}} \tag{A8.6}$$

$$dE^U = \frac{e^U_{\bar{U}^U} \frac{\partial D_{NT}}{\partial \beta}}{- e^U_{P_N \bar{U}^U} R^U_{E^U} + e^U_{I^U} R^U_{P_N \bar{U}^U}} \tag{A8.7}$$

where

$$R^U_{E^U} = w > 0$$

$$\frac{\partial D_{NT}}{\partial \beta} > 0$$

$R^U_{P_N E^U}$ = Rybczynski effect so the sign depends on factor intensities as stated earlier in the chapter.

From the assumptions made in the text, it follows that

$$d\bar{U}^U > 0 \quad \text{and} \quad dE^U > 0$$

as

$$e^U_{\bar{U}^U} \frac{\partial D_{NT}}{\partial \beta} > 0 \quad \text{and} \quad e^U_{P_N \bar{U}^U} R^U_{E^U} + e^U_{I^U} R^U_{P_N \bar{U}^U} > 0$$

A8.2. Rural region

In the case of the rural region, we now introduce an expenditure function and a revenue function and at the point of equilibrium they must be equal to each other, hence,

$$e^R[P, P_{NR}, \bar{U}^R] = R^R[P, P_{NR}; \bar{K}^R, E^R] \tag{A8.8}$$

Note that in the rural area, P_{NR} is flexible, hence, relative prices are important in this region. This is the flexi-price part of the model.

The market clearing equation for the rural non-traded good follows from differentiation of the balance condition with respect to P_{NR}:

$$e^R_{P_{NR}}[P, P_{NR}, \bar{U}^R] = R^R_{P_{NR}}[P, P_{Nr}; \bar{K}^R, E^R] \tag{A8.9}$$

which states that the demand for the rural non-traded good equals the supply of the non-traded good. By taking the second order derivative of the market clearing Equation (A8.9) we obtain

$$e^{R}_{P_{NR}\bar{U}^R}\, d\bar{U}^R - R^{R}_{P_{NR}E^R}\, dE^R = 0 \tag{A8.10}$$

From Equation (8.10) in the text, we know that

$$E^{U}d\lambda + dE^{R} = -(1+\lambda)dE^{U} \tag{A8.11}$$

The term dE^{U} has been solved for the urban region and from the assumptions already made it is positive.

Also from Equation (8.9) in the text we know that

$$(1+\lambda)dw_r + w_r\, d\lambda = 0 \tag{A8.12}$$

and

$$dw_r + \frac{\theta_{Kr}}{|\theta|^{R}}\, dP_{Nr} = 0 \tag{A8.13}$$

Finally from Equation (A8.8) we know that

$$e^{R}_{\bar{U}^R}d\bar{U}^R - R^{R}_{E^R}dE^R = 0 \tag{A8.14}$$

This gives us the following system:

$$
\begin{pmatrix}
e^{R}_{\bar{U}^R} & -R^{R}_{E^R} & 0 & 0 & 0 \\[2mm]
0 & 0 & 1 & \dfrac{\theta_{Kr}}{|\theta|^{R}} & 0 \\[2mm]
0 & 0 & (I+\lambda) & 0 & w_r \\[2mm]
0 & 1 & E^{U} & 0 & 0 \\[2mm]
e^{R}_{P_{NR}\bar{U}^R} & 0 & 0 & -R^{R}_{P_{NR}Er} & 0
\end{pmatrix}
\begin{pmatrix}
d\bar{U}^R \\[2mm]
dE^R \\[2mm]
d\lambda \\[2mm]
dP_{NR} \\[2mm]
dw_r
\end{pmatrix}
=
\begin{bmatrix}
0 \\[2mm]
0 \\[2mm]
0 \\[2mm]
-(1+\lambda)E^{U} \\[2mm]
0
\end{bmatrix}
\tag{A8.15}
$$

This system is equivalent to the system in Equation (8.26). The solution to this is left as an exercise for the reader. This shows how the GHT system can be represented in terms of duality and then manipulated.

References

Batra, R.N. and A.C. Seth (1977), "Unemployment, tariffs and the theory of international trade", *Journal of International Economics*, Vol. 7, pp. 295–306.

Brecher, R. (1974), "Minimum wage rates and the pure theory of international trade", *Quarterly Journal of Economics*, Vol. 88, pp. 98–116.

Corden, W.M. and J.P. Neary (1982), "Booming sector and de-industrialisation in a small open economy", *Economic Journal*, Vol. 92, pp. 825–848.

Hazari, B.R. and P.M. Sgro (1996), "International trade and regional development", *Pacific Economic Review*, Vol. 1, pp. 239–250.

Hazari, B.R. and P.M. Sgro (2001), *Migration, Unemployment and Trade*, Hingham, MA: Kluwer.

Hazari, B.R., J.J. Nowak, M. Salhi and D. Zdravevsski (2003), "Tourism and regional immiserization", *Pacific Economic Review*, Vol. 8(3), pp. 269–278.

CHAPTER 9

Tourism, Increasing Returns and Welfare

9.1. Introduction

In Chapters 2–8 we have generally assumed that most sectors under consideration are characterized by constant returns to scale. The idea of increasing returns to scale was introduced in Chapter 3 where we dealt with monopoly production of the non-traded good. It was established that tourism may benefit domestic residents by allowing the exploitation of increasing returns to scale – in particular by ensuring that the commodity is produced (in other words, the commodity in question may not be produced in the absence of tourism). However, increasing returns to scale were not modelled explicitly.

In this chapter a tourist boom and its consequences are examined in a three-sector model of trade consisting of two internationally traded and one non-traded good. An important feature of the model is that the manufacturing good is produced with increasing returns to scale while the other goods are produced under constant returns to scale. As has been stated throughout this book, a large proportion of a tourist's consumption is generally of non-traded goods and services and this consumption interacts with other sectors in a general equilibrium setting. The model used in this chapter captures the interdependence and interaction between tourism and the rest of the economy, in particular agriculture and manufacturing. This is important in view of the public debate on the effects of tourism, as it highlights the problem of competition for resources between two export-earning activities, agriculture and tourism. Furthermore, there is a concern as to whether tourism promotes or hinders the development of the manufacturing sector. Using this model, we analyse the effect of an increase in tourism boom on structural adjustment, factor and product prices and, most importantly, resident welfare. We again show that an expansion in tourism may be immiserizing. This occurs because of two effects. The first, a favourable effect, is due to an increase in the relative price of the non-traded. The second, a negative effect, is due to an efficiency loss that occurs in the presence of increasing returns to scale in manufacturing. If this second effect outweighs the first effect, resident immiserization occurs.[1]

9.2. The model

Our analysis uses a hybrid of the specific factor and Heckscher–Ohlin (HO) models under the assumption of full employment. The economy consists of three sectors: a non-traded goods sector producing X_N, an agricultural sector producing an exportable good X_A, and a manufacturing sector producing an importable good X_M. We assume that the traded goods are produced in a small open economy, hence, the terms of trade are given exogenously. It is assumed that commodities X_j ($j = N, A$) are produced under constant returns to scale and X_M with increasing returns to scale. The production functions for the agriculture and non-traded goods sectors can be written as follows:

$$X_j = F_j(L_j, T_j), \qquad j = A, N \qquad (9.1)$$

where L_j and T_j represent allocations of labour and land, respectively, utilized in the jth sector.[2] Agriculture and tourism use labour and land, hence, compete for land with each other. However, labour is used in the manufacturing sector and all the three sectors compete for labour. These production functions exhibit

---

[1] In the 'Dutch Disease' literature, Corden and Neary (1982) and Neary and van Wijnbergen (1986) have emphasized the detrimental consequences of a booming traded good sector and other traded good sectors, especially on manufacturing industry. In our model, since the foreign tourists consume the local non-traded good, the booming sector is the non-traded sector, which makes our analysis different from the 'Dutch Disease' model, although structural effects may still exist.

[2] Several studies stress the competition for the use of land and labor between agriculture and tourism, see Bryden (1973), Latimer (1986) and Telfer and Wall (1996).

positive and diminishing marginal products and constant returns to scale.

In the manufacturing sector, the production functions for a typical firm and the industry as a whole are as follows:

$$x_M^i = g_M^i(X_M)F_M^i(l_M^i, k_M^i), \qquad i = 1, 2, ..., N \qquad (9.2a)$$

and

$$X_M = G_M(L_M, K_M) = g_M(X_M)F_M(L_M, K_M) \qquad (9.2b)$$

where x_M^i is a typical firm's output of the manufactured good and X_M the total output in the manufacturing sector. The terms l_M^i and k_M^i are labour and capital employed by a typical firm in this sector and L_M and K_M are the total labour and specific capital employed in this sector. The increasing returns to scale in our model are output generated and are external to the firm and internal to the industry. This is a standard assumption in trade theory. These assumptions ensure that perfect competition prevails at the level of the firm and that the economy produces along its social transformation curve. Also note that the production function for the manufacturing sector, X_M, is multiplicatively separable.

The production function F_M in Equation (9.2b) is linearly homogenous in inputs. The increasing returns to scale are captured by the term $g_M(X_M)$ which is a positive function defined on the open interval $]0, +\infty[$ and is twice differentiable. This type of increasing returns to scale is considered to be 'neutral' in the sense that the capital intensity in production is independent of the scale of production. This is also a standard assumption in trade theory. Further, it is assumed that X_M is homothetic in L_M and K_M.

Using the production function X_M defined in Equation (9.2b), the rate of returns to scale in elasticity terms, e_M, is specified as

$$e_M = (dg_M/dX_M)(X_M/g_M) = F_M(L_M, K_M)g_M'(X_M) \qquad (9.3)$$

where e_M is defined over the open interval $]0, 1[$ in the case of increasing returns to scale.

The resource utilization conditions are specified as follows:

$$a_{LA}X_A + a_{LN}X_N = L_{AN} = \bar{L} - L_M \qquad (9.4)$$

$$a_{TA}X_A + a_{TN}X_N = \bar{T} \qquad (9.5)$$

$$a_{LM}X_M = L_M \tag{9.6}$$

$$a_{KM}X_M = K_M = \bar{K} \tag{9.7}$$

where the a_{ij}s denote the variable input coefficients, L_{AN} the total amount of labour used in the agriculture and non-traded goods sectors and L_M the amount of labour used in the manufacturing sectors. The terms $\bar{L}$, $\bar{T}$ and $\bar{K}$ are the inelastically supplied factors labour, land and capital, respectively. Note that the subset of sectors A and N forms a Heckscher–Ohlin structure with an endogenous labour supply [Equations (9.4) and (9.5)]. The endogenous labour supply $(\bar{L} - L_M)$ is determined by the amount of labour used in the manufacturing sector.

Under the assumption of profit maximization, interior solution and competitive markets, the price side of our model is as follows:

$$a_{LA}w + a_{TA}\Pi = 1 \tag{9.8}$$

$$a_{LN}w + a_{TN}\Pi = P_N \tag{9.9}$$

$$a_{LM}w + a_{KM}r = P \tag{9.10}$$

where P_N and P are the relative price of the non-traded and manufactured good, respectively; w, Π and r are the wage rate, rental on land and the rental on capital. The agriculture good has been chosen as the numeraire. Assuming a small open economy, the terms of trade, P, is given from outside. The relative price of the non-traded good, P_N, is determined domestically by the forces of demand and supply.

The quasi-concave aggregate utility function for the residents is

$$U = U(D_A, D_M, D_N) \tag{9.11}$$

where D_j ($j = A, M, N$) denotes the demand for the agriculture, manufactured and non-traded goods, respectively, by the residents.

Given utility maximization, it follows (from the equilibrium conditions) that

$$\frac{\partial U}{\partial D_A} = \frac{1}{P_M}\frac{\partial U}{\partial D_M} = \frac{1}{P_N}\frac{\partial U}{\partial D_N} \tag{9.12}$$

where $\partial U/\partial D_j$ ($j = A, M, N$) denotes marginal utility.

The demand for the non-traded good consists of resident demand (D_N) and tourist demand (D_{NT}) which can be written as follows:

$$D_N = D_N(P, P_N, Y) \tag{9.13}$$

$$D_{NT} = D_{NT}(P, P_N, \Delta) \tag{9.14}$$

where Y is resident income and Δ a shift parameter. All goods in consumption are substitutes and normal. We assume that $\partial D_{NT}/\partial \Delta > 0$ so that a tourist boom in our model is captured by an exogenous increase in Δ.

The market clearing conditions for the non-traded good and the resident budget constraint are as follows:

$$D_N + D_{NT} = X_N \tag{9.15}$$

$$Y = PX_M + P_N X_N + X_A = P_N D_N + PD_M + D_A \tag{9.16}$$

It is useful to represent the above model by using two diagrams, which highlight the interaction among the sectors and the factors of production. We represent the initial equilibrium of the model in Figure 9.1 where in quadrant II, the unit cost function for the agricultural sector is drawn as a P_A in the space (w, Π). Also shown are the isocost curves for the agriculture (given $P_A = 1$) and non-traded goods sector P_N^0. These curves are drawn under the assumption that the non-traded goods sector is labour intensive.

Figure 9.1. Initial equilibrium of the model – the factor market

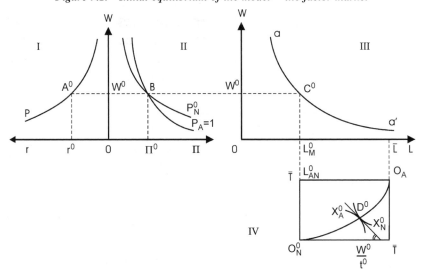

Given a solution for P_N from the non-traded good market (see Figure 9.2, quadrant II), we can determine the equilibrium values of w and Π as shown by w^0 and Π^0. In quadrant I, we have the isocost curve for the manufacturing sector P whose price is internationally given for the small-country case. The equilibrium solution for w^0 also determines the equilibrium value of r as shown by r^0.

In quadrant III, the curve aa' is the marginal product of labour curve in the manufacturing sector. The mathematical conditions necessary for this case are derived in Section 9.3. Generally, the marginal product curve for an increasing returns to scale technology can have any shape (Panagariya, 1986). From quadrant III, the equilibrium value w^0 enables us to determine the employment level

Figure 9.2.   Initial equilibrium of the model – the goods market

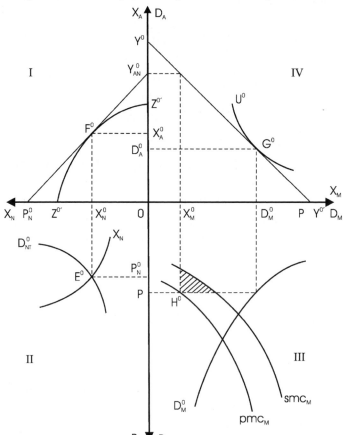

L_M^0 in the manufacturing sector. Since OL_M^0 of total labour supply is used in the manufacturing sector, the residual $\bar{L} - OL_M^0$ determines the supply of labour for the other two sectors, L_{AN}^0.

Given this residual supply L_{AN}^0 and the quantity of land, $\bar{T}$, we can draw the Edgeworth–Bowley box in quadrant IV of Figure 9.1. Also illustrated is the contract curve $O_A O_N^0$ drawn under the assumption that the non-traded good sector is labour intensive. Given the equilibrium wage/rental ratio on land determined in quadrant II, we can identify the point $D^0(X_A^0, X_N^0)$ on the contract curve which determines the allocation of labour and land between the two sectors, agriculture and non-traded goods. From the factor allocation in quadrant IV of Figure 9.1, we can derive the production possibility curve $Z^0 Z^{0\prime}$ for goods X_A and X_N in quadrant I of Figure 9.2, given the quantity of labour L_{AN}^0. In quadrant II of Figure 9.2, we have drawn the tourist demand curve D_{NT} and the non-traded good supply curve X_N. Note that for illustrative purposes only, we have made the simplifying assumption that residents do not consume the non-traded good. The actual results in the model presented in the following section are derived for the general case of both resident and tourist demand for the non-traded good. The equilibrium price and quantity are shown as P_N^0 and X_N^0. In quadrant I, given P_N^0, we can determine the production point $F^0(X_A^0, X_N^0)$ while in quadrant III, we have the demand (D_M^0) and private (pmc$_M$) and social (smc$_M$) marginal cost curves for the manufacturing sector. Note that the axes are labelled X_M, D_M and P. Given the international price P, to satisfy the demand D_M^0, we import $D_M^0 X_M^0$ of the manufacturing good. Due to the increasing returns to scale technology in this sector, the social marginal cost curve is below the private marginal cost curve, giving rise to a welfare loss represented by the shaded area. While in quadrant IV, we determine resident welfare. The national income budget line is represented by the line $Y^0 Y^{0\prime}$ while its slope is determined by the relative price ratio P. The vertical intercept of this budget line OY^0 is made up of the sum of $X_A^0 + P_N^0 X_N^0 + P X_M^0$, the values of which can be read from quadrant I and III. Also illustrated in quadrant I of Figure 9.2 is OY_{AN}^0 which represents the income generated in the Heckscher–Ohlin subset of the economy. Given the resident utility function U defined in Equation (9.11), with the restriction that resident consumption of the non-traded good is zero, we can determine the social indifference curve U_0 with equilibrium at G^0. Note that the G^0 includes the imports $D_M^0 X_M^0$ of the manufactured good derived in quadrant III.

9.3. Results

In this section, we present the implications of a tourist boom on relative prices, outputs, factor incomes and resident welfare. The tourism boom is captured by change in Δ in Equation (9.14).

By totally differentiating the cost Equations (9.8) and (9.9) which make up the Heckscher–Ohlin bloc, we obtain the standard Stolper–Samuelson result:

$$\hat{w} = \frac{\theta_{TA}}{|\theta|}\hat{P}_N \tag{9.17}$$

$$\hat{\Pi} = -\frac{\theta_{LA}}{|\theta|}\hat{P}_N \tag{9.18}$$

$$\hat{r} = \frac{-\theta_{LM}\theta_{TA}\hat{P}_N}{\theta_{KM}|\theta|} \tag{9.19}$$

where the θ_{ij}s are the cost shares, the $^\wedge$ notation denotes relative changes and $|\theta| = \theta_{LN} - \theta_{LA} = \theta_{TA} - \theta_{TN}$ describes the labour/land factor intensity which is positive for the case where the non-traded good is labour intensive vis-à-vis the agriculture good. Thus, if the relative price of the non-traded good, P_N, rises then w rises and Π falls. The price of the factor used intensely in its production, rises and falls.

Totally differentiating Equations (9.2b) and (9.10), using Equation (9.3) and after some manipulation, we obtain

$$e_M \hat{X}_M = \theta_{LM}\hat{w} + \theta_{KM}\hat{r} \tag{9.20}$$

From Equations (9.7) and (9.17)–(9.19), we obtain the following expression for $\hat{X}_M$:

$$\hat{X}_M = -\phi_M \hat{P}_N \tag{9.21}$$

where

$$\phi_M = \frac{\theta_{LM}\theta_{TA}}{(1 - e_M)\xi_M |\theta|}$$

$$\xi_M = \left(\frac{e_M}{1 - e_M} \right) \theta_{LM} - \frac{\theta_{KM}}{\sigma^M}$$

and σ^j is the elasticity of substitution between the primary factors in sector j. The term ξ_M is the elasticity of the marginal physical product of labour with respect to a change in labour in X_M and is assumed to be negative for stability.

From Equations (9.6) and (9.21), we obtain the following expression for change in the labour demand in the manufacturing sector:

$$\hat{L}_M = - \frac{\theta_{TA}}{|\theta|(\xi_M)} \hat{P}_N \tag{9.22}$$

By using Equation (9.22), we have the change in the labour supply for the agriculture and non-traded goods sectors:

$$\hat{L}_{AN} = - \frac{\mu_M}{\mu_{AN}} \frac{\theta_{TA}}{|\theta|\xi_M} \hat{P}_N \tag{9.23}$$

where μ_j $(j = M, A, N)$ is the labour share in j, e.g. $\mu_{AN} = L_{AN}/\bar{L}$.

From the full employment conditions in the Heckscher–Ohlin subset, Equations (9.4), (9.5) and (9.23), we obtain the following output changes for sectors X_A and X_N.

$$\hat{X}_A = -\phi_A \hat{P}_N \tag{9.24}$$

$$\hat{X}_N = \phi_N \hat{P}_N \tag{9.25}$$

where

$$\phi_j = \left[(\lambda_{Li}\wp_T + \lambda_{Ti}\wp_L) - \lambda_{Ti} \frac{\mu_M}{\mu_{AN}} \frac{\theta_{TA}}{\xi_M} \right] \frac{1}{|\theta||\lambda|},$$

$$i, j = A, N, \quad i \neq j$$

The term ϕ_j is the price elasticity of supply in sector j; λ_{Li} and λ_{Ti} are factor shares defined in sectors X_A and X_N. For example,

$$\lambda_{LA} = L_A/L_{AN}, \qquad \lambda_{TN} = T_N/\bar{T}$$

Note that $|\lambda| = \lambda_{LN} - \lambda_{TN} = \lambda_{TA} - \lambda_{LA}$ has the same sign as $|\theta|$ since there are no distortions in the labour market. The term $\wp_i$, $i = T, L$, denotes the elasticity of factor i in sector A and N with respect to (t/w) at constant outputs and factor endowments.

From the full employment conditions (9.4), (9.6) and (9.7), the production function (9.2b), and using the definition of e_M, we obtain the following relationship between the slope of the production possibility surface and relative prices:

$$\mathrm{d}X_A + P_N\,\mathrm{d}X_N + P_M\,\mathrm{d}X_M = e_M\,\mathrm{d}X_M \qquad (9.26)$$

Note that due to the presence of a distortion (here as increasing returns to scale), there is a non-tangency between the production possibility surface and relative prices.

Using Equations (9.11), (9.12), (9.16) and (9.26) we obtain the following expression for the change in resident welfare:

$$\hat{y} = \gamma_N\hat{D}_N + \gamma_M\hat{D}_M + \gamma_A\hat{D}_A = \psi\hat{P}_N, \qquad (9.27)$$

where

$$\psi = \left[\delta_{NT} + \left(\frac{e_M}{1 - e_M} \right) \frac{\theta_{TA}}{|\theta|} \frac{\delta_M\theta_{LM}}{\xi_M} \right] \lessgtr 0$$

δ_{NT} is the share of international tourist demand in national income and δ_M the share of manufacturing output in national income.

By differentiating Equations (9.13)–(9.15), we obtain:

$$\hat{X}_N = \hat{D}_{NT}\alpha_{NT} + \hat{D}_N\alpha_N \qquad (9.28)$$

where

$$\alpha_N = D_N/X_N, \qquad \alpha_{NT} = D_{NT}/X_N.$$

$$\hat{D}_{NT} = -\varepsilon_{NT}\hat{P}_N + \beta_{NT}\hat{\Delta} \qquad (9.29)$$

$$\hat{D}_N = -\varepsilon_N\hat{P}_N + \eta_N\hat{y} \qquad (9.30)$$

where $\varepsilon_i > 0$ $(i = N, NT)$ is the compensated price elasticity of demand, η_N the resident income elasticity of the non-traded goods and β_{NT} measures the sensitivity of the tourist demand to the tourist shock.

Using Equations (9.25) and (9.27)–(9.30) we obtain:

$$\hat{P}_N = (\alpha_{NT}\beta_{NT}/\Omega)\hat{\Delta} \qquad (9.31)$$

where $\Omega = \phi_N + \alpha_{NT}\varepsilon_{NT} + \alpha_N\varepsilon_N - \alpha_N\varepsilon_N\Psi$ is the excess supply elasticity of the non-traded good in general equilibrium and is positive for stability in this market.

From the above equations, we are now able to describe the consequences of an increase in tourism on the key variables.

Irrespective of the labour intensity of the non-traded goods sector, its price and output always increase and the output of the agricultural sector falls. In our model, P_N, as the relative price of an export is the tertiary terms of trade.

The response of the other key variables depends on the labour intensity of the non-traded goods sector. If this sector is labour intensive ($|\theta| > 0$), the wage rate increases and both the rental on land and capital fall. Due to the wage increase (and resultant increase in costs), the output of the manufacturing sector falls. Note that the tourist expansion comes at a cost to the manufacturing sector. Moreover, as the manufacturing output was already sub-optimal at the initial market equilibrium (due to the increasing returns to scale), this decrease in output worsens the welfare loss [second term in square brackets of Ψ in Equation (9.27)]. This welfare loss can outweigh the welfare gain [captured by δ_{NT} in Ψ in Equation (9.27)] due to the terms-of-trade effect [$\hat{P}_N > 0$]. Hence, resident welfare (income) may fall as a result of the increase in tourism. This may be a plausible hypothesis for small open economies of developed countries. On the other hand, 'green tourism' which consumes more land than labour would be welfare enhancing for residents.

If the non-traded goods is land intensive ($|\theta| < 0$), the wage rate falls, the rental on capital and land rise and the outputs of both X_M and X_N rise. Hence, the expansion in tourism helps the development of the manufacturing sector. Resident welfare (income) rises as both the effects referred to above are positive. That is, the terms-of-trade effect is still favourable while the expansion of the manufacturing sector reduces the welfare loss at the market equilibrium.

It will be useful to use Figures 9.1 and 9.2 to illustrate some of the results. We will illustrate the case of immiserizing growth. In quadrant II of Figure 9.4, the increase in tourism induces an increase in P_N. Recall that, for illustrative purposes only, we assume that residents do not consume X_N. By the Stolper–Samuelson effect the wage rate, w, increases at the expense of the rental rates on land as described in quadrant II of Figure 9.3. The manufacturing sector reduces its demand for labour as shown in quadrant III of Figure 9.3, which results in an increased labour supply for the HOS subset of the economy (X_A and X_N). In quadrant IV of Figure 9.3, we have represented both the

Figure 9.3.   Increase in tourism and factor markets

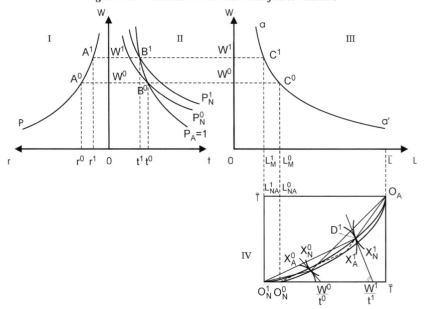

factor prices and the labour supply effects on outputs X_A and X_N. The expansion of X_N and contraction of X_A production are illustrated in quadrant I of Figure 9.4 by the shift in the production point from F^0 to F^1. We can identify the terms of trade and increased labour supply effects on resident income in quadrant I of Figure 9.4 by the distance $Y_{AN}^0 Y_{AN}^1$.

As a result of the increases in P_N, both the (pmc$_M$) and (smc$_M$) curves shift to the left with the pmc$_M$ curve shifting more than the (smc$_M$) curve because the private firm in X_M do not internalize the effects of the increasing returns to scale. As a result, the welfare loss (represented by the shaded area) becomes largest. This increase in the welfare loss outweighs the increase in income from the terms-of-trade effect as illustrated by the movement from the social indifference curve U^0 to U^1 in quadrant IV of Figure 9.4.

9.4. Conclusion

It is frequently asserted that international tourism may be costly to the host country. A great deal of attention has been paid to the most obvious costs due to externalities associated with tourism activity

Figure 9.4.   Increase in tourism and welfare

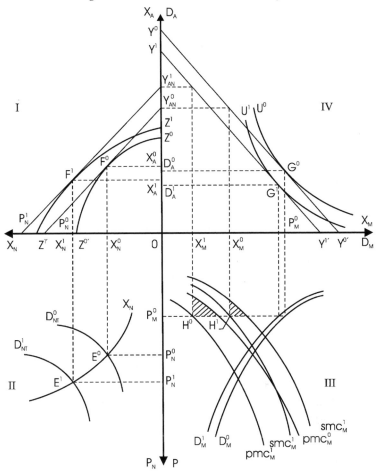

(pollution, congestion and sociocultural impacts). However, a general equilibrium analysis of the effects of tourism on structural adjustment and welfare in the presence of externalities is lacking. This chapter addresses this problem.

Under certain conditions, welfare and manufacturing output may fall as a result of increased tourism. This can occur when the non-traded tourism sector is more labour intensive than the agricultural traded sector. The empirical evidence on factor intensities suggests that this case is more likely to prevail and this theoretical possibility should therefore be taken seriously.

As is well known, the distortion literature establishes that a tax-cum-subsidy policy is required to correct the distortion. As noted earlier, due to the monopoly power in trade, tourism tax receipts are another source of taxation revenue, which could be used to subsidize the manufacturing sector.

References

Bryden, J.M. (1973), *Tourism and Development: A Case Study of the Commonwealth Caribbean*, London: Cambridge University Press.

Corden, W.M. and J.P. Neary (1982), "Booming sector and de-industrialisation in a small open economy", *Economic Journal*, Vol. 92, pp. 825–848.

Latimer, H. (1986), "Developing island economies: tourism v agriculture", *Tourism Management*, Vol. 6, pp. 32–42.

Neary, J.P. and S. Van Wijnbergen (eds) (1986), *Natural Resources and the Macroeconomy*, Oxford, Basil, Blackwell.

Panagariya, A. (1986), "Increasing returns and the specific factor model", *Southern Economic Journal*, Vol. 86, pp. 1–17.

Telfer, D.J. and G. Wall (1996), "Linkages between tourism and food productions", *Annals of Tourism Research*, Vol. 23(3), pp. 635–653.

CHAPTER 10

Tourism and Growth in a Dynamic Model of Trade

10.1. Introduction

The analysis so far has concentrated on the impact of increased tourism on resident welfare in a static framework and different types of market imperfections. It is time to depart from static models and construct a dynamic model of trade and tourism. In this chapter we analyse the impact of domestic capital accumulation and changes in the terms of trade on per capita consumption in the context of such a model. This represents a variation of the model in Hazari and Sgro (1995). The analysis is in the tradition of descriptive growth theory while in the following chapter an optimizing framework is used to study this problem.

In the dynamic framework of this chapter, tourism exports are assumed to be used to purchase foreign capital. This should be clearly distinguished from models of foreign ownership of capital where repatriation payments are made from the capital receiving country and ownership remains in the hands of foreign countries. This growth model is driven by the expansion in tourism along with other traditional variables used in descriptive growth theory. Spain is an excellent example of using tourism revenue to purchase foreign capital to add to domestic capital formation.

Descriptive growth theory begins with the Harrod (1942) and Domar (1946) growth model which was extended in the pioneering paper of Solow (1956). This paper by Solow not only solved some of the problems associated with the Harrod–Domar model but also explained the six stylized facts of Kaldor (1963).[1] The Solow model is rooted in the neoclassical production function and assumes a constant savings rate. A somewhat pessimistic prediction of the Solow model is that in the absence of technological progress, per capita growth must come to an end. The model also predicts that the lower the level of real per capita income the faster is the growth rate – hence, the faster is convergence to the steady-state level of the variables involved (given identical parametric values of other variables). While the Solow growth model deals with a closed economy, there are several ways of opening this model to trade and in this chapter a two-sector version of the model is used to incorporate trade and tourism.

As stated earlier, we explore the possibility of using tourism receipts to purchase foreign capital that adds to domestic capital accumulation. Such additions may help to reduce the need for high domestic savings rates for the economy to converge to a balanced growth path of the closed economy. As has been the case in the static modelling, we again assume the country to be small in traded goods but it has monopoly power in trade in the tourism sector. The Samuelson (1965) framework is exploited to set up a model in which two goods are produced: a capital and a non-traded consumption good.[2] The domestic economy not only imports capital but also another consumption good. Thus, there are two produced goods: a capital and a non-traded consumption good; two imported goods: a capital good that is imported and identical with the domestic good and a final good which is imported. This model is a variation on the dependency model of Chapter 3. Total capital accumulation consists of domestic and foreign capital.

---

[1] These six stylized facts are per capita output grows over time; per capita physical capital grows over time; the rental on capital is constant over time; capital–output ratio is constant over time; the shares of labour and capital remain constant over time, and finally there is a difference in the growth rates of output per worker across countries.

[2] Samuelson (1965) sets up a model of international trade in which the non-traded goods sector only produced capital goods which were utilized by the traded goods sector. This chapter is a forerunner of the Komiya (1967) paper where the non-traded good is used for consumption purposes only. Samuelson did not establish the steady-state growth path for his model as he was only interested in establishing interest rate equalization. However, it is relatively simple to establish the steady-state properties of the Samuelson model.

The results of the model establish as to how an exogenously given rate of growth in the tourism sector generates steady-state growth and a faster convergence to the domestic steady state without tourism. This faster convergence is generated by tourism acting as a time-saving device allowing the domestic population to consume now rather than later and this feature is brought out in our results.[3]

10.2. The model

10.2.1. Short-run (momentary) equilibrium

The tourist-receiving country produces two goods: X_i $(i = N, K)$. The commodity, X_N, is the consumption good and X_K the capital good. The model is written in continuous time. The production functions for these goods are given below and satisfy the usual conditions imposed on F_i as postulated in this book:

$$X_N = F_N[K_N^d + K_N^f, L_N] = L_N f_N(k_N) \tag{10.1}$$

$$X_K = F_K[K_K^d + K_K^f, L_K] = L_K f_K(k_K) \tag{10.2}$$

where K_j and L_j $(j = N, K)$ represent the capital and labour allocation to the sectors and k_j $(j = N, K)$ the capital–labour ratios in each sector. The superscripts of d and f on K refers to domestic and foreign.

In per capita terms these functions can be written as

$$x_N = l_N f_N(k_N) \tag{10.3}$$

$$x_K = l_K f_K(k_K) \tag{10.4}$$

where l_N and l_K represent the share of labour allocated to each sector, i.e. $l_N = L_N/\bar{L}$ and $l_K = L_K/\bar{L}$.

Note also that the relative price of the non-traded consumption good, P_N, is determined endogenously by domestic and foreign demand. Total demand is made up of the consumption by domestic consumers and tourists. From the assumptions of profit

---

[3] Similar results can also be obtained via rapid export growth with monopoly power in trade.

maximization and the existence of an interior equilibrium it follows that

$$w = P_N[f_N(k_N) - k_N f'_N(k_N)] = f_K(k_K) - k_K f'_K(k_K) \tag{10.5}$$

$$r = P_N f'_N(k_N) = f'_K(k_K) \tag{10.6}$$

where w, r and P_N denote the real wage, real rental on capital and the relative price of the non-traded consumption good in terms of the capital good. We shall present the large-country case and derive the results for the small-country case as a subset.

The following relationships are based on the material in Chapter 2 with the notation introduced in this chapter:

$$\omega = \frac{w}{r} = \frac{f_N(k_N)}{f'_N(k_N)} - k_N = \frac{f_K(k_K)}{f'_K(k_K)} - k_K \tag{10.7}$$

and

$$P_N = \frac{f'_K(k_K)}{f'_N(k_N)} \tag{10.8}$$

where f'_K and f'_N denote the marginal product of capital in the relevant sector.

It is assumed that the country imports capital, hence, the factor endowment condition for capital requires that

$$l_N k_N + l_K k_K = k^d + k^f = \tilde{k} \tag{10.9}$$

where k^d represents the ratio of aggregate domestic capital to labour and k^f the ratio of imported capital to labour. The term $\tilde{k}$ shows the overall or aggregate capital–labour ratio. Labour is fully employed, hence, it follows that

$$l_N + l_K = 1 \tag{10.10}$$

National income accounting requires that savings must equal the output of the capital goods – both newly produced and purchased overseas. Following the Solow convention of descriptive growth theory, it is assumed that a constant proportion of income is saved, hence:

$$sY = X_K + \dot{K}^F \tag{10.11}$$

where s denotes the constant average and marginal savings rate. Equation (10.11) in per capita terms can be written as[4]

$$sy = \frac{X_K}{L} + \frac{\dot{K}^F}{L} \tag{10.12}$$

where $y = Y/L$ denotes per capita income. Lower case letters will be used to denote per capita variables. Per capita income from the factor side is defined as

$$y = w + r\tilde{k} \tag{10.13}$$

Since savings equals investment, Equation (10.11) can be rewritten in the following form by making use of Equation (10.13):

$$x_K = l_K f'_K(\omega + k_K) = sy - \frac{\dot{K}^F}{L} \tag{10.14}$$

Solutions for l_N and l_K in terms of sectoral and aggregate capital labour ratios can be obtained from Equations (10.9) and (10.10) as given below:

$$l_N = \frac{k_K - \tilde{k}}{k_K - k_N} \tag{10.15}$$

$$l_K = \frac{\tilde{k} - k_N}{k_K - k_N} \tag{10.16}$$

where $\tilde{k} = k^d + k^f$. It will be assumed that factor intensities do not reverse and that l_N and l_K are positive at all relevant factor price ratios.[5] Equation (10.14) can be rewritten as

$$\tilde{k}\left(\frac{r(\omega + k_K)}{(k_K - k_N)} - sr\right) - \frac{rk_N(\omega + k_K)}{(k_K - k_N)} - s\omega r + \frac{\dot{K}^F}{L} = 0 \tag{10.17}$$

As is the practice in growth theory, we first obtain a unique momentary equilibrium which requires that ω and $\tilde{k}$ are related monotonically with each other.

---

[4] The balance equation is $Y = P_N X_N + X_K + \dot{K}^F + M_1$, where M_1 denote imports. Rewriting the balance equation, we obtain $Y - P_N X_N - M_1 = X_K + \dot{K}^F$ and the LHS is the same as sY, hence $sY = X_K + \dot{K}^F$.

[5] For factor intensity reversals, see Hazari (1986).

By differentiating Equation (10.17) with respect to and using the definition of elasticity of substitution between capital and labour:

$$\sigma_i(\omega) = (\omega/k_i)\frac{dk_i}{d\omega} \qquad (i = N, k)$$

we obtain

$$\frac{d\tilde{k}}{d\omega} = \frac{c(\omega)\sigma_K(\omega) + d(\omega)\sigma N(\omega) + e(\omega)}{\omega a(\omega)b(\omega)} \tag{10.18}$$

where

$$a(\omega) = \omega + sk_N + (1 - s)k_K$$

$$b(\omega) = (1 - s)\omega k_N + k_K(s\omega + k_C)$$

$$c(\omega) = k_K(1 - s)(\omega + k_N)^2$$

$$d(\omega) = k_C s(\omega + k_K)^2$$

$$e(\omega) = \omega(k_K - k_N)^2 s(1 - s)^2.$$

Since a, b, c, d and e are all positive, it follows that $d\tilde{k}/d\omega > 0$, in other words, $\tilde{k}$ and ω are uniquely related. Therefore, for any $\tilde{k}$ the solution of the entire system is uniquely determined.

10.2.2. Long-run equilibrium

Recall that we have assumed that the country receives tourists who, together with domestic residents, consume the non-traded good. We have also assumed that the country imports consumer goods which are not produced domestically. Let the growth in tourist demand for the non-traded goods be given by

$$\dot{K}^F = E^T = P_N^\eta e^{ut} \quad \text{with } \eta < 0, \ 1 + \eta > 0 \tag{10.19}$$

where η is the constant price elasticity of demand.[6] Tourism is growing at the exogenously given rate of u. The value of $\eta \neq \infty$ represents the case of monopoly power arising from trade in tourism. This is further elaborated in the following chapter. The demand for

---

[6] Uzawa (1963) and Hanson (1971) have shown that for a fixed savings rate, the income elasticities of demand are zero.

imports is given by

$$M_1 = P_1 e^{\lambda \tau} \tag{10.20}$$

The term λ is the exogenously given rate of the growth in demand for imports by domestic residents.

We are now in a position to write our balance-of-payments constraint as

$$P_N^\eta e^{ut} = e^{\lambda \tau} + \dot{K}^F \tag{10.21}$$

where the left-hand side shows the value of exports and the right-hand side the value of imports of consumer and capital goods over time. This equation ensures that the balance-of-payments condition holds in a dynamic framework.

From the previous section of this chapter we know that there are two sources of capital accumulation, domestic and foreign. The domestic supply of capital is contingent upon domestic output of capital goods while the purchases of imported capital depends on the rate of growth of exports as shown in Equation (10.21). The left-hand side of Equation (10.21) shows the growth in exports (which in our model consists of growth in tourism via the consumption of the non-traded goods). The right-hand side shows the growth in imports which consist of the growth of the importable consumption good and imported capital.[7] The importable good is not produced domestically as is the case in Chapter 2 of this book.

We assume that the initial stock of labour equals unity ($L_0 = 1$) and the labour force grows at an exogenously given rate of n:

$$L(t) = e^{nt} \tag{10.22}$$

The rate of accumulation for domestic capital is given by

$$\dot{k}^d = x_k - nk^d \tag{10.23}$$

---

[7] Note that we have ignored depreciation of capital. This could be introduced in the usual manner. It should be pointed out that depreciation of capital may be quite high in the non-traded goods sector as many services which are consumed are durable consumption goods like hotels and resorts which require constant refurbishing.

By substituting from Equations (10.13) and (10.14) the above equations can be rewritten as

$$\dot{k}^{d} = s(\omega + k^{d})r - \frac{\dot{K}^{F}}{L} - nk^{d} \tag{10.24}$$

From Equation (10.21) we can substitute for $\dot{K}^{F}$ assuming that $\lambda = u = n$ to obtain:

$$\dot{k}^{d} = s(\omega + \tilde{k})r - (P_{N}^{\eta} - 1) - nk^{d} \tag{10.25}$$

It is assumed that the country imports foreign capital. This requires that $(P_{N}^{\eta} - 1) > 0$. This condition will be maintained throughout this chapter. Furthermore, for the sake of analytical simplicity, all the growth rates will be set equal to each other, therefore, $\lambda = u = n$. Using Equation (10.21) we can rewrite Equation (10.25) as

$$\dot{\tilde{k}} = \dot{k}^{d} + \dot{k}^{F} = s(\omega + \tilde{k})r - n\tilde{k} \tag{10.26}$$

Along the balanced growth path $\dot{\tilde{k}}/\tilde{k} = 0$. Hence, it follows that

$$\frac{s(\omega + \tilde{k})r}{\tilde{k}} = n \tag{10.27}$$

In the closed-economy case, the steady-state growth path is given by the equation:

$$\frac{s(\omega + k^{d})r}{k^{d}} = n \tag{10.28}$$

The impact of tourism can be captured by examining Equations (10.27) and (10.28). Since $(P_{N}^{\eta} - 1) > 0$, $\dot{k}^{F} > 0$, therefore, the left-hand side of Equation (10.27) captures the impact of tourism. In the first term, $\tilde{k}$ has risen due to the capital inflow. Assuming a constant P_{N} and using the Rybczynski theorem, r and ω are constant. Given that Equations (10.27) and (10.28) are equal at steady state, s, must be lower after the capital inflow to maintain the equality. That is, tourism acts as a time-saving device which allows consumers to consume more now (reduce s) rather than later. We can illustrate Equation (10.26) in Figure 10.1 where the steady-state value of $\tilde{k}$ is denoted as $\tilde{k}^{*}$. The steady-state value of k^{d} in the case of no foreign capital inflow will be below $\tilde{k}^{*}$, say k^{d*} since $\tilde{k} = k^{d} + k^{F}$.

Figure 10.1.   Steady state with tourism

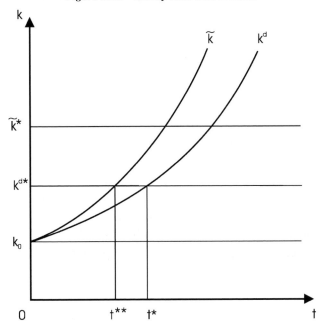

We can also illustrate that the economy will grow at a faster rate with foreign capital inflow than without. From Equation (10.23) we can write:

$$\dot{k}^d = l_k f_k(k^d) - nk^d$$

or

$$\dot{k}^d = k_0 e^{\lambda t} \tag{10.29}$$

where $\lambda = l_k f_k(k^d) - n$. This k^d grows over time depending on the value of λ. In the case of tourists, Equation (10.29) changes to

$$\dot{\tilde{k}} = k_0 e^{\lambda' t} \tag{10.30}$$

where $\lambda' = l_k f_k(\tilde{k}) - n$.

We may compute the time required to reach k^{d*} (denoted by t^*) by using Equation (10.29) as

$$t^* = (\log k^{d*}/k_0)/\lambda \tag{10.31}$$

Similarly, one can compute the time required to reach k^{d*} with foreign capital by examining the time taken to reach $\tilde{k}^*$. The time required to reach $\tilde{k}^*$ is

$$\tilde{t}^* = (\log \tilde{k}^*/k_0)/\lambda' \qquad (10.32)$$

This $\tilde{t}^*$ may be to the left or right of t^*. What is clear is that starting from k_0, the time-path of capital accumulation to reach k^{d*} is steeper with foreign capital inflow and that k^{d*} will be reached at $t^{**} < t^*$. This is illustrated in Figure 10.1.

10.3. Conclusion

This chapter shows the benefits of tourism in a dynamic model. These benefits arise because tourism can add to growth and act as a time-saving device for the domestic population.[8] That is, it allows the domestic population to consume more now rather than later.

References

Domar, E.D. (1946), "Capital expansion, rate of growth and employment", *Econometrics*, Vol. 4(2), pp. 137–147.

Harrod, R.F. (1942), *Towards a Dynamic Economics: Some Recent Developments of Economic Theory and Their Application to Policy*, London: Macmillan.

Hanson, J.A. (1971), *Growth in Open Economics*, New York: Springer.

Hazari, B.R. (1986), *International Trade: Theoretical Issues*, London: Croon Helm.

Hazari, B.R. and P.M. Sgro (1995), "Tourism and growth in a dynamic model of trade", *Journal of International Trade and Economic Development*, Vol. 4, pp. 243–252, Special Issues on the Four Little Dragons.

Kaldor, N. (1963), "Capital accumulation and economic growth", in: F.A. Lutz and D.C. Hague, editors, *Proceedings of a Conference Held by the International Economics Association*, London: Macmillan.

Komiya, R. (1967), "Non-traded goods and the pure theory of international trade", *International Economic Review*, Vol. 8, pp. 132–152.

---

[8] In a distortionary model, it is possible for the economy to decay. An example of decay in the long run is provided in Sgro and Takayama (1981). This model shows the impact of minimum wage on the growth process in an economy. As this is a second best model it is our conjecture that such phenomena may arise in distortionary models where optimal policies are not used. The assumption of a variable r gives rise to monopoly power in trade.

Samuelson, P.A. (1965), "Equalisation by trade of interest rate along with the real wage", in: R.E. Baldwin, editor, *Trade, Growth and Balance of Payments in Honour of Gottfried Haberler*, Chicago, IL: Rand McNally.

Sgro, P.M. and A. Takayama (1981), "On the long-run growth effects of a minimum wage for a two sector economy", *Economic Record*, pp. 180–185.

Solow, R.M. (1956), "A contribution to the theory of economic growth", *Quarterly Journal of Economics*, Vol. 70(1), pp. 65–94.

Uzawa, H. (1963), "In a two-sector model of economic growth II", *Review of Economic Studies*, pp. 105–118.

CHAPTER 11

Optimal Growth and Tourism

11.1. Introduction

The previous chapter was concerned with modelling growth and tourism in terms of descriptive growth theory. This chapter extends the interrelationship between tourism and growth to a Ramsey (1928) framework with monopoly power in trade and indispensability of foreign capital in the production process. We maximize a social welfare function and ask the question of how an economy might ideally evolve if the savings decision is endogenous, that is, we are interested in optimal economic growth not just how an economy might evolve when an arbitrary savings rule is prescribed (descriptive growth theory). Typical examples of economies where foreign capital is indispensable in production are countries that can attract tourists due to its natural and cultural heritage (for example, many countries in Africa) but are unable to utilize the production technology only with domestic capital. The model presented here may also be applied to developed countries such as Spain where growth has been led by tourism. This chapter provides a rationale for the Spanish strategy of using tourism to promote growth.

The basic intuition underlying our model relies on the importance of tourism as a means of purchasing capital goods rather than obtaining them via foreign direct investment (FDI). The logic of this strategy has already been stated in the previous chapter. Spain is the archetypical example of a country where economic development and industrialization have been achieved since the early 1960s via imports of capital goods mainly financed by tourism receipts (Sinclair and Bote Gomez, 1996).[1]

---

[1] According to Sinclair and Bote Gomez (1996, p. 91), 'Net earnings from tourism…have played a key role in financing Spain's industrialization process'. Also Spain's GDP rate of growth was on average 7.1% per year between 1960 and 1970 while it was only 5.5% for France, 5.3% for Italy, 5.2% for the Netherlands and 4.4% for Germany (World Bank, 1982). Further, according to Sinclair and Bote Gomez (1996, p. 95), this Spain's 'economic miracle' '…could not have occurred in the absence of receipts from tourism'.

Other examples of the importance of international tourism for economic growth via the financing of capital good imports are provided by emerging Asian countries, Singapore, Hong Kong and Korea (Pye and Lin, 1983).

An important finding of this chapter is to show how growth can be self-sustaining without involving the processes associated with modern endogenous growth theory.[2] Several models have established that international trade affects the growth of an economy, mainly through innovation, research and development activity, FDI or accumulation of human capital. In contrast to these models we describe a mechanism of international transmission of growth through trade and terms-of-trade movements. In keeping with the theme of this book, it is established that a country may import sustainable growth through trade in a differentiated product for which it has monopoly power in trade.

11.2. Tourism and growth

We utilize a variation of the two-sector growth model of Chapter 10 to examine the effects of tourism on optimal growth. The good X_K is again treated as a capital good and X_N as a non-traded consumption good which is consumed by both domestic residents and tourists. In contrast to the previous chapter where foreign capital was a perfect substitute for domestic capital and used in both sectors, in this chapter, purchased foreign capital is specific to the capital goods sector X_K and is treated as an indispensable factor of production. The two types of capital used in the production of X_K are assumed to be imperfect substitutes. Foreign capital is considered to be indispensable in the production process; hence, it must be imported by promoting and selling part of the domestic product. These exports take the form of international tourism. As stated earlier, without any consumer mobility, the domestic good would be purely non-traded.

---

[2] Note that Lee (1995) and Mazumdar (2001) provided empirical evidences on the importance of imported capital goods for growth. Using panel data, the latter found that investment in domestically produced equipment reduces the growth rate while investment in imported equipment increases it, especially for developing countries.

The technology of this economy is described by the two Cobb–Douglas production functions, which are given below in intensive form:

$$x_K = l_K k_{dK}^\alpha k_i^\gamma \tag{11.1}$$

$$x_N = l_N k_{dN}^\beta \tag{11.2}$$

where x_i $(i = K, N)$ denotes per capita output of the ith sector, k_{di} the domestic capital–labour ratios and k_i the imported capital–labour ratio in the capital good sector. The terms l_i $(i = K, N)$ denote the proportion of labour used in each sector and sum to unity.

The gross investment in domestic (i_d) and imported (i_i) capital in intensive form is given by

$$i_d = \dot{k}_d + (n + \delta)k_d \tag{11.3}$$

$$i_i = \dot{k}_i + (n + \delta)k_i \tag{11.4}$$

This formulation has been taken from Barro and Sala-i-Martin (2004) and i_i plays a role similar to the human capital accumulation equation in endogenous growth theory.

For analytical simplicity, both domestic capital and imported capital are assumed to depreciate at the same rate δ. The term n denotes the exogenously given rate of growth of the domestic labour force. The national income equation in per capita terms is given below

$$y = c + i_d + \tilde{e} \tag{11.5}$$

where $\tilde{e}$ denotes exports in per capita terms. Recall that these exports are assumed to consist solely of international tourism and are used for importing foreign capital goods only. Commodity x_K is assumed to be the numeraire good, hence:

$$P_N \tilde{e} = i_i \tag{11.6}$$

Let P_N denote the relative price of the non-traded good and is determined endogenously from the market clearing condition:

$$\tilde{e} = \tilde{e}^D = P_N^\eta e^{(\zeta m - n)t} \tag{11.7}$$

$\tilde{e}^D$ is the foreign demand expressed in terms of domestic labour for tourism services, ζ and η are, respectively, the income and price elasticities.[3] The term $m(>0)$ is the exogenous rate of growth for the foreign country. The own-price elasticity η is assumed to be negative ($\eta < 0$) and it is clear from Equation (11.7) that the host country has monopoly power in trade provided ($\eta \neq -\infty$).

Using Equations (11.4) and (11.6), the accumulation equation for imported capital is given by

$$k_i = P_N \tilde{e} - (n + \delta)k_i \tag{11.8}$$

It is assumed for analytical convenience that households and producers are not separated from each other. Each infinite-lived family firm possesses perfect foresight and wishes to maximize an additively separable intertemporal utility function U given by

$$U = \int_0^\infty \left[\frac{c^{1-\tau} - 1}{1 - \tau} \right] e^{-\rho t} \, \mathrm{d}t \tag{11.9}$$

where c is the consumption per capita of domestic output and the term $\rho(>0)$ denotes the rate of discount (time preference). This type of utility function is standard in endogenous growth theory.

We assume that the representative firm takes the relative price of the non-traded good P_N as given and selects the investment plan that maximizes intertemporal utility Equation (11.9) subject to the technology and budget constraints. They ignore the presence of monopoly power in trade. Using Equations (11.9), (11.2) and (11.5), and the capital accumulation Equations (11.3), (11.4) and (11.8), the Hamiltonian expression for this system is given below:

$$J = \left[\frac{c^{1-\tau} - 1}{1 - \tau} \right] e^{-\rho t} + \nu[i_d - (n + \delta)k_d] + \mu[P_N \tilde{e} - (n + \delta)k_i]$$
$$+ \lambda[R(P_N, 1, k_d, k_i) - c - i_d - \tilde{e}] \tag{11.10}$$

---

[3] For example, an early study by Gray (1966) estimated per capita income elasticities of 5.13 for US demand for tourism in the rest of the world and of 6.6 for Canadian demand. Uysal and Crompton (1984) provided a set of income elasticities from 1.59 to 6.07 for arrivals in Turkey from a range of origins, whereas Gunadhi and Boey (1986) provided values of 0.81–7.3 for Singapore. Syriopoulos (1995) estimated an income elasticity of 3.32 for US demand for Portuguese tourism and 2.85 for German demand. More recently, Lanza *et al.* (2003) found an average of the expenditure elasticities around 3 for 13 European countries (4.02 for France, 4.76 for Austria).

where ν and μ are shadow prices associated with $\dot{k}_d$ and $\dot{k}_i$, respectively, and λ is the Lagrange multiplier associated with the budget constraint. Note that the real national income, y, has been expressed in terms of the revenue function $R(P_N, 1, k_d, k_i)$.[4] The first-order conditions for maximization are

$$\frac{\partial J}{\partial c} = c^{-\tau}e^{-\rho t} - \lambda = 0 \tag{11.11}$$

$$\frac{\partial J}{\partial i_d} = \nu - \lambda = 0 \tag{11.12}$$

$$\frac{\partial J}{\partial x} = \mu P_N - \lambda = 0 \tag{11.13}$$

$$\frac{\partial J}{\partial k_d} = -\nu(n+\delta) + \lambda R_{kd} = -\dot{\nu} \tag{11.14}$$

$$\frac{\partial J}{\partial k_i} = -\mu(n+\delta) + \lambda R_{ki} = -\dot{\mu} \tag{11.15}$$

The transversality conditions of the system are

$$\lim_{t\to\infty} k_d\, \nu = 0 \tag{11.16}$$

$$\lim_{t\to\infty} k_i\, \mu = 0 \tag{11.17}$$

By using Equations (11.12) and (11.13), Equations (11.14) and (11.15) can be rewritten as

$$\frac{\dot{\nu}}{\nu} = n + \delta - \frac{R_{kd}}{R} \tag{11.18}$$

$$\frac{\dot{\mu}}{\mu} = n + \delta - \frac{P_N R_{ki}}{R} \tag{11.19}$$

where R_{kd}/R is the gross average product of domestic capital and $P_N R_{ki}/R$ is the gross average product of imported capital.

By differentiating Equations (11.11) and (11.13) with respect to time, and using Equations (11.18) and (11.19), we obtain the following expressions for proportional changes in consumption and

---

[4] An excellent example of the use of revenue functions in growth theory is in Dixit (1976).

the relative price of the non-traded good:

$$\frac{\dot{c}}{c} = \frac{\dfrac{R_{kd}}{R} - (n + \delta + \rho)}{\tau} \tag{11.20}$$

$$\frac{\dot{P}_N}{P_N} = \frac{\gamma R_{pk}}{k_i} - \beta \frac{R_{PN}}{k_d} \tag{11.21}$$

Note that R_{kd}/R has been redefined via the revenue function and that in the revenue function $P_K = 1$. In a similar manner R_{ki} has been defined. These are the average products of the two types of capital. In this chapter, we are only interested in steady-state solutions and therefore neglect all transitional dynamics.

A steady state is defined as a situation in which c and P_N grow at a constant rate. For a steady-state equilibrium both the average products have to be constant. It follows from Equations (11.20) and (11.21) that the average products of capital are constant over time, if and only if

$$\frac{\dot{x}_K}{x_K} = \frac{\dot{k}_d}{k_d} \tag{11.22}$$

$$\frac{\dot{P}_N}{P_N} + \frac{\dot{x}_K}{x_K} = \frac{\dot{k}_i}{k_i} \tag{11.23}$$

Solving Equation (11.23) and explicitly using properties of the production function we obtain:

$$\frac{\dot{P}_N}{P_N} = (1 - \gamma)\frac{\dot{k}_i}{k_i} \tag{11.24}$$

Therefore, the terms of trade are a function of imported capital accumulation. The rate of growth of the imported capital stock $(\dot{k}_i/k_i)$ is determined from Equations (11.7) and (11.8) as

$$\frac{\dot{k}_i}{k_i} = \frac{P_N^{1+\eta} e^{(\zeta m - n)t}}{k_i} - (n + \delta) \tag{11.25}$$

The constancy of the capital stock at steady state implies that

$$\frac{\dot{k_i}}{k_i} = (1 + \eta)\frac{\dot{P_N}}{P_N} + \zeta m - n \tag{11.26}$$

Now by substituting the expression from Equation (11.24) into Equation (11.26), we get

$$\frac{\dot{k_i}}{k_i} = \frac{(\zeta m - n)}{\Delta} \tag{11.27}$$

where $\Delta = (\gamma(1 + \eta) - \eta)$ is assumed positive.

From Equations (11.24)–(11.27) we obtain:

$$\frac{\dot{P_N}}{P_N} = \frac{(1 - \gamma) - (\zeta m - n)}{\Delta} \tag{11.28}$$

$$\frac{\dot{k_d}}{k_d} = \frac{A(\zeta m - n)}{\Delta} \tag{11.29}$$

where

$$A = \frac{\alpha_1 + \alpha_2(1 - \gamma)}{\alpha_d}$$

The terms

$$\alpha_1 = \frac{rk_i}{y}, \qquad \alpha_2 = \frac{Px_N}{y}, \qquad \alpha_d = \frac{rk_d}{y}$$

From these equations, we can establish the following propositions.

Proposition 11.1. *The presence of monopoly power in trade (i.e. $\eta \neq -\infty$) is a necessary condition for the domestic economy to experience long-run sustained growth.*

For the small-country case ($\eta = -\infty$) the economy is stationary in the long run. This proposition clearly shows that if tourism gives rise to monopoly power in trade, then it enables the host country to purchase foreign capital to generate growth. Note that this result also applies to other goods in which a country may have monopoly power in trade. However, many small countries possess monopoly power in trade due to the differentiated nature of the goods that tourists consume.

Proposition 11.2. *If Proposition 11.1 holds and an optimal tariff is not used, then the domestic economy grows (decays) in the long run as the growth rate, ζm, of its tourism export demand is larger (smaller) than the growth rate of its labour force, n.*

Thus, although the technology exhibits diminishing returns to scale in the quantities of the two capital inputs, a domestic economy can experience long-run sustained growth (decay) provided it has uncorrected monopoly power in trade for its exports and the foreign economy's growth is strong (weak). If $\zeta m - n > 0$, the income effect causes the demand for its exports (per head) to grow continuously and therefore its terms of trade to also improve continuously. Domestic firms are able to import increasing amounts of foreign capital goods over time. This growing net investment in imported capital ensures that per capita output increases along with accumulation in domestic capital. This accumulation does not lead to a decline of the domestic real rate of return as the phenomenon of diminishing returns to domestic capital is compensated by the constant rise in imported capital and movements in the terms of trade. Therefore, tourism enables the host country to import growth from abroad. In this case it delivers sustained growth without the usual assumptions associated with endogenous growth theory. There is here a mechanism of international transmission of growth from one country (the tourism services importer) to another (the tourism services exporter) through trade and terms-of-trade movements without any technological progress, R&D activity or accumulation of human capital.

The degree of the monopoly power in trade, as measured by the price elasticity of the export demand, exerts a strong influence on the magnitude of this transmission; the less elastic its export demand (and therefore the more differentiated its tourism product), the more the host country can benefit from the foreign country's growth (see η in Δ). In the case of a small country ($\eta \to -\infty$), the absence of monopoly power in trade prevents the domestic economy from any growth and condemns it to stagnation.

Proposition 11.3. *In view of the impact of the price elasticity of the export demand on the rate of growth, the host country should increase the degree of differentiation of its tourism services.*

The policy advice of this proposition stands in sharp contrast to practitioners in tourism who are often obsessed with the idea of competitive tourism.

It is important to note that trade in tourism services can also lead to decay in the domestic economy. This occurs if the foreign economic growth is not strong enough relative to the domestic demographic expansion. The income effect is then negative, causing a fall in the demand for the domestic exports and deterioration in its terms of trade. The mechanism described above is reversed, leading to domestic capital decumulation and a continuous decrease in per capita output. Of course, this case also is conditional on the presence of a monopoly power in trade, while in Sgro and Takayama (1981) decay is due to the presence of a minimum wage distortion. However, both results are related to the presence of a distortion in the economy.

11.3. Optimal taxation of tourism in growth

We now proceed to correct the monopoly power in trade which is ignored by private agents who maximize utility by taking the foreign rate of transformation as given exogenously. The government is aware of the presence of monopoly power and implements policies to correct it so that decay does not occur in the economy and it stays on a sustained growth path.

To derive this dynamic optimal tariff, we use a subset of our two-sector model and assume that only one good is produced for both consumption and investment purposes.[5] Assume that we produce only one good with Cobb–Douglas type technology which in per

---

[5] Bhagwati (1968) pointed out that in the static framework, even in the presence of an optimal tariff, growth may be immiserizing. This immiserization can only be removed by re-adjusting the level of the optimal tariff. Following on this intuition, in this chapter we provide an equation for adjusting the optimal tariff in a dynamic framework.

capita terms is given below:

$$x = k_d^{\alpha} k_i^{\beta}, \qquad 0 < \alpha + \beta < 1 \tag{11.30}$$

From the corresponding Hamiltonian, we can derive the following solution:

$$\frac{\dot{c}}{c} = \frac{\alpha \Psi_d - (n + \delta + \rho)}{\tau} \tag{11.31}$$

where Ψ_d is the gross average product of domestic capital and

$$\frac{\dot{k}_i}{k_i} = \frac{(\zeta m - n)(1 - \alpha)}{\Delta} \tag{11.32}$$

when $\Delta \equiv \beta - \eta(1 - \alpha - \beta) > 0$. We can also obtain the following solutions for

$$\frac{\dot{k}_d}{k_d} = \frac{\dot{x}}{x} = \frac{\dot{\tilde{e}}}{\tilde{e}} = \frac{\dot{c}}{c} = \frac{\beta(\zeta m - n)}{\Delta} \tag{11.33}$$

$$\frac{\dot{P}_N}{P_N} = \frac{(1 - \alpha - \beta)(\zeta m - n)}{\Delta} \tag{11.34}$$

Propositions 11.1–11.3 can be easily derived for this model.

The government recognizes the country's monopoly power in trade for tourism services and then imposes an optimal tariff. The government takes into account the influence of the volume of exports on P_N and incorporates the price formation mechanism in the maximization problem. The equilibrium terms of trade P can be expressed from Equation (11.7) as

$$P_N = \tilde{e}^{1/\eta} e^{(n - \zeta m)t/\eta} \tag{11.35}$$

After substituting P_N into the accumulation equation of imported capital (11.8), the Hamiltonian expression becomes

$$J = \left[\frac{c^{1-\tau} - 1}{1 - \tau} \right] e^{-\rho t} + \nu[i_d - (n + \delta)k_d] + \mu[\tilde{e}^{(\eta+1)/\eta} e^{(n - \zeta m)t/\eta}$$
$$- (n + \delta)k_i] + \lambda[k_d^{\alpha} k_i^{\beta} - c - i_d - \tilde{e}] \tag{11.36}$$

From the static case we know that the optimal tariff is given by $t^* = 1/(\eta - 1)$ for the function used in this chapter. For this the absolute value of η is used.

The first-order conditions are similar to those already presented except for the derivative of J with respect to $\tilde{e}$ which now becomes

$$\frac{\partial J}{\partial \tilde{e}} = \mu\left(\frac{1+\eta}{\eta}\right)\tilde{e}^{1/\eta}e^{(n-\zeta m)t/\eta} = \lambda \qquad (11.37)$$

The dynamics of the optimal tariff are obtained by differentiating Equation (11.37) with respect to optimal t and solving to obtain

$$\frac{\dot{t}^*}{t} = \frac{\alpha\Psi_D - \Psi_i\beta + (\zeta m - n)/\eta}{\partial\tilde{e}/\partial t} \qquad (11.38)$$

where $\Psi_i = P_N x/k_i$ is the gross average product of imported capital. The growth path in the presence of an optimal tariff is derived by using the equation given below:

$$\frac{\dot{k}_i}{k_i} = \frac{x^{1/\eta}e^{(\zeta m-n)(1-1/\eta)t}}{k_i} - (\eta + \delta) \qquad (11.39)$$

To solve for the accumulation equation, we differentiate Equation (11.39) and by setting $\dot{k}_i/k_i = 0$:

$$\frac{\dot{k}_i}{k_i} = (\zeta m - n)\left(\frac{1}{1+t^*}\right) \qquad (11.40)$$

Thus, if $(\zeta m - n) > 0$, then the optimal tariff should be maintained at t^* and the static gains translate into the dynamic context. However, if $(\zeta m - n) < 0$, then we require that $t^* < -1$ so that the second terms become negative and $\dot{k}_i/k_i > 0$. This implies that exports need to be subsidized. The Chinese scheme of import duty rebate is an example of such a policy.

11.4. Conclusion

International tourism has been recognized as a major provider of foreign currency earnings and therefore an essential means of economic development and growth through financing imports of capital goods. While a considerable amount of empirical evidence has been accumulated, no theoretical model has been provided to explain this phenomenon. We have built a simple and highly stylized growth model to explain this empirical result. The necessary condition to import long-run sustained growth from abroad is the possession of some monopoly power in trade. Therefore, any product for which the domestic economy has some market power is able to promote growth. Nevertheless, the model is particularly well suited to tourism because consumption of non-traded goods necessarily gives market power to the host country. This was formally demonstrated in Chapter 4. A simple but essential policy recommendation is that a host country ought to seek to increase the degree of differentiation of its tourism product, the more differentiated it is, the higher is the potential for increasing the economy's long-run growth rate. In line with distortion theory, monopoly power in trade should be corrected in both the static and dynamic context.

References

Barro, R.J. and X. Sala-i-Martin (2004), *Economic Growth*, Cambridge, MA: MIT Press.

Bhagwati, J. (1968), "Distortions and immiserizing growth: a generalization", *Review of Economic Studies*, Vol. 25, pp. 201–205.

Dixit, A. (1976), *The Theory of Equilibrium Growth*, Oxford: Oxford University Press.

Gray, H.P. (1966), "The demand for international travel by the United States and Canada", *International Economic Review*, Vol. 7(1), pp. 83–92.

Gunadhi, H. and C.K. Boey (1986), "Demand elasticities of tourism in Singapore", *Tourism Management*, Vol. 7(4), pp. 239–253.

Lanza, A., P. Temple and G. Urga (2003), "The implications of tourism specialisation in the long run: an econometric analysis for 13 OECD economies", *Tourism Management*, Vol. 24, pp. 315–321.

Lee, J. (1995), "Capital goods imports and long-run growth", *Journal of Development Economics*, Vol. 48(1), pp. 91–110.

Mazumdar, J. (2001), "Imported machinery and growth in LDCs", *Journal of Development Economics*, Vol. 65, pp. 209–224.

Pye, E.A. and T.B. Lin (eds.) (1983), *Tourism in Asia: The Economic Impact*, Singapore: Singapore University Press.

Ramsay, F.P. (1928), "A mathematical theory of saving", *Economics Journal*, Vol. 38, pp. 543–559.

Sgro, P.M. and A. Takayama (1981), "On the long-run growth effects of a minimum wage for a two-sector economy", *Economic Record*, Vol. 57, pp. 180–185.

Sinclair, M.T. and V. Bote Gomez (1996), "Tourism, the Spanish economy and the balance of payments", in: M. Barke, M. Newton and J. Towner, editors, *Tourism in Spain: Critical Perspectives*, Chapter 4, Wallingford: CAB International.

Syriopoulos, T. (1995), "A dynamic model of demand for Mediterranean tourism", *International Review of Applied Economics*, Vol. 9(3), pp. 318–336.

Uysal, M. and J.L. Crompton (1984), "Determinants of demand for international tourist flows in Turkey", *Tourism Management*, Vol. 5(4), pp. 288–297.

World Bank (1982), *World Development Report*, Washington, DC (Table 2).

CHAPTER 12

Competition for Tourism in the OECD Countries

12.1. Introduction

In the preceding 11 chapters we have incorporated tourism in the pure theory of international trade. However, no attempt had been made to study tourism from the point of view of applied economics (the empirical side). In this chapter, based on Hazari *et al.* (2003), we provide an example of some empirical work that can be done in this area. In spite of our finding that differentiated products are the key to promoting tourism, there exists a large body of literature that emphasizes competitiveness in tourism.[1]

The purpose of this chapter is to examine, for a set of 19 OECD destination countries, two aspects of their competitiveness in tourism- and travel-related services. The first concerns their external competitiveness, that is, ground plus travel components of the tourism industry (both downstream and upstream). The second concerns their tourism comparative advantages including some findings relating to possible economic and social explanations of their specialization.

Most previous studies of service activities in the OECD countries suggest there is no policy emphasis for specializing in this area of activity. It is also suggested that there is no difference between specialization in manufactured goods and tourism services. Our empirical analysis shows first that some OECD countries may be highly specialized in tourism services and second, that such specialization in manufactured goods and tourism may not be connected with each other.

---

[1] Doubts on this hypothesis have also been shown in empirical work by Ulubasoglu and Hazari (2004) which is an interesting application of Zipf's law to tourism.

12.2. Competitiveness in tourism

This section investigates the competitiveness in tourism of the OECD countries (for which data are available). We construct indices of tourism competitiveness that will enable us to discern whether a country is more competitive in comparison to another country. We now proceed to define competitiveness. The external competitiveness of a country's tourism industry is defined as that country's competitive ability to retain or increase its market share of tourism exports in terms of ground and travel components. This rather general concept encompasses price differentials, exchange rate movements, productivity levels of various components of the tourism industry (transport, accommodation, tour services, restaurants and entertainment) and qualitative factors affecting the attractiveness of a destination.

In order to analyse country i's net performance in tourism, we calculate the following index:

$$CR_{tj} = \frac{X_{tj}/M_{tj}}{X_{tz}/M_{tz}} \tag{12.1}$$

where X_{tj} denotes exports of tourism services by country j, M_{tj} the imports of tourism services by country j, X_{tz} the total exports of tourism services from the reference area and M_{tz} the total imports of tourism services from the reference area.[2]

The numerator of Equation (12.1) shows the exports of tourism divided by the imports of tourism in country j as a share of the total tourism exports of the region divided by total imports of the region (this is the denominator of Equation (12.1)). We can distinguish three cases:

Case 1: $CR_{tj} = 1$; country j will be said to have no competitive advantage in tourism.

Case 2: $CR_{tj} > 1$; in this case, country j is said to have competitive advantage in tourism relative to the reference area z.

---

[2] Market shares are expressed in value terms, since there are no data on the volume-price distribution in traded services.

Case 3: $CR_{tj} < 1$; in this case, the country is said to have no comparative advantage to the reference area z.

Figure 12.1 shows that the USA is the only country that over time has become heavily involved in the tourism industry. This finding is consistent with that of CEPII (1998) which noted that 'travel flows are the service operations in which the inertia of established positions seems to be greatest'. This supposedly confirms the importance of cultural heritage and family visitation for these countries, which compensate for low price competitiveness. The USA's increasing competitiveness in tourism and the relative decline of Italy and the UK are undoubtedly the major factors in the changes that have taken place in tourism in this sub-group. France and Spain, on the other hand, seem to be maintaining their respective positions in the sub-group (Figure 12.2).

In the case of the intermediate OECD tourist destinations, a different guiding principle seems to have emerged (this is the second sub-group of countries). The overall lack of movement in the hierarchy of the first sub-sample is replaced here by livelier competition between the countries. Since the early 1980s, countries such as Australia (Figure 12.3) and, to a lesser extent, Ireland and New Zealand (Figure 12.4) have become increasingly involved in tourism, while there has been a decline in the external

Figure 12.1. Evolution of tourism competitiveness in the United States (1980–1997)

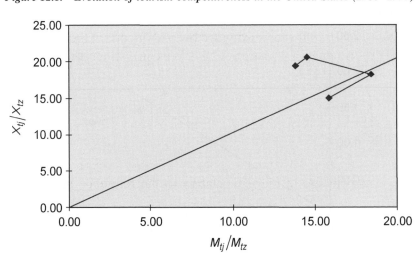

Figure 12.2.   Evolution of tourism competitiveness (European countries) (1980–1997)

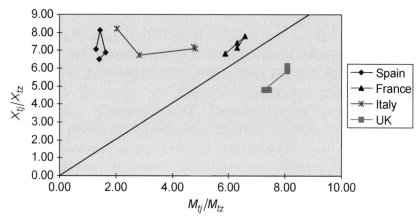

competitiveness of destinations such as Greece, Mexico and Switzerland (Figure 12.5).

In summary, these findings provide some evidence of competition in tourism between these OECD countries. This competition leads us to investigate the question of competitiveness in tourism and travel components in greater detail. Let us turn first to the role played by fluctuations in real exchange rates (RERs) in determining a country's competitiveness.

Figure 12.3.   Evolution of tourism competitiveness in Australia (1980–1997)

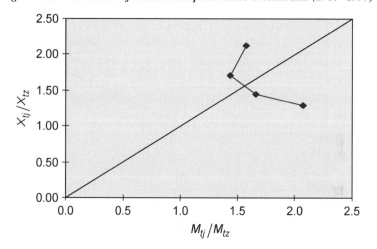

Figure 12.4. Evolution of tourism competitiveness (Ireland/New Zealand) (1980–1997)

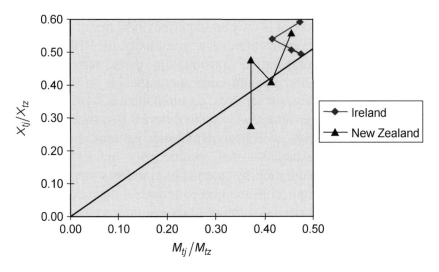

12.3. Real exchange rates and destination competitiveness

Once the measures of overall competitiveness have been developed, it is useful to examine how a destination's competitive position changes with regard to certain variables. An important variable in this context is the RER.

Generally, competitiveness is considered to have two components: a 'price' and a 'non-price' component. The RER impacts

Figure 12.5. Evolution of tourism competitiveness (Switzerland/Mexico/ Greece) (1980–1997)

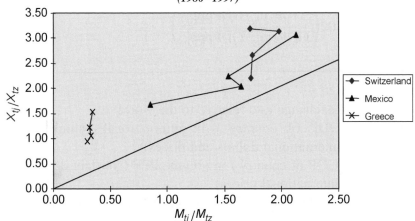

on the first. The second non-price component (quality, brand image and marketing) exerts considerable influence on trade in tourist services. Furthermore, it is only an imperfect indicator of the factors likely to affect price competitiveness. Admittedly, the RER provides information on comparative consumption costs, but it is also necessary to take into account costs more specific to the tourism industry, such as transport services, accommodation, food, drink and entertainment and to attach weights to different goods and services consumed by tourists to reflect purchasing patterns. In addition, consumer theory establishes that specific price indices should be calculated for consumption by international tourists, depending on their country of origin, consumption patterns and the nature of their destinations. This extremely arduous task requires a volume of data that is difficult to obtain for such a large sample of countries and for such a long observation period. It also turns out that the results obtained do not generally warrant the effort required. RERs provide an efficient mapping of these price indices and can be used as excellent representation of individual indices. Therefore, in the present investigation of external tourism competitiveness we will confine ourselves to using the RER calculated by the CEPII. The advantage of this is that it draws on a comparison of real incomes in the country and abroad that is based on an evaluation in terms of purchasing power parities (PPPs). More precisely, it consists of a comparison of the relationships between GDP in current dollars and GDP in PPP, both for the country in question and the world as a whole:

$$RER_j = 100 \left(\frac{GDPcur_j / GDPppp_j}{GDPcur_m / GDPppp_m} \right) \qquad (12.2)$$

where

RER_j = real exchange rate relative to the world
$GDPcur_j$ = GDP of country j in international value (current international dollars and prices)
$GDPppp_j$ = GDP of country j in volume PPP (constant dollars and international prices)
$GDPcur_m$ = world GDP in international value (current internationaldollars and prices)

GDPppp$_m$ = world GDP in volume PPP (constant international dollars andprices)

Here a rise (fall) in the RER$_j$ reflects a real appreciation (depreciation) in the currency of country j. Table 12.1 shows that during the period 1980–1997 there were pronounced fluctuations in the RER, which were caused, inter alia, by appreciation and subsequent depreciation of the dollar and the emergence of two blocs of countries in the European Union. The currency fluctuations have had an impact on the indicator of the countries' competitive positions in the tourism industry (Table 12.2), which is defined as the ratio of the tourism balance in the 'travel' and 'transport of passengers' items of each country's balance of payments to total international trade flows in tourism. Thus,

$$POS_{vj} = \frac{X_{vj} - M_{vj}}{\left(\dfrac{X_{v\bullet} + M_{v\bullet}}{2}\right)} \tag{12.3}$$

where X_{vj} and M_{vj} are the country's earnings from and expenditure on tourism and transport of passengers and $X_{v\bullet}$ and $M_{v\bullet}$ are total international earnings from and expenditure on tourism and transport of passengers.

Examination of the graphs in Figure 12.6 comparing these two ratios (RER$_j$ and POS$_{vj}$) shows that for most countries they moved in opposite direction: appreciation of the RER$_j$ is usually reflected in a fall in the POS$_{vj}$, and vice versa.[3] In general, the under- or overvaluation of a country's currency has a fundamental impact on a country's competitiveness. It should be noted that the change in the competitive position of certain countries, such as the USA, Canada, Australia and New Zealand, is a result not only of currency depreciation but also of the fall in airfares that followed airline deregulation. The expected links between RER$_j$ and POS$_{vj}$ emerge clearly from this initial investigation of price competitiveness of a tourist destination.[4]

---

[3] Here it reflects an increase in the prices of tourist services in country j relative to international prices.

[4] These tests were conducted on an initial sample of 19 countries and two sub-groups, in each case for the period 1980–1997.

Table 12.1　Real exchange rates data

	1980	1981	1982	1983	1984	1985	1986	1987	1988	1989	1990	1991	1992	1993	1994	1995	1996	1997
Australia	123.90	137.52	139.09	137.33	140.38	119.20	107.35	110.42	125.68	135.67	130.67	129.75	119.07	112.48	119.31	116.05	127.14	128.96
Canada	114.62	123.30	134.48	44.84	139.80	137.48	121.49	121.35	128.15	138.30	135.43	137.77	127.06	121.66	113.54	108.25	111.79	115.87
South Korea	72.27	75.69	77.46	78.81	77.21	76.28	69.36	71.05	80.06	90.97	88.31	91.43	87.43	89.99	92.66	95.29	95.85	88.66
Spain	102.0	89.1	88.0	77.4	76.1	77.3	91.8	100.5	105.6	110.3	128.0	130.9	136.3	115.1	111.2	117.2	120.7	111.5
USA	106.4	117.3	128.4	137.7	142.2	148.0	133.6	125.6	122.5	126.6	123.0	124.5	122.6	126.9	126.7	121.1	125.6	134.0
France	138.2	120.3	115.0	111.6	103.3	106.9	128.7	139.0	135.8	129.8	146.1	141.9	148.4	143.1	145.0	153.1	153.5	142.2
Greece	96.2	88.6	94.8	87.9	81.5	78.8	80.5	86.5	89.6	88.7	102.0	103.7	109.4	103.0	105.4	112.3	118.9	118.8
Italy	100.0	89.7	91.0	95.8	91.2	92.0	111.9	124.3	124.2	124.0	142.3	144.2	145.8	120.0	118.4	115.1	129.4	126.0
Ireland	122.5	112.7	118.0	117.5	107.6	111.0	132.6	136.2	135.4	131.7	142.0	137.0	141.9	129.4	129.4	130.2	133.2	135.2
Japan	115.3	123.4	114.7	125.7	127.3	130.2	165.2	175.4	187.2	175.7	159.4	171.4	178.0	205.5	218.8	220.8	192.8	182.7
Mexico	70.2	83.0	59.9	55.0	61.9	63.6	40.8	39.5	44.9	52.0	54.3	60.7	65.0	71.2	69.6	47.1	52.3	62.5
Norway	173.0	168.0	170.1	165.3	155.1	155.8	158.0	168.8	172.0	170.0	181.3	174.7	174.2	157.0	153.9	165.7	172.2	169.1
New Zealand	95.73	98.63	97.26	95.99	86.51	86.64	95.55	109.90	124.27	118.76	113.17	107.96	98.35	101.61	110.70	117.66	127.50	128.58
Netherlands	145.5	122.1	124.0	121.6	108.2	107.0	128.0	139.9	136.2	127.3	141.2	137.6	143.6	139.5	142.4	153.4	150.1	138.6
Portugal	61.95	59.26	57.11	52.42	48.81	51.35	62.06	66.03	69.11	70.49	81.56	87.99	100.07	89.00	90.90	99.09	101.43	96.09
UK	126.1	121.5	117.4	110.1	99.6	102.4	106.3	113.2	122.7	119.8	128.8	132.8	132.7	117.8	119.4	117.9	121.7	137.4
Switzerland	153.3	138.3	147.3	150.2	137.1	135.0	167.4	188.8	185.8	169.7	194.0	194.1	195.2	192.0	206.2	225.0	219.6	195.5

Reference area: world.
Source: CHELEM.

Table 12.2 Evolution of the countries' positions (POS_{vj}) in the tourism industry

	1980	1981	1982	1983	1984	1985	1986	1987	1988	1989	1990	1991	1992	1993	1994	1995	1996	1997
Australia	-0.71	-0.69	-0.79	-0.64	-0.82	-0.57	-0.26	-0.04	0.40	-0.10	0.01	0.29	0.28	0.52	0.68	0.77	0.82	0.73
Canada	-0.76	-0.58	-0.66	-1.26	-0.99	-0.89	-0.29	-0.78	-0.88	-1.26	-1.81	-2.03	-1.76	-1.53	-0.92	-0.60	-0.62	-0.64
South Korea	0.02	0.01	-0.14	0.04	0.09	0.16	0.70	0.97	0.98	0.45	0.16	-0.14	-0.17	-0.19	-0.35	-0.32	-0.65	-0.56
Spain	5.81	5.79	6.49	6.42	6.70	6.61	7.92	7.80	7.26	6.22	5.67	5.57	5.59	4.95	5.29	5.57	5.64	5.53
USA	0.18	3.42	2.38	0.28	-2.98	-3.58	-1.00	-0.79	0.99	3.75	4.60	7.57	7.82	8.34	6.98	7.22	7.68	7.85
France	2.26	1.51	1.94	3.12	3.23	3.16	2.41	2.06	2.09	2.94	3.14	3.43	3.78	3.57	3.31	2.97	2.64	2.83
Greece	1.44	1.54	1.22	0.88	0.95	0.98	1.01	1.07	0.85	0.55	0.59	0.60	0.69	0.78	0.84	0.74	0.63	0.61
Ireland	0.00	-0.02	0.01	0.04	0.07	0.11	-0.02	0.01	0.02	0.04	0.12	0.14	0.09	0.12	0.06	0.05	0.07	0.09
Italy	7.14	5.83	6.93	7.74	6.31	6.02	5.16	4.57	3.20	2.42	2.43	2.41	1.32	2.28	3.27	3.68	3.55	3.25
Japan	-4.00	-3.93	-3.56	-3.89	-3.55	-3.41	-4.34	-5.29	-8.11	-9.18	-8.44	-7.89	-7.74	-7.76	-8.24	-8.88	-8.23	-7.13
Mexico	0.14	-0.74	0.48	1.26	1.13	0.64	0.64	0.72	0.44	0.27	0.00	0.06	-0.01	0.20	0.31	0.80	0.89	0.92
New Zealand	-0.31	-0.27	-0.25	-0.17	-0.09	-0.01	0.04	0.13	0.01	0.03	0.03	0.03	0.04	0.08	0.14	0.27	0.24	0.16
Netherlands	-2.61	-1.67	-1.58	-1.76	-1.35	-1.45	-1.82	-2.02	-1.77	-1.43	-1.27	-1.28	-1.22	-1.18	-1.19	-1.35	-1.25	-1.00
Portugal	0.87	0.79	0.65	0.64	0.71	0.83	0.91	1.05	0.96	1.00	1.06	1.03	0.85	0.72	0.74	0.72	0.63	0.60
UK	0.52	-0.58	-0.83	-0.15	-0.08	0.70	-0.60	-1.01	-1.84	-1.86	-1.50	-1.78	-1.93	-1.75	-2.12	-1.50	-1.53	-1.87
Switzerland	0.80	0.94	0.87	1.12	1.02	0.85	0.84	0.83	0.57	0.50	0.61	0.75	0.67	0.55	0.59	0.54	0.36	0.34

Reference area: world.
Source: own calculations using the CHELEM database (2000).

Figure 12.6.   Tourism price competitiveness for various OECD destination countries

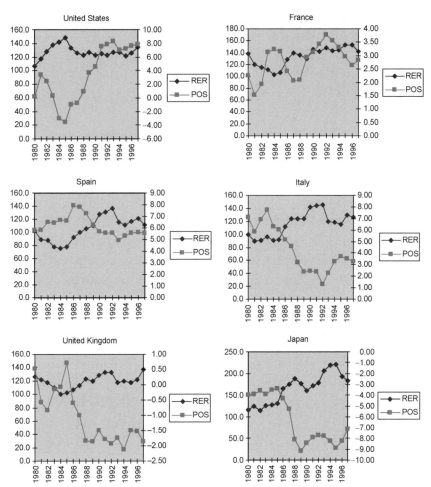

12.4. Econometric analysis of tourism specialization

In Section 12.2, we described the general framework within which tourist flows take place and assessed the external competitiveness in tourism of several countries. Furthermore the existence of a link between the RER and countries' competitive position was established. In the present section, we will first examine the countries' specialization on the ground component of the tourism industry by means of the Balassa (1965) index and second, conduct an econometric analysis of the evolution of the countries' specialization

Figure 12.6 (continued)

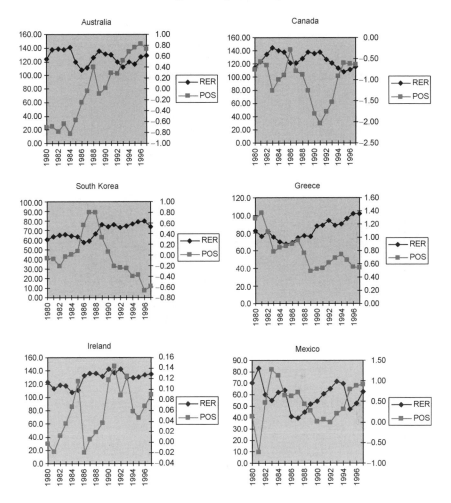

in tourism and evaluate what causes these changes. Examination of a country's specialization reveals its medium-term internal and external competitiveness. It is, therefore, structural in nature and its measurement should reveal the fundamental characteristics of the economy by separating it from short-term macroeconomic trends.

The empirical findings on specialization in tourism show that a number of hypotheses can be verified. First, that specialization in tourism is not independent of a country's economic structure and second that the quality and dynamics of specialization differ from one country to the next (or from one sub-group to the next).

Figure 12.6 (continued)

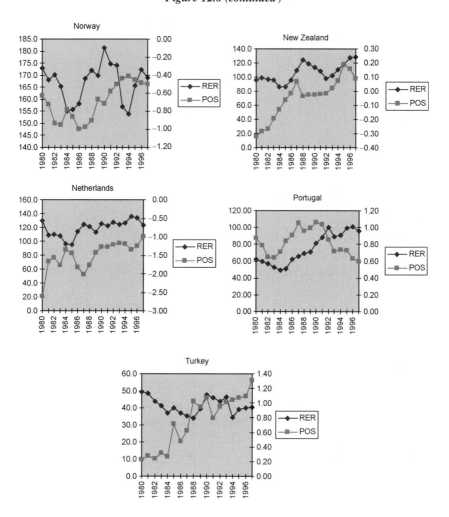

Moreover, the econometric results obtained from the panel data indicate that tourism does not necessarily evolve in the same way in all countries. As we shall see, its evolution is a function of price competitiveness; the degree of specialization in passenger transportation; the level of domestic demand for tourist services and the destination's degree of maturity.

12.4.1. Analysis of the countries' specialization in tourism

There are many indicators of national specialization in the international trade literature and one of these is the Balassa-revealed comparative advantage (RCA) index. According to this index, the degree of comparative advantage or disadvantage of activity i is estimated on the basis of the relationship between the share of activity i in the total exports of country j and the share of that same activity relative to zone z:

$$\mathrm{RCA}_{ij} = \frac{X_{ij}/X_{\bullet j}}{X_{iz}/X_{\bullet z}} \times 100 \qquad (12.4)$$

where X_{ij} denotes exports of the product (service) i by country j, $X_{\bullet j}$ the total exports of goods and services from country j, X_{iz} the total exports from the reference area of product (or service) i and $X_{\bullet z}$ the total exports of goods and services from the reference area z. If the index is greater than 100, the country is specialized in the good (service) i, since it exports relatively more of the good (service) than the reference zone. It therefore has a comparative advantage in that activity. If the index is smaller than 100, the country is not specialized and it therefore has a comparative disadvantage. Thus, this is a method of indirect calculation that can be used to determine the kind of activities in which individual countries have comparative advantage.

In both tourism and goods, there are pronounced differences in the degree of specialization among the countries. The emphasis in this section will be on identifying the forces underlying the comparative advantage of the 'downstream' segments of the tourism industry such as accommodation, catering and attractions, which are included in the 'travel' item of the balance of payments.

An analysis of Table 12.3 shows that both rich (USA, France, Italy, UK and Australia) and less rich OECD countries (Spain, Portugal, New Zealand and Turkey) are specialized in these 'downstream' segments of the tourism industry. This implies that there are several sources of RCA$_{ij}$ in tourism.[5] The OECD countries that have the highest market shares in travel are not necessarily those that are most specialized in the 'downstream' segments of the tourism industry. For example, the USA, France, Italy, Spain and, to

---

[5] Factor endowments could be the basic components of the production of tourism products. They correspond to the general factors required for the functioning of the whole economy (human resources, capital and infrastructure resources), and to specific factors to the tourism sector such as certain natural, artistic and cultural heritage.

Table 12.3   Travel-revealed comparative advantage (RCA) indices

	1980	1981	1982	1983	1984	1985	1986	1987	1988	1989	1990	1991	1992	1993	1994	1995	1996	1997
Australia	106.40	119.12	117.42	124.06	110.66	102.24	110.38	125.60	154.03	137.53	142.18	141.26	132.85	143.71	166.34	180.69	182.14	175.44
Canada	81.87	83.47	82.82	81.55	72.19	72.86	78.22	70.74	68.71	69.77	70.92	73.15	63.56	58.14	56.94	58.08	58.72	57.82
South Korea	44.9	44.7	47.3	49.9	48.5	54.0	74.0	75.3	80.8	81.9	71.9	57.6	46.8	46.8	46.5	56.2	50.9	46.8
Spain	521.76	494.55	503.01	484.09	469.57	454.48	498.08	473.82	450.68	407.93	370.66	345.96	339.36	317.09	311.69	307.51	299.22	294.41
USA	93.39	121.65	125.20	117.33	151.86	151.90	152.58	148.68	142.36	150.34	154.37	156.23	154.32	155.73	150.39	148.67	150.75	146.83
France	129.93	118.56	124.54	130.19	130.24	126.86	112.40	111.42	112.49	122.25	118.44	119.04	120.49	123.62	126.08	122.33	123.86	124.61
Greece	514.24	505.94	463.28	380.60	402.96	430.21	443.13	410.98	382.18	317.49	331.39	295.31	335.26	375.60	417.96	428.97	390.60	414.53
Ireland	145.21	129.26	126.52	113.48	98.86	101.93	89.89	86.17	83.82	80.96	90.83	88.35	77.23	73.57	74.30	72.01	71.88	68.51
Iceland	46.19	41.65	54.12	54.57	70.40	74.48	72.90	81.50	95.98	97.72	120.77	111.76	102.20	106.56	105.12	119.50	106.34	105.14
Italy	221.91	181.92	203.41	215.24	194.20	182.01	155.31	150.18	137.17	121.07	124.71	138.66	149.95	152.32	155.21	154.36	149.04	156.24
Japan	10.49	10.01	10.98	11.30	11.12	12.04	11.93	14.88	17.24	17.67	18.41	15.77	14.23	13.13	12.21	10.50	13.94	14.78
Mexico	341.13	280.27	218.50	208.46	214.84	195.88	216.11	194.72	195.09	199.27	188.85	187.92	166.02	150.74	139.18	111.40	103.70	101.77
Norway	67.09	66.42	66.33	60.81	55.25	59.11	76.92	77.69	79.89	62.19	55.61	56.29	60.70	61.43	70.12	64.52	55.51	54.14
New Zealand	80.2	88.2	84.7	94.0	124.9	130.2	155.2	180.1	157.9	156.6	147.0	143.4	134.2	140.3	163.5	208.0	205.9	191.6
Netherlands	59.95	57.16	58.35	52.87	52.56	4.41	49.94	49.78	45.93	45.34	43.06	47.71	51.27	48.54	45.84	47.36	46.36	47.56
Portugal	414.5	396.8	346.3	304.5	301.4	310.3	298.1	311.8	295.0	282.7	275.1	279.1	236.2	267.0	254.0	241.1	226.8	230.2
UK	114.11	102.48	100.82	114.09	109.86	113.56	107.32	106.96	101.53	99.58	98.12	85.90	86.91	88.86	87.62	97.48	90.78	92.22
Switzerland	157.26	154.79	163.73	179.44	162.69	152.51	139.99	147.58	137.82	129.64	127.51	132.85	122.57	118.07	123.70	123.68	117.61	127.36
Turkey	216.98	151.45	110.63	121.93	125.14	206.22	169.20	189.81	237.36	246.18	255.58	195.79	226.70	226.24	230.54	218.22	198.53	219.87

Reference area: world.
Source: own calculations using the CHELEM database (2000).

a lesser extent, the UK are in the first rank of world tourism destinations (in terms of foreign exchange earnings from tourism and number of international visitors). Nevertheless, their RCAs on the ground component of the tourism industry are relatively modest compared with other countries with more modest market shares but higher RCA_{ij} (Greece, Portugal, Turkey, Australia and New Zealand).[6] Hence, not surprisingly the results are inconclusive.

12.4.2. Econometric analysis of the interface between specialization and level of development in tourism

Our earlier investigation enabled us to characterize the general framework within which tourist flows take place and to assess the state of competitiveness and specialization in tourism of certain OECD countries. In particular, we were able to show the existence of a link between the effects of RERs and that of the countries' competitive positions in tourism. The aim of this section is to use some of the findings presented above for an econometric analysis of the evolution of specialization in tourism.

12.4.2.1. Specifying the model

The econometric analysis undertaken here adopts a different perspective from previous studies and constitutes, to the best of our knowledge, the first attempt to analyse the tourism specialization by including the role of monetary and real variables, for example, RERs (monetary) and consumption advantage (real).

The construction of a database from an initial sample of OECD countries (and then from two sub-groups) enabled us to carry out regressions on panel data. It should be noted that, in practice, the panel data model does not produce interesting results unless identifying restrictions reflecting the various hypotheses to be tested are imposed on the structure. As in any type of regression, these hypotheses relate to the nature of the exogenous variables and the properties of the random term. For each hypothesis about

---

[6] Incidentally, this finding is consistent with that of Peterson (1988, p. 362) who, in his comparison of the market shares in exports of tourist services and the comparative advantages in tourism of countries such as the USA, Greece and Spain, reaches the same conclusion as we do. In his article, he states: 'Thus for all three countries their competitive ability, as measured by the value of their export shares, differed significantly from the pattern of competitiveness highlighted by their RCA indices'.

behavioural heterogeneity, there is a corresponding model and method of calculation. The choice of specification depends on the type of economic question that is to be investigated. We will see how, in our model, the large number of observations enabled us to identify and measure fixed effects, the omission of which could have led to bias in the calculations. However, before examining the results of our calculations, let us first present the equation for the model.

The function for estimation can be expressed as follows:

$$\text{RCARV} = f(\text{SGNPI}, \text{SRCATR}, \text{RER}, \text{CHOPM}, \text{TIRM})$$

This function states that the consumption advantage in tourism (RCARV) is a function of income per capita (SGNPI), the revealed competitive advantage in international passenger transport (SRCATR), the real exchange rate (RER), the hotel function rate (CHPOPM) and the tourist density function (TIRM).

The actual equation adopted is linear, as it is in many econometric applications, which makes it well suited to econometric analysis of panel data, and is given below:

$$\text{RCARV}_{jt} = b_1 \text{SGNP1}_{jt} + b_2 \text{SRCATR}_{jt} + b_3 \text{RER}_{j(t-1)}$$
$$+ b_4 \text{CHPOPM}_{jt} + b_5 \text{TIRM}_{jt} + \alpha_j + \beta_t + U_{jt} \quad (12.5)$$

All the variables used are double indexed. Index j represents the country, while index t represents the year in question; b_j = structural coefficients; α_j = the specific effect (country dummy); β_t = temporal dummy and U_{jt} = the random error term; $t = 1980,\ldots,1997$ and $j = 1,\ldots,N$. [$N = 19$ (sample 1); $N = 5$ (sub-samples 2 and 3), Table 12.4].

The variable RCARV_{jt}, to be explained equates to specialization in the 'downstream' segment of the tourism industry (accommodation, tour services, food and beverage, entertainment, etc.) (accommodation–catering–social and cultural activities), which is usually considered labour intensive and 'less progressive'.[7] This latter assumption may be justified in terms of the importance of services in tourist expenditure and to the fact that, over a long period, productivity growth in tourism has lagged behind that in manufacturing and transport services. In our model, this

[7] For further details of this concept, cf. Lanza *et al.* (2003).

Table 12.4   *List of countries*

Sample 1 (Initial Group)		Sub-sample 2 (Sub-group of Mediterranean Tourist Countries)	Sub-sample 3 (Sub-group of North American and Asia-Pacific Countries)
(1) Australia	(11) Japan	(1) Spain	(1) Australia
(2) Canada	(12) Mexico	(2) France	(2) Canada
(3) South Korea	(13) Norway	(3) Greece	(3) South Korea
(4) Spain	(14) New Zealand	(4) Italy	(4) USA
(5) USA	(15) Netherlands	(5) Portugal	(5) Japan
(6) France	(16) Portugal	(6) Turkey	(6) Mexico
(7) Greece	(17) UK		(7) New Zealand
(8) Ireland	(18) Switzerland		
(9) Iceland	(19) Turkey		
(10) Italy			

'downstream' specialization is expressed on the basis of Balassa's index of comparative advantages $(SRCAV_j)$.[8]

The changes in the consumption advantage index over time $(RCARV_{jt})$ are explained by the following exogenous variables.[9]

Income per capita $(SGNP1_{jt})$. This is the gross national product per inhabitant of country *j* for the year *t* in current dollars. GNP per capita is used because it is readily available measurement across different countries, and is widely accepted as being a good indicator of a nation's income (or personal disposable income) and a major economic determinant of domestic and international tourism spending.

The real exchange rate $(RER_{j(t-1)})$. This is the CEPII RER relative to the rest of the world. As suggested by the theory of PPP, the long-run exchange rate can be a good proxy for the relative cost of living in destination countries. It is argued that potential visitors are well informed on exchange rates but relatively uninformed on general price levels in destination countries. Prior to travel, affordability may therefore be judged by exchange rate movements rather than by shifts in general price levels. In our regressions, this variable is lagged by one period in order to take account of adjustment lags.

---

[8] The $SACRV_j$ indicator is based on the 'travel' item. Here, the reference zone is the world as a whole.

[9] From a general point of view, our variables are derived from three databases (*World Development Indicators* 1999 from the World Bank, the CEPII's CHELEM 2000 database and the World Tourism Organization's statistical yearbooks).

The revealed comparative advantage in international passenger transport $(SRCATR_{jt})$.[10] This is the index of specialization in the 'upstream' segment of international passenger transport, which is capital intensive in character. This indicator can be used to develop an analysis of specialization in tourism based on the international segmentation of production.

$$SRCATR_{jt} = \frac{X_{ij}/X_{\bullet j}}{X_{iz}/X_{\bullet z}} \times 100$$

where X_{ij} denotes exports of international passenger transport services by country j, $X_{\bullet j}$ the total exports of goods and services from country j, X_{iz} the total exports of international passenger transport services from the reference area and $X_{\bullet z}$ the total exports of real goods and services from the reference area z.

The hotel function rate (CHPOPM). This is a ratio of accommodation supply to host population, which is based on the dual relationship between the number of guest rooms available and the population of country j and that of the reference zone. This simple index can give a fairly good estimate of the relative importance of tourism in country j, because the number of rooms determines the number of people directly employed in this sector. For most international standard hotels, the ratio of rooms to employees range from 0.5 to 2.0 (Oppermann and Sung Chon, 1997), often depending on the availability and cost of labour. A high $CHPOPM_{jt}$ implies that a relatively high proportion of the local population in country j works in the hospitality industry. Hence, the higher the hospitality function index, the more important is tourism's role in job creation in the local economy.[11]

$$CHPOPM_{jt} = \frac{Room_{jt}/Population_{jt}}{Room_{zt}/Population_{zt}} \times 100$$

---

[10] This is the indicator of specialization in international passenger transport, as accounted under the 'services to passengers' heading.

[11] This index is the most useful tool for examining tourist activity in countries where most accommodation is in the form of hotels and motels. However, it should be interpreted with caution where there are large spatial variations in the type of accommodation available (camping, campervans).

The tourist density rate (TIRM_{jt}). This is the relationship between the number of international tourists visiting country j and its permanent population and that of the reference area. This rate captures the number of tourists as a proportion of the population vis-à-vis the tourism population in the reference area:

$$\text{TIRM}_{jt} = \frac{\text{Tourists}_{jt}/\text{Population}_{jt}}{\text{Tourists}_{zt}/\text{Population}_{zt}} \times 100$$

These indicators provide a basis for subsequent evaluation of the level of international tourism for OECD countries and estimation of the optimal level of the corresponding supply of hotel rooms.

12.4.3. Panel regression results

For the econometric estimation, the standard panel technique was used. First of all, we test the significance of group effects with an F-test. So the hypothesis that the country effects are the same is rejected.[12] Second, we use the fixed effects approach or the random-effects approach. The Hausman test values show the first one should be used. In this way, the bias derived from the existence of country effects correlated with the explanatory variables is avoided and the within-group estimator is the only consistent estimator.

Table 12.5 shows the results of the estimates obtained using the fixed-effects method (*within*). The test was first conducted on the entire group of 19 countries and then on two sub-groups of countries (European countries in the Mediterranean Basin and countries in the Asia-Pacific region and North America). By this means, three samples containing 32 countries in all were obtained.

Despite the reservations that must be expressed with regard to any empirical analysis of international tourism, the results are promising; overall, the variables are significant at the 5% level and only one of the three adjusted coefficients of determination (R^2_{adjust}) is less than 89%. Furthermore, the results seem to confirm the argument that the influence of the explanatory variables adopted is not the same for all the countries (or sub-groups of countries). In particular, it would seem that for the group as a whole (sample 1) and the sub-sample of North American and Asia-Pacific countries

---

[12] The F-test takes values between 36.89 and 79.39 for the three samples.

Table 12.5 Regression results with panel data

	Sample 1	Sub-sample 2	Sub-sample 3
SGNP1	0.35×10^{-2}* (4.42)	0.64×10^{-2}** (1.79)	0.55×10^{-2}* (5.09)
SACRTR	0.09* (4.83)	0.22* (3.57)	0.06* (3.10)
RER(−1)	−0.84* (−5.23)	−3.55* (−5.05)	−0.70* (−3.20)
TIRM	−0.05 (−0.68)	−0.14 (−0.56)	0.51* (2.08)
CHPOPM	0.07* (2.34)	0.07 (1.07)	0.049 (0.07)
Adjusted R^2 from *within* estimation	0.92	0.89	0.86
Fisher	79.31	36.95	43.89
Hausman	27.62	15.89	15.41
Number of observations	323	102	119

In the interest of clarity, the temporal dummies are not shown in the table.
*Significance level of 5%; t-values in parentheses.
**Significance level of 10%.

(sub-sample 3), the evolution of the specialization in tourism is positively correlated (albeit weakly) with the level of income per capita GNP (SGNP1). An explanation for this positive result draws on Linder's (1961) representative demand theory, in which a country's international specialization is said to depend on the existence of a sufficiently high level of domestic demand. This is especially the case, it would seem, in the countries in sub-sample 3, since their estimated coefficient of the level of per capita GNP (SGNP1), has a positive sign is statistically significant at the 5% level and has a value greater than that for the initial sample 1 $(0.55 \times 10^{-2} > 0.35 \times 10^{-2})$.

The estimated coefficients of SGNP1 suggest that, for these two samples, international demand for tourism seems to supplement demand at national level. In the group of Mediterranean tourist countries (sub-sample 2), on the other hand, the level of per capita GNP does not seem to influence the countries' level of specialization in tourism at the 5% level, since the estimated coefficient for SGNP1 is not statistically significant. In these countries, domestic demand for tourism seems to have less influence on the evolution of the specialization in tourism than in the other two samples. From this point of view, it seems quite logical to attribute part of the dynamism of their tourism specialization to foreign demand from international tourists.

As far as the estimated coefficients for the index of international specialization in passenger transport (SRCATR) are concerned, they are all significant and have a positive sign (albeit with a higher coefficient for countries in sub-sample 2). Thus, these countries are specializing across a broad range of tourist industries.

The estimated coefficient of price competitiveness $RER(-1)$ also proves to be significant in all three cases and has the expected sign (negative): appreciation of the RER has an adverse impact on a country's specialization in tourism. Furthermore, fluctuations in the RER seem to play a more important role in the Mediterranean OECD countries. This greater sensitivity to relative prices is certainly indicative of a tourism specialization based on products that are both more substitutable and exposed to greater competition than those of the countries in sub-sample 3. This finding corroborates one of our initial hypotheses, namely that travellers are sensitive to relative prices but not indifferent to the nature of the destination. Econometric analysis confirms the initial intuition that there is a general relationship between specialization in tourism and relative prices but also shows that the strength of this relationship differs depending on the group of countries under consideration.

Regarding the hotel function indicator (CHOPM), the coefficients in all three cases are relatively weakly positive, with only one being statistically significant at the 5% level (initial group). The estimated coefficients for this employment indicator seem to have no effect at all on the tourism specialization in sub-groups 2 and 3 in the 'downstream' segment. Again this could be another example of Linder's representative demand theory.

Finally, the results of the estimated coefficients for the tourism density rate (TIRM), a social variable, are as follows. First, this variable is not significant in two of the three samples analysed (initial group and the Mediterranean countries group). Second, its sign changes (it is negative in the case of the initial sample and of sub-sample 2 and positive in the case of sub-sample 3). The estimated coefficient is significant only for the American and Asia-Pacific countries group. For the countries in sub-sample 2, the estimated coefficient of TIRM is negative (but not significant), which would perhaps indicate that these countries are in the stagnation (or even the decline) phase. This result leads us to recommend that the authorities in the Mediterranean OECD countries should put a temporary cap on the number of international visitors and therefore restrict the number of permits issued for the construction of new establishments and even cut back on promotional campaigns abroad. This does not, however, mean that the number of rooms should not be modified. To put it simply, these modifications should be qualitative rather than quantitative in nature (quality driven and further differentiation).

Better specification of the model would have required the introduction of other indicators in order to evaluate the overall dimensions of the tourism/environment interface. Indeed, determining the desirable level of international tourism for a given country is a complex task. This varies from one country to another and is the subject of much debate. According to the literature, determining the optimal carrying capacity requires consideration of three components: physical capacity, environmental capacity and social capacity. Unfortunately, relevant data encompassing the full spectrum of these three components are unavailable at an international level. Consequently, our analysis of the general relationship between the level of specialization in tourism and OECD countries' carrying capacity is confined to the social dimension.

12.5. Conclusion

Empirical analysis of tourism in OECD countries provides us with a comprehensive overview of two aspects of the various countries' competitiveness. First, it is shown that a well-known size effect makes the large OECD countries major players in terms of tourism market shares, as they are in international trade in goods. Short-term competitiveness effects show a certain degree of similarity with trade in goods. Despite the statistical difficulties, the influence of the RER on the countries' positions in the tourism market has been shown. Depreciation stimulates a country's tourism industry by making other destinations more expensive and increasing the competitiveness of the local destination. These results support the notion that the RER is one of the key variables of competitiveness in international tourism. Further, even if tourism remains, to a large extent, governed by the existence of certain resources (sea, sun, mountains and cultural heritage), other factors also play an important role. These, of course, include technological factors, which serve to differentiate the nature of tourism comparative advantages, as well as the social dimension, the destination's degree of maturity, the level of domestic demand for tourism (Linder effect), the price competitiveness and dominance of the transport segment. The econometric analysis of panel data demonstrated the relevance and relative importance of these last factors. Moreover, it revealed that their impact differs depending on the level of development of a country's tourism industry.

References

Belassa, B. (1965), "Tariff protection in industrial countries: an evaluation", *Journal of Political Economy*, Vol. 73(6), pp. 573–594.

CEPII (1998), *Compétitivité des Nations*, Paris: Economica.

Hazari, B.R., M. Sahli and P.M. Sgro (2003), Tourism specialization: an economic analysis of 19 OECD destination countries. Mimeographed.

Lanza, A., P. Temple and G. Urga (2003), "The implications of tourism specialisation in the long-run: an economic analysis for 13 OECD economies", *Tourism Management*, Vol. 24, pp. 315–321.

Linder, S.B. (1961), *An Essay on Trade and Transformation*, New York: Wiley.

Opperman, M. and K. Sung Chon (1997), *Tourism in Developing Countries*, New York: International Thomson Business Press.

Peterson, J.C. (1988), "Export shares and revealed comparative advantage: a study of international travel", *Applied Economics*, Vol. 20, pp. 351–365.

Ulubasoglu, M. and B.R. Hazari (2004), "Zipf's law strikes again: the case of tourism", *Journal of Economic Geography*, Vol. 4, pp. 459–472.

INDEX

Footnotes are indicated by n after the page number